DATE DUE

Fumbling
the
Future

Fumbling the Future

How Xerox Invented, Then Ignored, the First Personal Computer

Douglas K. Smith and
Robert C. Alexander

William Morrow and Company, Inc.
New York

Library of Congress Cataloging-in-Publication Data

Alexander, Robert C.
    Fumbling the future : how Xerox invented, then ignored, the first personal computer/Robert C. Alexander, Douglas K. Smith.
        p. cm.
    Includes index.
    ISBN 0-688-06959-2
    1. Xerox Corporation. 2. Microcomputers. I. Smith, Douglas K.
II. Title.
HD9802.3.U64X472   1988
338.7'68644—dc19   88-12822
                                                                     CIP

Printed in the United States of America

First Edition

1 2 3 4 5 6 7 8 9 10

BOOK DESIGN BY MARK STEIN STUDIOS

In memory of Cameron M. Smith,
who loved books, and Paul L. Alexander,
who loved radios

Acknowledgments

We are grateful to Harvey Ginsberg, our editor, for his confidence, guidance, and good judgment.

In addition to Joy Harris, our agent, we would also like to thank Margot Alexander; John Alexander; David Falk; Alexa Greenstadt's father, Alan; Todd Kushnir and his parents, Alan and Carole; Margie O'Driscoll; Laura Handman; Julien Phillips; Mark Singer; Alena Smith; Eben Smith; Jane Simkin Smith; Stanley Stempler; Bob Tavetian; Chuck Thacker; Laird Townsend; and John Whitney.

Contents

The Commercial

Here is a three-part trivia question about televised personal computer advertising:
Name the companies responsible for

1. The longest playing series of personal computer commercials?
2. The most creative single commercial?
3. The first personal computer commercial?

Answering part one is easy. IBM's "Charlie Chaplin" ads ran for more than six years. They were entertaining, effective, and nearly impossible to avoid. Identifying Apple as the maker of the most creative commercial may be more challenging. Apple showed the ad just once, during the second half of the 1984 Super Bowl. Nonetheless, some people consider it the most impressive corporate identity commercial in history. Now for the last piece of the puzzle. Who televised the first personal computer commercial? This is not a trick question. It wasn't IBM, and it wasn't Apple.

It was Xerox.

Xerox is not a name most personal computer consumers, let alone general television audiences, associate with the multibillion dollar personal computing industry. Fifteen years after it invented the world's first personal computing system, and long after it portrayed that system in a 1979 commercial, Xerox still means "copy" to most people. Had it succeeded in marketing the computers shown in the commercial, however, Xerox might have meant more than copiers—much more.

Unlike Xerox, IBM, of course, always has been synonymous with computers. By far the most dominant personal computer advertising promotes the IBM PC. In it, a contemporary actor plays Charlie Chaplin playing his renowned tramp. The little man with derby, moustache, baggy trousers, and awkward walk twitters and jerks his way through the delightful discovery that computers can be useful and even fun for real people. IBM has spent massively on the campaign, as much to build interest in personal computing itself as to identify IBM's product as the standard in the industry.

In contrast to the IBM barrage, the memorable Apple commercial was more like a proclamation. Less than a decade after being incorporated in the garage workshop of two kids in their twenties, Apple Computer stood out as the Fortune 500 corporation best positioned to challenge IBM's dominance in personal computing. The brash, young California company selected 1984 and the Super Bowl to broadcast its commercial, a video morality play celebrating the glory of iconoclastic individualism and condemning the sinister threat of organizations whose power oppresses rather than liberates the human spirit. Using imagery without words, Apple drew the battle line clearly between itself and IBM.

There might have been a third competitor. In 1973, more than three years before Steve Wozniak of Apple soldered together a circuit board that qualified as a computer in name only, researchers at Xerox's Palo Alto Research Center (PARC) flipped the switch on the Alto, the first computer ever designed and built for the dedicated use of a single person. Long before Wozniak, prodded by his friend and partner Steve Jobs, went on to build his second computer—the famous Apple II, credited with changing forever the American home and workplace—and even longer before IBM implemented a crash strategy for breaking into and then dominating the personal computer industry, Xerox employees ranging from scientists to secretaries were using personal computers that, in many respects, were superior to any system sold in the market before 1984, the year of the Apple Super Bowl commercial.

The scientists at Xerox PARC created more than a personal computer. They designed, built, and used a complete system of hardware and software that fundamentally altered the nature of computing itself. Along the way, an impressive list of digital "firsts" came out of PARC. In addition to the Alto computer, PARC inventors made the first graphics-oriented monitor, the first hand-held "mouse" inputting device simple enough for a child, the first word processing program for nonexpert users, the first local area communications network, the first object-oriented programming language, and the first laser printer.

They called this entirely new approach to computing "personal distributed computing." Their design and philosophy challenged accepted wisdom about the relationship between people and digital processors. Mainline computer people scoffed at the notion of one computer for each person; the Xerox team built the Alto. Traditional computer applications centered on number and data manipulation; the Xerox team focused on words, design, and communications. By the mid-seventies, PARC had crafted a framework of machines and programs that were "personal" because they were individually controlled, and "distributed" because they were linked through networks to shared resources and knowledge. The entire system—of people, machines, and programs—advanced human productivity through computing tools in ways paralleled only by the exploitation of pencil, paper, printing press, and telephone.

Xerox, however, did not convert either the vision or the implementation of personal distributed computing into the commercial success and recognition now enjoyed by Apple and IBM. It's not that Xerox failed to profit financially from its innovative technology. The company's laser printer business is thriving, and its latest generation of copiers incorporates technology developed at PARC. But these successes related easily to the world of imaging well-known at Xerox. By comparison, the greater possibility to define and dominate the unfamiliar business of personal computing smoldered unproductively within the company for more than a decade, frustrating far more of the organization than it inspired.

The Alto confronted Xerox with the unknown. When Xerox established PARC in 1970, there was no market for personal computers. There were no compact disc players, no Walkmen, no portable telephones, no digital watches, no VCRs, no video camcorders, no personal copiers. Not even the now ubiquitous pocket calculator had been introduced yet to the marketplace. Furthermore, from the time of its invention in the late 1940s through the end of the 1970s, computer technology remained unaffordable, inaccessible, and useless to most people. Computers were owned by corporations and universities, not individuals; operating the technology required a knowledge of protocols as formalized and arcane as any used in international diplomacy; and, all the effort yielded results for a narrow set of applications. For the most part, computers manipulated numbers in ways and with speeds helpful only to scientists, engineers, and accountants. Not surprisingly, popular films and novels depicted the technology as enigmatic and those who understood it as weird.

Except for the perception, all of this had changed by the time IBM introduced its personal computer in 1981. Consequently, IBM emphasized consumer education in its marketing strategy. If the Charlie Chaplin tramp could own a PC, the machine must be affordable. If he could operate one, the technology must be accessible. And if he could use a computer to better himself commercially and, yes, even romantically, then it must be useful.

The campaign was a remarkable success. By 1987, Americans had purchased more than twenty-five million personal computers. The machines were owned by one of every six households, and their absence in an office was far more remarkable than their presence. Children considered the technology routine. IBM's name was so identified with personal computing that IBM PC knockoffs, known as "clones," were grabbing a big share of the market for their United States and Asian manufacturers—so big that IBM ultimately changed its advertising strategy. The Charlie Chaplin character began touting the uniqueness of IBM products instead of merely demonstrating the wonders of personal computing in general.

IBM's early promotions made sense for a number of reasons. First, people did not have to be sold on the idea that IBM could make a good computer. Next, since IBM was the only personal computer manufacturer in the early 1980s willing and able to advertise extensively on television, it had no competition for what advertisers call the "share of voice." Television viewers simply didn't see or hear that much about the competition. As a result, IBM could educate consumers while relying on sheer omnipresence to associate its product with a safe and wise choice. Finally, the approach succeeded because, by 1981, enough personal computer hardware and software was available in the marketplace to back up the discovery claims made by IBM's little tramp.

Only five years earlier that had not been the case. The first personal computing products appeared in the mid-seventies and had limited appeal. They were sold by small electronics firms and individual hobbyists through clubs, direct mail, and word of mouth to other hobbyists and tinkerers. Wozniak's Apple I typified the early merchandise. It was an unpackaged circuit board wired by Wozniak so that a purchaser could hook it up to a power supply (not included), connect a tape cassette for input (not included), a television for output (not included), and then set about writing programs (not included) to fit within the Apple I's limited internal memory. Millions of Americans preferred spending their time in other ways.

Within a few years, however, astonishing advances in integrated circuitry provided the critical raw materials needed by hobbyists and others to build bigger, better, and more useful computing tools. Personal computer memories, speed, and power expanded. Disc drives, keyboards, mice, monitors, and printers were added. And, most important, programmers began writing routines to make the machines appealing to people other than tinkerers.

At first, many programmers focused on games. But by 1979, data base management, word processing, and the electronic spreadsheet all had been invented. With the emergence of these applications, large numbers of people realized that the small computers could help them manage information more productively, write and type better, and think more clearly. The personal computing market, having rung up its first sale in 1975, measured revenues in the billions of dollars by 1981.

Few opportunities have ever burst onto the scene so suddenly and with such force. To thrive on the shock of such an explosion required not only good, responsive products but the faith and hustle to profit from them. Apple had that magic combination. Theirs was the classic American business story starring two high school graduates with little money, no economic training, and big dreams. Wozniak built and improved the product; Jobs provided the faith and the hustle. When Jobs's energy exceeded his understanding, he recruited more experienced manufacturing, marketing, and financial managers to guide Apple through its rapid expansion.

By 1984, the year George Orwell predicted would witness a tyranny of computers in the hands of evil men, Apple Computer, like the personal computing industry at large, held out the opposite promise. Apple marked the event with its Super Bowl commercial. The ad begins with several indistinguishable cohorts of gray-clad ideological slaves marching in lockstep toward a great hall. Once inside, they take instruction from a larger-than-life image projected on a screen at the head of the auditorium. In the midst of this lifeless, impersonal scene, a powerfully built woman, dressed in bright colors and wielding a sledgehammer, charges into the hall and spins herself around and around and around, frightening the brainwashed masses. With each of her revolutions, the tension grows in the great hall until, finally, at the end of the piece, she launches her weapon directly at the big screen.

The commercial's imagery richly conveyed Apple's perspective on its history, computers, and IBM. Perhaps more subtly, the television time purchased told as much about Apple the corporation. Super Bowl minutes are the most expensive advertising time in the world. Apple may have had an antiestablishment past, but its economic power in 1984 was as conventional and formidable as the beer, car, and financial services companies who also sponsored the annual football championship. The Super Bowl spot marked Apple's arrival; it was only the second company in history to have reached a billion dollars in sales in less than ten years on the merits of a new technology.

The first was Xerox. Less than a decade after the 1959 introduction of its revolutionary office copier, Xerox went over the billion dollar mark and claimed a position, along with IBM, as one of America's leading office products companies. By 1970, competition between the two giants seemed inevitable as each rushed into the technology of the other—IBM into copiers, and Xerox into computers. At the time, business computers were stationed in corporate back offices, handling the work of accountants and statisticians. No one expected them to stay there. So, in addition to taking on IBM in back office computing, Xerox established its Palo Alto Research Center to invent systems that could support executives, secretaries, salesmen, and production managers in what became known as the "office of the future."

The remarkable group of scientists and engineers who joined PARC responded with the Alto personal distributed computing system. Xerox's 1979 commercial demonstrates how the Alto functioned in an office setting. We see friendly "Bill," a balding middle-aged executive with a warm smile, arrive at work, grab a cup of coffee, and head for his office, saying good morning to people on the way. When Bill gets to his desk, he flips on his Alto computer, grins, and greets it with a "Morning, Fred." "Fred" the computer flashes the appropriate response: "Good morning, Bill."

Bill asks, "What's the mail this morning?" and then scans a list showing the times and origins of messages he has received since leaving work the day before. "This one looks interesting," says Bill. "Let's, ah, take a look at this." He selects the desired message with the aid of his mouse, and the full text fills one section of Fred's monitor.

After reading it, Bill tells Fred, "I'm going to need a couple of copies of this." Bill presses a button that controls an off-camera laser printer, and the commercial cuts to some time later when a secretary delivers Bill the paper copies he's requested from the printer. He thanks the secretary, then turns back to the computer saying, "Oh, and thank you, Fred. You know, Fred, I think everyone on the routing list should see this." So Bill pushes a few more buttons, sending electronic copies of the message down the hall, around the corner, and across the country.

The commercial highlights many parts of the Xerox system including the graphics-rich Alto screen, the mouse, the word processing program, the laser printer, and, most prominently, the system's communications capabilities. It's an effective ad—other than the Xerox name, nothing about it would surprise a television audience even if it were shown today.

But in 1979, despite airing the spot several times, Xerox decided against marketing the Alto system. By then the organization barely resembled the buoyant company that a decade earlier had challenged both IBM and the office of the future. External factors including fierce competition, government antagonism, and economic recession all marked Xerox's slide—from overconfidence to loss of confidence. Internal forces were even more combustible, as the company's research, finance, and marketing groups each pursued a separate vision of the "right" Xerox future. In the end, the company that invented the first version of a personal computing future found itself struggling to recapture the advantages of its copier past.

In one fundamental respect, neither economists nor business people would consider the corporate histories behind the three different personal computer commercials that remarkable. Of course IBM waited for personal computers to move beyond hobbyist circles before entering and dominating the market. It's a well known strategy for firms with established economic power to take advantage of the innovation and product testing done by others. Of course a start-up like Apple flourished. Rags-to-riches entrepreneurs are among the most cherished citizens in capitalist economies. Of course Xerox stumbled.

But why? Why do corporations find it so difficult to replicate earlier successes in new and unrelated fields? How could Xerox, sired by one radical technology, bring forth yet another extraordinary invention, only to fumble away most of the economic opportunity it promised? It doesn't have to happen this way. One clue to why it did happen to Xerox, and why it's now occurring but shouldn't be at other corporations, is found in the conclusion of the Alto commercial. We cut to quitting time for a final dialogue between "Bill" and "Fred" the computer:

> Bill (tired): "Anything else?"
> Fred: A richly detailed bouquet of daisies spreads across the screen.
> Bill (puzzled): "Flowers? What flowers?"
> Fred: "Your anniversary is tonight."
> Bill (chagrined): "My anniversary. I forgot."
> Fred: "It's okay. We're only human."

Marketing:
The
Architecture
of
Information

Chapter

1

When Joe Wilson named Peter McColough to succeed him as chief executive officer of Xerox Corporation in 1968, both men knew McColough would never squander Wilson's legacy through idleness. McColough proclaimed that his biggest challenge would be "to keep our momentum even though it's on a different order of magnitude now." Momentum. It was a word with unprecedented meaning to the first company in history to ride a new technology to a billion dollars in sales in less than ten years. It was also a code word in circulation at Xerox since the mid-sixties, when McColough's mentor Wilson had carefully selected "momentum" to signify an insistence that his original dream, to build a great company, had been neither satisfied nor forgotten with the triumph of xerography. Joe Wilson wanted more. So did Peter McColough.

They recognized that Xerox, for all its present glory, was essentially a one-product company. To keep their employees in jobs and their shareholders in dividends, the two executives were determined to do more than protect Xerox's prosperous copier franchise. Both Wilson, who remained as chairman of Xerox, and McColough wanted to diversify the company into noncopier businesses in order to provide balance for the day of competitive reckoning that ultimately arrives for all monopolies and would surely come for Xerox.

Wilson and McColough worried not so much about the copier competition they could see (and were beating further into the ground with each passing day), but about the technological threat beyond their line of sight. Having emerged from obscurity themselves, on the strength of xerography, to take control of the copier industry, they feared some equally radical and unknown technology might spring forth to condemn xerography to the same fate xerography had already cast upon carbon paper. Momentum also required moving beyond xerography into new products and markets. Three areas were targeted—computers, education, and medicine—of which the first was considered by far the most critical, especially to Wilson. Joe Wilson believed Xerox's destiny was to become a world-class communications company, and he was convinced that couldn't be done without computers.

The xerography boom hardly had begun when Wilson told McColough: "Look, we're only communicating graphic information. Things that have been written down that you can copy and send from one person to another so they can share that information. But in looking at the future, all information is not going to be graphic. The computer is coming along. The computer handles information in a totally different way, in digital form. And if we're going to be big ten years or twenty years out we've also got to be able to handle information in digital form as well as graphic form."

At the time he became chief executive of Xerox, McColough didn't understand much about computers. But then, he hadn't known *anything* about xerography fourteen years earlier when he joined the Haloid Company, as Xerox was known before 1960. In 1968, neither he nor Wilson nor, for that matter, anyone else could have predicted the emergence of personal computers or the $100 billion in revenues personal computing would spin out in its first decade of business. Computers, in the late 1960s, were too large and expensive to be owned or operated by single individuals. And they were far too specialized to be accessible to masses of laymen. Not even science fiction writers had yet coined the phrase "personal computer."

But McColough didn't require specific insights into the future of computing to agree with Wilson that Xerox had to acquire or develop digital capability. He knew IBM was preparing to enter the copier field and, to respond, Xerox had to get into computers. Furthermore, growth in the computer industry was explosive, feeding off the same limitless phenomenon Wilson ascribed to copying. "Ours is a business with infinite possibilities," he said often, "because we serve all industries, all professions, every kind of enterprise." Finally, digital technology was changing as rapidly as Xerox's sales and profits. And to Peter McColough change signaled opportunity, and opportunity required action instead of reflection.

Boldness was the hallmark of McColough's career. He took the first of many daring steps in his life after graduating from law school in his native Nova Scotia in 1947. His years at law school had convinced him that in the choice between lawyer and client, he would rather be the client. As a result, he recalls, "I went to get my papers admitting me to the bar in Canada at noon and returned right to my job as a concrete inspector to make some money to go to the Harvard Graduate School of Business Administration."

After graduating from Harvard in 1949, McColough joined the Lehigh Navigation Coal Sales Company in Philadelphia as a salesman. There he met the woman he would marry and threw himself into his new job. Enthusiasm and hard work paid off; by thirty-one, he had been named vice president of sales. McColough, however, wanted more from life than a promising career in coal.

He put together a resume and mailed it to a management recruiter. The headhunter sent him to Rochester for an interview with the Haloid Company, a small photographic paper and supply firm. Five years in the comfortable, well equipped offices of Lehigh Navigation left McColough unprepared for the scene that greeted him in Rochester. Every spare dollar at Haloid was being thrown into the research and development of a process the company called xerography. Managers shared uncarpeted rooms, worked at secondhand desks, and answered their own phones.

On meeting John Hartnett, Haloid's head of sales, McColough immediately noticed the workman's lunch pail perched on the recycled orange crate Hartnett employed as a bookshelf. Business had to be bad at Haloid, very bad. Hartnett took him on a tour of the Haloid plant and showed him the Model A Copier, the company's first attempted product based on xerography. It looked like a clunker to McColough. As he tried to follow Hartnett's complicated description of how the machine operated, he may have suspected he was hearing a good explanation for why the company's chief salesman was packing his own lunch.

If what McColough saw at Haloid that morning struck him as unimpressive, what he saw later that day changed his life. He met Haloid's president Joe Wilson and came away inspired. "He was home sick with a cold," recalls McColough of his interview at Wilson's house. "He began to outline what he had in mind for this company and by the end of the afternoon I became sold on his ideas about Haloid's revolutionary copying process. It was all promise and no performance, but I was taken with the opportunity. I would have accepted a job offer right then, but it didn't come through for a few days."

McColough's first assignment was managing the company's

service center in Chicago, a responsibility soon expanded to cover
the other service centers around the country. As he traveled from
center to center, McColough repeatedly experienced a sense of
déjà vu that brought back his first morning in John Hartnett's
office. The "service centers" were nothing but glorified storage
rooms. Boston was typical. A cautious climb up three creaking
flights of stairs in an ancient building rewarded a potential customer with the sight of a small loft crowded with cartons of sen-
sitized paper, boxes of photographic supplies, and all the other
materials Haloid then distributed to the trade.

Joe Wilson's vision of xerography would not take flight on the
wings of such warehouses. McColough lobbied to pry loose some
money from research and development for the complete overhaul
of Haloid's sales and service function. First, the service centers
required renovation. "Our machines," he pointed out to Wilson
and others at Haloid, "are too big and complicated to be carried
into a customer's office. We have to bring the customer to see the
machine in our own quarters. That means we've got to have modern, spacious, attractive demonstration rooms. The longer we wait
to make the change, the more we're going to lose."

In addition, he argued that Haloid must hire and train a large,
national direct sales force if the company hoped to take advantage
of xerography. In the late fifties, most office product companies
sold their machines through independent dealers instead of directly to customers. Since dealers worked on a commission basis,
they had to represent several manufacturers to make a profit.
Haloid's dry, plain paper copying machines, however, would be
far more complex to sell and service than other copiers then in
the marketplace. As a result, McColough reasoned, dealers were
unlikely to invest in the time, effort, education, and parts essential
to provide Haloid customers with top flight sales and service.

"To sell machines," McColough insisted, "we need salesmen
and demonstrators who are trained for the jobs. We need service
people who will keep the machines in perfect order. We need
distribution centers that can provide new parts and everything
else a machine needs in equipment and replacements. In other
words, we need a completely new and larger chain of branch
offices—places geared to xerography instead of simply selling
photographic materials."

Wilson bought McColough's logic and gave him the job of
building the new sales and service force, a task McColough did

so well it would later be called a masterpiece of industrial organization. The young executive's move to the tiny Rochester company began to pay off, at least in terms of career advancement and responsibility. In 1957, McColough was made manager of marketing. Two years later, he became general manager of sales.

That year, 1959, Haloid's thirteen year struggle with the development of xerography produced the first prototype of the long awaited plain paper office copier. Going from a prototype that works in the lab to an assembly process capable of turning out dependable and reliable machines for customers is, however, a big, expensive step. The rule of thumb most manufacturers follow says that for every dollar spent on researching a new technology, ten dollars will have to be spent on developing product; and, for every ten dollars spent on product development, one hundred dollars will have to be invested in the manufacturing and marketing capability necessary to introduce the product to customers.

Haloid already had sunk millions of dollars into research and development. Talk among the company's board members turned to finding a better capitalized corporation to take on the next burden. Wilson reluctantly contacted a number of companies, including IBM. IBM hired a consulting firm, Arthur D. Little, to study the copier market and advise it on how to respond to Haloid's request for help. Wilson, in turn, asked McColough to lead a Haloid team that would advise him whether or not to accept any forthcoming offer.

After five of the most exciting years of his life, McColough was damned if he was going to recommend sharing the promise of xerography with anyone, especially IBM. He wasn't alone. "The younger guys in the group didn't want to sell. Basically, we felt that we should not give that machine to IBM because it would kill our future."

As it happened, McColough and the others never had to face that bleak prospect. Based on extensive financial and market analysis, Arthur D. Little projected that no more than five thousand of the new Haloid machines would sell. Neither IBM nor any of the other contacted companies was interested in Haloid's offer. Instead, Wilson convinced his board to increase their stake in xerography by issuing and selling enough stock to pay for the required manufacturing capability. A year later, the then Haloid-Xerox Company introduced the 914 Copier. McColough was ecstatic. "We shipped our first 914 on March 1, 1960. About six months later, after we saw the customer acceptance, we knew we had a real winner."

McColough's national sales force, considered by some extravagant for a small company, was trained, in place, and ready to move when the first 914 television commercials began to run. In 1959, the company's final year before the 914, Haloid-Xerox had sales of $32 million. The next year, as customers got their first look at the copiers on television and in person, sales jumped nearly 16 percent. Nice. But nothing compared to what would follow.

In 1961, the first full year of the 914, Xerox sales were $61 million. In 1962, sales hit $104 million. In 1963, $176 million. In 1964, $280 million. In 1965, $393 million. In 1966, $534 million. In 1967, $701 million. And in 1968, the ninth year of the 914, Xerox sales reached $1.125 billion. Over the same period, annual profits soared from $2.5 million to $138 million.

None of Xerox's senior managers, including Wilson, had predicted numbers like those. Everyone had underestimated the power of copiers as communications tools. One chronicler of the copying madness that swept the country in the sixties cited bridal gift lists, property receipts for jailed suspects, hospital laboratory reports, brokerage firm hot tips, and copyright violations as just some of the many ingenious ways people used the Xerox technology. By 1965, Xerox estimated that 9.5 billion copies were being made annually. A year later, the company adjusted the figure up to 14 billion. As a result of its unique product and the capacity of McColough's sales and service team, virtually all of the business belonged to Xerox.

In 1966, Wilson named McColough president. For the first time in his business career, McColough had to broaden his attention from sales to general management. As he did so, he discovered an unexpected side to Xerox's rapidly rising sales numbers: other parts of the company were out of control. In only seven years, Xerox had manufactured and placed 190,000 copiers. Total employment had jumped from 900 to more than 24,000. Some managers were hiring 50 to 100 people every month, and interviewing at least 30 people a day just to fill the jobs required by Xerox's growth. Since the introduction of the 914 Copier, Xerox had erected twenty-four buildings in the Rochester area, with three more under construction the year McColough became president.

Gaining an administrative grip on Xerox's prosperity was an

enviable problem, but a problem nonetheless. "The company was exploding so rapidly," said McColough, "that we didn't have systems and controls. In fact, just about that time, I was concerned that we couldn't pay our bills even or pay our salesmen. Not because we didn't have money, but our records were so lousy. The whole system was falling apart. We couldn't even bill our customers."

McColough knew he needed help, and Wilson agreed. But when he looked around the executive suite in Rochester, McColough saw few people he considered up to the task. Too many senior executives were caught in small company habits. The management challenge of the fifties—to keep Haloid solvent while developing and marketing xerography—had limited relevance to the financial and administrative obstacles now confronting Xerox. Although his colleagues may have expected the scope of their jobs to expand with the company's fortunes, McColough feared their expectations outstripped their abilities.

In an unpopular move, he decided to hire outsiders. Xerox had broken into the ranks of the Fortune 500 in 1962. Four years later the company was well inside the top two hundred. McColough persuaded Wilson they ought to look to other Fortune 500 corporations for the talent needed to bring management control to Xerox. Eventually they brought in nearly a dozen top people from companies like Ford, IBM, and General Motors.

By 1968, the new management team had introduced a series of systems and controls to save Xerox's rocketlike rise from turning into a huge Roman candle. Wilson and McColough turned more confidently to the task of diversification. Through acquisition and internal development, they had made progress in two of the three noncopier business areas targeted for growth: medicine and education. But the most important of the three, computers, remained elusive. In 1965, Xerox had approached Digital Equipment Corporation without success. Later, Xerox had held a series of inconclusive talks with Scientific Data Systems, but hadn't been impressed enough to move forward.

McColough was determined to get a computer company. Inquiries were made at Control Data, then Burroughs. Neither was interested. Consternation was mounting at Xerox headquarters when an investment banker asked McColough to consider the acquisition of Commercial Investment Trust, a large financial services firm.

No one at Xerox ever had touted financial services as a way to build a great communications company. Nevertheless, in a by then characteristic move, McColough seized the moment. He was persuaded that CIT's significant cash resources could help fund Xerox's entry into computers, and were reason enough to proceed. McColough negotiated a deal—only to see it fall through shortly before the closing.

As 1968 turned to 1969, Xerox still wasn't in the computer business. A dismayed McColough began to hear voices. "The pressure was on from all through the organization," he recalls. " 'Dammit McColough,' they all said, 'You got to buy your computer company.' The only ball game left in town was Scientific Data Systems. The thing that made me the most nervous was that I saw no options and I knew we had to have digital capability."

McColough took the initiative. He called Max Palevsky, the head of Scientific Data Systems, and arranged to meet him and his partners. Palevsky's company, like the other computer concerns approached by Xerox, was small, relative to IBM, but profitable—in 1968, SDS earned $10 million on sales of $100 million. At the meeting, McColough announced that he wanted to buy SDS and would pay Palevsky and the others more than $900 million worth of Xerox stock for the privilege. The deal was done in less than two weeks.

People at Xerox, at SDS, and on Wall Street were shocked by the audacious price. In purchasing SDS, Xerox was buying the earnings power of a going business concern, not a capital appreciation opportunity in real estate, art, or gold. Yet the bill for the acquisition was *ninety-two times* greater than SDS's earnings in 1968, until then its best year ever. If SDS income never changed, Xerox would receive a skimpy one percent annual return on its investment. At the time, savings accounts yielded more than four times that much. To make sense as an acquisition, Xerox's new computer division would have to multiply its results severalfold. The odds were long.

Nonetheless, McColough moved confidently forward. He believed strongly that Xerox could help SDS grow. The El Segundo, California, computer maker was selling its products mainly to engineering and scientific customers. McColough intended to change that by taking advantage of Xerox's established marketing presence in the nation's business offices. In his opinion, SDS was bound to make highly profitable inroads into the commercial data processing market dominated by IBM.

Furthermore, Xerox had the financial resources to fund a major research effort to take advantage of the rapid pace of change in digital technology. Research could produce the kind of major opportunity that might justify the high price paid for SDS. Haloid had spent huge sums on the research and development of xerography when other, more risk averse companies had shied away. And if Haloid alumni like Peter McColough should have learned anything, it was that investment in research, and the courage and commitment to follow it through, had their own rewards.

As for the doubters and critics, McColough had heard them before. Those questioning the wisdom of the SDS acquisition only echoed voices from long ago when he left the law and Canada for a business career in the United States, when he quit a comfortable position at the coal company to join Wilson's crusade, when he argued for a first class sales and service organization years before the 914 Copier was ready for the market, and when he went outside the company to bring in a professional team of managers. The doubters and critics could not see what McColough saw. His job was to build the great communications corporation of Joe Wilson's dreams. The SDS price measured far more than the computer company's value; it calibrated McColough's boundless confidence in himself, in his company, and, most important, in the future.

Chapter

2

ollowing the announcement of the Scientific Data Systems deal, Jack Goldman, head of research at Xerox, recommended to Peter McColough that the company set up a new digital technology research center. SDS had no such facility; Xerox would have to start with a clean slate. Cost, however, was irrelevant to Goldman. He argued that combining a research initiative with the SDS investment was essential to give Xerox the chance at another commercial revolution, one he hoped would be even bigger than xerography.

Goldman also warned McColough that the copier business might become vulnerable to computers if Xerox failed to pursue long range digital research. Computer systems could process, store, *and print* information. Although contemporary computer printing produced low quality images, Goldman knew that improvements were inevitable. When people could press computer buttons as easily as copier buttons and get as many high grade copies as they needed, Xerox's revenues would surely suffer. Instead of ignoring the threat, Goldman wanted Xerox to lead the way by developing a machine based half on xerography and half on digital technology. That would require research.

Jack Goldman shared easily in Peter McColough's dreams for the future. A poker playing physicist, Goldman believed innovation was dealt from two decks—science and commerce—with the pot going to the company that played its hand the best. A few months before the SDS agreement, he had accepted McColough's offer to leave Ford Motor Company for Xerox because, after a long career at the auto maker, he was convinced that Ford's financially oriented management had all but thrown down their cards while McColough and Xerox were still eager to gamble.

The only negative in the Xerox opportunity was the number of ex-Ford financial people McColough had hired to control the copier boom. In Goldman's opinion, Ford had been ruined by such accountants. After World War II, Henry Ford II invited a group of statistically oriented financial men to help him turn around his company. The group succeeded, but then went too far. By 1968, when Goldman left the company, Ford decision makers were so risk averse and numbers-bound that meaningful change seemed impossible. To Goldman, Ford-trained financial managers had become nothing more than bean counters bound to a regimen of heartless formulas without factors for enthusiasm, faith, or finesse.

McColough and Xerox, on the other hand, appeared willing to raise the ante while holding less than a royal flush in spades. And with good reason—in the late sixties, Xerox was the very symbol of dramatic economic growth based on daring innovation. Most of us identify "innovation" with invention, employing the terms interchangeably to describe newness and change. But just as "momentum" meant something quite special to Peter Mc-Colough, "innovation" described more than invention to Jack Goldman.

About inventions Goldman once wrote, "The familiar cartoon representation of the inventive spark as a bolt of lightning striking or an electric bulb flashing near the head of the inventor is not far off the mark. Invention can result from a flash of genius or painstaking pursuit of a technical response to an identified or perceived need—sometimes perceived only by the inventor himself." However arrived at, inventions come from the dedicated effort to make brilliant insight work in practice at least one time. They are manned flight and the Wright brothers, telephony and Bell, xerography and Chester Carlson.

Carlson was a classic inventor. He grew up in Washington, Mexico, and California, an only child whose parents' bad health kept the family moving in search of salubrious climates and, as a result, largely out of work. Carlson's early schooling was erratic and often solitary. His mother died when he was seventeen, his father seven years later. In between, he worked his way through a junior college, then Cal Tech, obtaining a degree in physics. But when he graduated in 1930, he couldn't get work as a physicist. Eventually he landed in the New York City patent office of a small electronics company.

He assembled patent applications. This required making copies of drawings and specifications, a task Carlson found tedious and boring. Frustration was his catalyst. Through that mystery known only to genius, Carlson decided to invent a simpler method of copying.

He studied everything he could find about photography, the chemistry of paper and paper treatment, the physics of light, and all known printing and copying processes. After months of research, he uncovered something truly intriguing—a property known as photoconductivity, the manner in which light affects the electrical conductivity of materials. If he could use light to cast an image, then rely on photoconductivity to capture and fasten the image to paper, Carlson believed he could invent a more efficient copying process.

That insight sparked Carlson's pursuit of what he called "electrophotography." Over the next three years, in addition to his patent job by day and law school by night, Carlson drove steadily toward his goal of making the electrophotographic process work. Finally, on October 22, 1938, he created a blurred but legible image—"10-22-38 Astoria"—on a piece of waxed paper. "10-22-38" was the date, and "Astoria" was the name of the apartment building housing Carlson's makeshift laboratory. Forty-seven years later, in 1985, this first image, together with the Xerox 914 Copier it ultimately inspired, would be placed in the permanent collection at the Smithsonian.

Carlson and his invention were both remarkable. Still, to Jack Goldman, stories like Carlson's are but the first step in the broader challenge to commercialize an inventor's original insight. That is what Goldman calls "innovation," the transformation of an invention *into a business*. It takes more than developing a reliable product. Purchasing, manufacturing, distribution, price, cost, packaging, consumer education, finance, insurance, warrantability, service—these issues and more can demand innovative solutions before a new business becomes viable. The effort is difficult enough when the product to be introduced—for example, the first food processor—provides an incremental and easily understood advance over the competition. But when the invention is as fundamental and novel as Carlson's electrophotography or, later, personal computing, the commitment, talent, organization, and leadership required must be truly extraordinary.

Inventors rarely can achieve commercial success on their own. Chester Carlson, for example, spent years trying to find a corporate sponsor for electrophotography. He failed. Only after a long series of refusals from the likes of General Electric, RCA, IBM, and Remington Rand, after driving himself to destitution and his wife to divorce, did Carlson finally persuade a private foundation in Ohio called the Battelle Memorial Institute to continue research on his invention.

For electrophotography, the path to innovation began in 1945, when Joe Wilson and John Dessauer, president and chief engineer, respectively, of the small Haloid Company, visited Battelle to investigate Carlson's process. Wilson was looking for expansion opportunities. Earlier that year, Dessauer had given him an abstract on electrophotography taken from the journal *Radio-Electronic Engineering*. After some preliminary investigation, the two men decided to go to Ohio for a firsthand look. The demonstration they saw was very manual and very messy, but it captivated Wilson, who exclaimed to Dessauer, "Of course it's got a million miles to go before it will be marketable. But when it does become marketable, we've got to be in the picture!"

Wilson's enthusiasm spurred years and years of hard, tough work by hundreds of dedicated people at Haloid. Engineers had to solve literally thousands of problems to make Carlson's invention into a product. And the nontechnical businesspeople, the factory managers, sales personnel, accountants, lawyers, and others, had to be just as creative and persistent.

In one of their first, and ultimately most profound, steps, they decided to change the name of the process. "Electrophotography" was too technical and not sufficiently proprietary. A language professor suggested "xerography," from the Greek *xēros*, for "dry," and *graphein*, "to write." Wilson much preferred this to other recommendations like "Kleen Kopy," "Dry Duplicator," and "Magic Printer"; and, "xerography" was adopted. Much later, Haloid changed its own name to Xerox to further identify the company with the new process. Both moves clearly worked. Today, xerography is an established science, and "Xerox" is used regularly as both verb and noun.

Wilson's team produced a variety of creative business solutions. They built Peter McColough's national direct sales force instead of relying on the traditional approach to distributing office products; they erected a wall of patent and license protection around xerography; they invested in land near Rochester far in advance of needing it in order to save on capital; they became one of the first companies not selling consumer oriented products like cars and soap to use television advertising. But perhaps the most ingenious of their innovations had to do with pricing and with the nature of what they would sell.

Haloid/Xerox chose to peddle copies instead of copiers. At the time the 914 Copier was introduced, competitive copying machines sold in the $300 to $400 range. The 914s, however, were far more complex and expensive pieces of equipment; selling them profitably would have required a price as much as one hundred times higher. While the Haloid/Xerox management group believed strongly in the superiority of their product, they doubted whether customers would find the value of clean, easy-to-read copies worth such a gaping price difference.

They cleverly finessed the price issue by leasing the machines instead of selling them, and letting the lease price fluctuate with use. Customers could try out a 914 Copier for ninety-five dollars a month, with the first two thousand copies free and a charge of just four cents per copy after that. Customers made no investment in the machines, and they had the right to return them after fifteen days. Few did.

Xerox reaped tremendous rewards from the scheme. Since copies were so easy to make, clean to handle and read, and useful in communications, the copy volume at the heart of Xerox's revenues exploded. In its first year of operation, the average 914 generated enough copies, and hence revenues, to pay for all of the manufacturing, sales, administration, and overhead costs associated with the machine. At the end of the year, of course, Xerox still owned the 914 because of the decision to lease instead of sell it. So the revenues generated by the next year's usage, typically even greater as the customer's appetite for copies expanded, were mostly profit. And the same held true for the year following that. And the next. And the next. And the next.

Naturally, Wilson's organization made a number of mistakes too. Perhaps the most instructive was the Model A Copier, Haloid's first attempt to market a product based on xerography. The Model A was really three machines connected by a person. The operator had to transfer a flat, heavy metal plate on which the copy image was created from each machine to the next for every single copy to be made. In all, there were thirty-nine manual steps, a process taking three minutes when everything worked according to an instruction manual that, like many of its genre, could fool you.

Wilson knew the Model A was crude. But after several years of working in isolation, having all suggestions and critiques of xerography come from Haloid or Battelle, he wanted to test the marketplace to find out if people working in offices would be interested enough in dry copying to buy it. He didn't have to wait long for the results. Without exception, test site users reported that the Model A was too difficult and complex to operate and the copies produced were too often illegible or otherwise defective.

The news shook the confidence of many Haloid board members and executives, including Dessauer. Wilson recognized the failure, but insisted to his colleagues that the real mistake would be to ignore the lessons of the experience. Users hadn't rejected xerography, only a rather poor attempt to implement it. In Wilson's opinion, the Model A fiasco could guide Haloid's effort to design and produce a better, more commercially acceptable office copier.

Even Wilson was surprised, however, when the Model A also turned out to be a stroke of good luck. In the midst of Wilson's effort to rally Haloid's spirits, a Battelle researcher called to report that someone had discovered a completely unexpected and quite promising application for the awkward machines. The Model A's could produce paper master plates used in high volume offset duplicating, and do it at a fraction of the time and cost required by existing methods. Furthermore, offset technicians, who were comfortable with complexity, were undaunted by the Model A's challenging procedures. Once Haloid announced and demonstrated the offset application, orders for machines began to roll in.

The unexpected use of the Model A was fortuitous. But then no organization, regardless of how creative and innovative, produces a major commercial breakthrough like xerography without some luck. It took Joe Wilson's company *fourteen years* from the day Wilson and Dessauer first looked at Carlson's electrophotography process until the introduction of the Xerox 914 Copier. The Haloid/Xerox people were very fortunate that, throughout those many years, the rest of the world was content to leave existing copying technology and markets unchanged.

It doesn't always happen this way. Often a number of different people and companies identify a technological opportunity more or less at the same time and work in competition to get a product out first. Henry Ford was only one of dozens of mechanically minded inventors hoping to build a business out of horseless carriages. In more recent times, several electronics giants concurrently recognized the chance to create and then market sophisticated home video recording and playback equipment. And personal computer ventures would tell a similar story.

Of course Haloid might have won any such hypothetical race to new copying technology. The point is they never had to worry about it. In part, this happened because Haloid owned the exclusive right to exploit Carlson's patents. But it was also true that no one else was much interested. Many people in both the business and scientific communities knew about the Haloid effort; some were even asked to participate. Unlike Joe Wilson, none of them saw enough promise in copying to invest the effort necessary to create any meaningful competition for xerography.

Still, fourteen years is a long time to hold body, soul, and organization together in pursuit of anything. And it is manifoldly more difficult when, as in the case of xerography and Haloid, the goal is unrelated to the existing business of the company trying to achieve it. By contrast, the classic entrepreneur starts out fresh. Henry Ford, for example, could pursue his vision of mass produced automobiles without having first to convince fellow executives and employees—already engaged in some other profitable activity—to pin their fortunes on his ambitions.

In this respect, Joe Wilson had a greater challenge. He not only had to convert a technology into a business, he had to change the organization that would do it. Haloid had been in the photographic supply business for half a century. Its employees had good jobs and futures in a field they knew and understood. To them, xerography was as novel a concept as it was to the rest of the world.

Wilson deliberately risked Haloid's established business for his office copier dream. Under his directive, Haloid spent $75 million on the development of the 914 Copier, more money than total company profits for the 1950s combined. Many at the company —from the board level on down—had doubts about the wisdom of Wilson's investment. To maintain their good will and constructive participation in his crusade, Wilson had to demonstrate consistently and persuasively that he knew what he wanted and how to get it, and that, while he willingly risked the past for the future, he still cared about the photographic supply business and the people who operated it.

In other words, Wilson had to *lead* a transformation at Haloid based on xerography. For him to succeed, his commitment had to be total, his business judgment unerring, and his faith absolute. As one Haloid veteran of the period said, "Xerography went through many stages in its development at which any sane management committee would have been justified in turning it down. There always had to be something extralogical about continuing."

In Jack Goldman's estimation, that element of faith distinguished the history of Haloid from the management of Ford. Nothing extralogical could survive the Ford tyranny of accountants. During his thirteen years at the car company, Goldman had built a first-class, nationally recognized research center that produced a variety of intriguing inventions including advanced work on fuel cells and the all-electric car. Nevertheless, Goldman's ambition to inspire the rest of Ford remained unfulfilled; financial people repeatedly passed up opportunities to transform his laboratory's inventions into innovations. The rejections left him as closed minded about financial analysts as he accused them of being toward nonnumeric, qualitative considerations.

When a headhunter told Goldman in 1968 about John Dessauer's intention to step down from the top research job at Xerox, Goldman wasted no time in getting on a plane to Rochester to meet Peter McColough. A year and a half earlier the same recruiter had suggested to Goldman that he consider a position reporting to Dessauer, but he wasn't interested. He wanted to be part of top management, to have, unlike at Ford, some voice in the decisions affecting the fate of research.

This time McColough told Goldman everything he hoped to hear. Xerox would become a world class company by repeating the success of xerography in other areas. In each case, McColough said, the strategy would turn on pursuing an innovation powerful enough to challenge entrenched industry leaders. As Dessauer's replacement, Goldman would become a board member and a key decision-maker on McColough's team.

McColough threw down his offer like a gauntlet. "Peter told me," says Goldman, " 'It's your head on the block, not mine. If I don't get the results I expect, your head is in the noose and I will be the hangman.' " It was the kind of tough talk the brassy and optimistic Goldman loved. The Xerox job meant money, stature, power—all of consequence to the Brooklyn-born son of immigrants. But most important, Peter McColough seemed to be a man of action who, like Goldman himself, was determined to work change in the world.

Goldman said yes to McColough and soon after called John Dessauer to arrange a visit to Xerox's research laboratory in Webster, New York, just outside of Rochester. Xerox's newly appointed research chief couldn't wait to meet the scientists and engineers who had pioneered xerography. And he was itching to find out how the Webster lab, among the country's ten best funded corporate research centers, utilized one of the world's newest scientific tools—the computer.

The first electronic digital computer was completed by an Army funded University of Pennsylvania team in 1945. At a hundred feet long, ten feet high, and three feet deep, and containing more than 100,000 separate components, the machine was as inelegant as its name, the Electronic Numerical Integrator and Calculator (ENIAC). Although unreliable, the ENIAC represented an acceptable solution to a dilemma that had vexed scientists and engineers for centuries: how to relieve the time and drudgery of complex or repetitive arithmetic calculations.

Before 1945, most attempts at this puzzle relied on analog, not digital, technology. Analog machines operate by measuring output as an unbroken, progressive reflection of input. Thus, for example, the speed of an automobile is continuously and completely analogous to the force applied to its gas and brake pedals. The most famous analog computer was one of the earliest, the slide rule invented in 1632. By matching number to length, the slide rule took advantage of the laws of logarithms to ease the pain of multiplication and division, adding lengths of sticks for the former, subtracting them for the latter. Subsequent analog inventions employed weight, volume, and voltage, in addition to length, to measure out answers to problems of calculation.

But two inherent limitations condemned analog computing devices. First, most analog computers were designed to solve specific mathematical tasks and either had no relevance to, or performed poorly on, other kinds of questions. For example, a slide rule would hinder, not help, someone totaling a grocery bill for dozens of items. Second, analog machines were imprecise. Output measuring input may work perfectly in theory, but in practice the calibrations on the device must have a finite limit to be readable. Again, the slide rule illustrates the difficulty. If the logarithms required by a particular multiplication fall somewhere in between the markings on the instrument, then the person solving the problem has to estimate the answer.

For computing, digital technology was superior to analog. The digital power source is a clocklike generator that dispatches bursts of electricity with each beat. Thus, instead of comparing number to length or weight or degree of turn, the digital method treats value the same way people do—one unit at a time. Tick tock. Tick tock. Tick tock. High voltage. Low voltage. High voltage. Low voltage. High voltage. Low voltage. One. Two. Three. Four. Five. Six.

This makes digital computers precise. Problem solving flexibility followed when one of the ENIAC's creators discovered that he could change the nature of the task to be calculated by rewriting the computer's instruction program (software) rather than having to redesign and rebuild the machine itself (hardware).

Like the ENIAC, the first commercially available computers were room sized, finicky, and expensive. But their reputation as powerful calculators spread rapidly. At Ford, Jack Goldman saw computers dramatically improve the working habits and productivity of the auto maker's scientists and engineers. He remembers that, when the new technology was first introduced, many people were uneasy, even afraid; by the time he left Ford, however, Goldman says his biggest job was fighting off requests for more and better computers.

Goldman did not expect Ford's appreciation of computers to be more advanced than that of "hi tech" Xerox. It was.

"In the course of my initial visit to Webster," he says, "I asked the man running the lab for Dessauer, 'What kind of computer facilities do you have here?' He answered, 'I don't really know. I guess we get time on the finance department's UNIVAC.' It was clear they had very little understanding of the world of digital technology. That was shocking to me!"

Webster's computer gap was Goldman's first surprise at Xerox; the news about the SDS acquisition was the second. He knew about McColough's determination to get digital capability for Xerox. Indeed, after his experience at the Webster lab, he'd encouraged it. But he had not expected his new boss to act either so soon or so secretively. Only a few months earlier, McColough had told Goldman he would be part of the senior management team at the company. Now Xerox announced the biggest acquisition in its history, in a field in which it had virtually no experience, and Goldman had been excluded from the councils making the move.

"Here I was," he exclaimed, "the chief technical officer of the corporation, and no one even told me what was going on until after the fact. Not that I could have evaluated the technical promise of SDS. My stock in trade was that I knew everyone in the world. It's not my brilliance that could have shown them the right thing to do, but I could network. It wouldn't have been any problem for me to get analyses about SDS from any number of experts on the potential of the company. But I wasn't asked."

How Peter McColough could have spent over $900 million of Xerox stock to buy a computer company without consulting his top scientist was a good question. Goldman, however, chose not to dwell on it, figuring that, as the new boy on the block, he wasn't quite in yet on the big decisions. Instead, he fastened on a pair of more optimistic implications of the acquisition.

Investing over ninety times earnings in a small, second-tier firm in an industry dominated by a monopolist never could be justified by Ford-style financial analysis. The ex-Ford finance and administration men who had joined Xerox in the late sixties must not have had the same control over policy in Rochester that their brethren did in Detroit. Clearly, McColough was the boss at Xerox, and the Bunyanesque bill for SDS reinforced Goldman's impression that McColough used more than numbers to make important decisions. Contrary to Ford, chutzpah apparently still counted for something at Xerox.

Furthermore, Goldman interpreted the SDS move as a strong signal by McColough to Xerox that computers would be as much a part of the company's future as copiers had been of its past. To pull it off would require major innovation grounded in fundamental research. Just as Wilson and Dessauer had changed Haloid with xerography, McColough and Goldman could now lead a digital transformation of Xerox. So instead of bemoaning his exclusion from the SDS decision, Goldman went to McColough and recommended the investment in a new research center. He was not at all surprised when McColough gave him a green light.

Chapter

3

A half dozen major items crowded Peter McColough's management agenda in early 1970. In addition to approving Jack Goldman's research proposal, McColough had followed the billion dollar SDS acquisition by transplanting Xerox's corporate headquarters from New York to Connecticut, ordering company lawyers to prepare a patent infringement suit against the anticipated IBM copier, directing SDS to alter its basic business strategy, and setting a company-wide target of $10 billion in revenues by 1980. It was a lot to ask.

Many at Xerox mistrusted their CEO's enthusiasm for change. Protecting the copier franchise made sense to them; diversifying into noncopier businesses did not. "If you're talking about diversification," went one typical opinion, "we are diversified in the best possible way. We do business with every industry in the country. If any one of them—or any ten of them—falls into a period of recession, we've still got all the others to deal with. Can you be more diversified than that?"

McColough readily countered such opinions. The copying industry might be recession proof, but Xerox would not monopolize it forever. Filed patent applications indicated that IBM's copier introduction was imminent. Furthermore, it was common knowledge in Rochester that Kodak engineers, just across town from Xerox, were developing a copying machine as well. While Xerox might hinder IBM and Kodak with legal challenges, the company's patent protection ultimately would have to expire. And when it did, competition was bound to reduce Xerox's 95 percent share of the plain paper copying market. Therefore, McColough's brief for diversification concluded, the company should prepare to offset any decline in copier employment and earnings with growth in noncopier businesses.

But while the logic against diversification was shallow, the emotional objections ran deep. Xerox was profoundly a copier company. For example, after introducing the 914 Copier, the company modified its correspondence format by replacing the traditional "cc" indicating one or more "carbon copies" of a letter or memorandum with an "xc" for "xerographic copies." Later, with the widespread adoption of xerography, Xerox went to the single "c"; "xc" being considered redundant. "Xerox" literally meant "copy" at Xerox. It was more than a matter of English usage. It reflected the corporation's underlying value structure.

Xerox's education, medical, and computer activities were popularly referred to inside the company as the "noncopier" businesses, and being defined by a negative frustrated their managers. McColough heard the grumbling. "Look," they'd say, "unless we work in Rochester we're second-class citizens. We don't get the same capital considerations for expansion. We don't get the same promotion opportunities." McColough hoped to dispel their concerns about fairness by transferring corporate headquarters to Stamford, Connecticut. He also wanted to send a message to the copier division that Xerox was more than a one-product company.

The symbolism of the headquarters move, however, contended with the reality of Xerox's bottom line. In 1969, worldwide copier revenues exceeded a billion dollars. By contrast, Xerox's largest diversification program before SDS, the Education Group, had yet to reach $100 million in sales. Furthermore, the copier business continued to grow at double digit rates, making it that much harder for the company's other enterprises to find their way out of financial footnotes and small print.

McColough expected SDS to correct the imbalance. "Our financial projections for Scientific Data Systems," he later wrote to Xerox board members, "showed their revenues growing from $101 million in 1968 to $330–400 [million] in 1973 for a compound growth rate of 27–32 percent. Net income was expected to grow at a similar rate." That kind of performance, in his opinion, required SDS to reshape the narrow strategy that had made it a winning company, a message he quickly conveyed to SDS's management. "These guys," says an engineer who worked with SDS throughout the period, "knew clearly that SDS had not been purchased to be a scientific computer company, but to help make Xerox into a large scale 'information' company. Xerox wanted to go head to head with IBM."

IBM dominated the computer industry in 1970, holding more than 70 percent of the market. They hadn't been the first computer company; that distinction went to Remington Rand in 1951 when it combined with the ENIAC's inventors to bring out a computer called the UNIVAC. But when IBM's first computer was introduced two years later, it rapidly took control of the business.

IBM's triumph was no accident. For decades, the company had monopolized the market for automated bookkeeping systems. In the competition to replace such electromechanical systems with computers, IBM had several advantages. First, it had a nationwide sales force already serving most of the customers looking to buy computers. Second, unlike Remington Rand and other newcomers, it already understood how to automate record keeping. Third, IBM (as Xerox did with copiers) leased instead of sold its equipment. Long after the machinery had paid for itself, rent checks kept rolling in, making it possible for IBM to finance computer development with interest free funds provided by customers instead of expensive money obtained from banks or other lenders.

Moreover, IBM exclusively controlled punch card equipment. Computers had threatened IBM's position because they far surpassed IBM's electromechanical tabulators in speed, accuracy, and versatility. But the new digital technology still relied on punch cards to input data and instructions. As a result, IBM could price its punch card equipment high and its computers low, relying on the profitability of the former to subsidize the introduction of the latter.

With all these advantages, IBM converted one monopoly into another. Perhaps unfairly so. In 1969, the U.S. Department of Justice filed a major antimonopoly suit against IBM. By then, however, it was too late for most companies that had tried to compete head on with IBM. For example, after a decade of trying, neither RCA nor GE had ever turned a single year's profit in the computer business. Within twenty-four months of the Justice Department action, each pulled out of the competition.

The computer companies that prospered did so by avoiding IBM. Some, like Digital Equipment Corporation, pioneered smaller, less expensive systems called minicomputers. Others marketed so-called "IBM compatible peripherals"—equipment and accessories that worked with IBM mainframe computers, but were cheaper or faster than the same items offered by IBM itself. Still others, like Scientific Data Systems, bypassed the commercial data processing segment dominated by IBM and sold to technical markets.

Scientists and engineers, unlike accountants, had no historic dependence on IBM, which put SDS on a fairer footing against the computer giant. Also, scientists and engineers wrote their own software. That freed SDS from the expense of programming, education, and support required to service commercial accounts. Finally, scientific computer applications did not require the full panoply of equipment found in corporate data processing centers. For SDS, fewer products meant fewer financial, production, inventory, and marketing burdens.

SDS's niche strategy worked nicely. But selling to scientists and engineers would not advance McColough's goal of transforming Xerox into a great communications company. After Xerox shareholders officially approved the acquisition in May of 1969, their chief executive immediately directed SDS to tackle the commercial segment of the computer market. "There was a goal," McColough said, "to try to see if we couldn't reach the No. 2 position in the industry."

The failure of GE, RCA, and others to compete across the board with IBM did not frighten McColough. Unlike them, Xerox had the cash-generating lease base, sales force, and customer relationships to match IBM. Furthermore, if Jack Goldman's proposed research center excelled, Xerox might get the chance to seize the initiative from IBM by rewriting the rules of where and how to compete for computer customers.

In the late sixties, computers came in two sizes, big and giant. They occupied so-called "back offices" where they counted, sorted, and calculated for those trained to operate and understand them. The technology, however, had little relevance to the communications environment Xerox knew best: the front offices of sales forces, production managers, finance and planning personnel, secretaries, and executives. McColough expected the reach of computers to expand, and he wanted Xerox research to lead the way.

In March of 1970, McColough scheduled a speech to The New York Society of Security Analysts in order to publicize the aggressive goals he'd set for Xerox and SDS. Joe Wilson had kicked off the copier crusade in front of the same body, and perhaps McColough hoped a similar beginning would produce a comparable ending.

Not surprisingly, he started the speech with a reference to Wilson. "Some of you," said the forty-seven-year-old CEO of Xerox, "probably remember a presentation made before this group in December of 1961 which began with an odd question: How high the moon?"

McColough recalled for the analysts that, at the time Wilson made the earlier speech, the Xerox office copier boom had just begun. Revenues and profits in 1961 were still well under $100 million and $10 million respectively. Nevertheless, the optimistic Wilson had concluded his address by asking, "Should our objective be to attain a billion dollars? Why not?"

McColough proudly reminded his audience that Wilson and Xerox had met and exceeded that target. He then proceeded to discuss the continuing importance of xerography, the company's forays into education, and its international operations—none of which, however, had brought the overflow crowd to the auditorium. Ten months had passed since Xerox, in the first major transaction under McColough's leadership, had swapped over 15 percent of its common stock for Scientific Data Systems. Wall Street considered the move controversial, and the analysts wanted to find out just what Peter McColough had in mind.

He obliged them. Success in copiers, McColough explained, had made it inevitable that Xerox would enter the computer business because both copiers and computers served the same ultimate demand for better, faster, and more powerful means to develop and communicate information. Yet, of the two technologies— copiers and computers—the latter clearly represented the larger opportunity. By the end of the decade, McColough noted, computer industry revenues would exceed $40 billion.

SDS was to be Xerox's ticket to participate in all that bounty. Furthermore, McColough stressed, the largest and fastest growing slice of the computer industry was in commercial data processing. Consequently, he announced that, while SDS would continue to sell to the scientific and engineering communities, the primary objective of Xerox's new computer subsidiary would be to establish a strong position in the business markets. And he confidently declared that SDS would be well supported in its new strategy by Xerox's marketing experience, Xerox's commitment, and Xerox's tremendous resources—the most precious of which was research.

"At Xerox," McColough continued, "R&D *has been, is,* and *will be* a way of life. Our company already owes much to the prompt exploitation of new technology." He then announced that Xerox would invest part of its $100 million annual research budget in a corporate laboratory devoted to discovering how digital technology and basic science could strengthen the company's role in computers and information processing.

"Knowledge," McColough told the analysts, "has already been projected as an industry in its own right, wrapped in the assurances of endless growth and self-renewing opportunity. But while it's easy to see 'the knowledge explosion' as a supreme tool, we too seldom see it as a potential tyrant.

"The hard reality, however, is that in attempting to gather, process, absorb, and disseminate information and knowledge today, we find ourselves living more and more in the confusion of tied-up telephones, computer printout, procedure manuals, stacked airplaines, unnecessary correspondence, meetings, mail, memoranda, and aging files marked 'Must Read.' " McColough might have added, but didn't, copies and copies and still more copies of several of the items on his list.

To him, information was part tale-bearer, part tumor. Making it truly useful to decision makers required the invention of tools to sort it out, organize it, and communicate it in timely and pertinent ways. In McColough's opinion, the office of 1980 would hardly resemble the one of 1970.

With that in mind, Xerox's chief executive articulated an extraordinary vision for his company and the world: "The basic purpose of Xerox Corporation is to find the best means to bring greater order and discipline to information. Thus our fundamental thrust, our common denominator, has evolved toward establishing leadership in what we call 'the architecture of information.'

"What we seek is to think of information itself as a natural and undeveloped environment which can be enclosed and made more habitable for the people who live and work within it.

"At the moment, of course, our purpose is still basically a concept. We are only now beginning to engage it; and it is no easy task. Undoubtedly, we'll find obstacles we've never encountered before and we'll make some mistakes. Yet today even a casual examination of Xerox reveals that we already have most of the raw materials of advanced architecture of information technology: computers, copiers, duplicators, microfilm, communications devices, education techniques, display and transmission systems, graphic and optic capabilities, heavy research, and global scope.

"Just think for a moment of combining those raw materials with the talents of some 55,000 people throughout the world. Can we conclude that the next decade at Xerox might be even more constructive than the last?"

Recalling Joe Wilson's how-high-the-moon speech once more, McColough declared, "The question may be different, but the answer is the same. Why not?"

Research:
The
Creation
of the
Alto

Chapter

4

*I*n 1970, "architecture of information" was elegant and inspirational phraseology. But what did it mean? According to a senior engineer then at Xerox, "McColough said that Xerox would tackle the question of how information is organized and how it works. There was no possibility that he knew or could know in business detail, market detail, or technical detail what that would encompass. Maybe he meant this, or maybe he meant that. McColough did exactly what he intended to do—set the climate and focus of discussion and initiative for the company."

The opening move belonged to research. A few months before McColough's speech, Jack Goldman recruited a long-standing acquaintance of his named George Pake to set up and manage the proposed Xerox research center. While Goldman could, and would, continue to speak at corporate headquarters on behalf of the effort he'd inspired, he had too many responsibilities as the company's chief scientist to operate the facility himself. He had to find someone else for that job, and Pake was his first choice.

Pake, like Goldman, was a physicist with limited understanding of computers or computer science. That didn't bother Goldman. Years of directing research at Ford had convinced him that managing a laboratory differed from conducting the research itself. The issues facing digital technology could be learned; the wisdom to choose the most promising projects and researchers could not. And he had tremendous confidence in Pake's judgment. "I had known George since we were youngsters together; we worked on our first jobs at Westinghouse during the War. He'd left Westinghouse to finish his Ph.D. at Harvard, but we were in related fields and remained friends. Pake was a formidable force in nuclear magnetic resonance, and I had a lot of regard for him and a lot of respect."

In 1969, after a long and distinguished academic career as a scholar and an administrator, George Pake was ready for a change. A mild mannered person who loathes confrontation, Pake had spent several years on the front lines of campus unrest during the 1960s, leaving him, in his word, fatigued. He resigned that summer as provost and executive vice-chancellor of Washington University in St. Louis, intending a return to academic research. But to Pake's surprise, Ford offered him the job Goldman had vacated. He refused.

Goldman had been thrilled to learn that Pake was considering a jump from academia to industry. Once Pake said no to Ford, Goldman acted quickly. With a flourish that impressed the professor, he hopped on a corporate jet and flew to St. Louis for an afternoon of hard selling. He described the extraordinary Xerox legacy of growth through research and innovation, a tradition he hoped Pake would help him perpetuate. The most urgent task, Goldman pitched, was to invent the information systems and technologies that Peter McColough expected to drive Xerox into the 1980s. Pake would get to build a multimillion dollar research center. From scratch. And, Goldman contended, with Xerox funding and Pake's leadership, the center someday was sure to compare to the legendary Bell Labs.

"I conveyed to him very seriously," recalls Goldman, "that this was not Ford, and Xerox meant business. That it wanted to enter a new field foreign to Xerox but a very important one for us, and that he was the guy to do it."

Pake agreed to meet McColough, who charmed the former provost. "I was in love with university life," recalls Pake. "It was a big struggle to leave the academic world. But I also knew this was a once in a lifetime opportunity to start a new research group for an enlightened institution. Peter McColough played a big part in my decision. Xerox had a solid tradition of supporting research, and McColough seemed to understand it very well and believe in it. When I told McColough and Goldman that it would take between five and ten years to get any results, neither one of them blanched at all. McColough just really seemed to understand that you don't get quick payoffs from research."

What Pake considered "enlightened" was indeed an atypical business attitude toward research. Many corporations have no research budgets at all. In others, what's called "research and development" is mostly the latter. Laboratory work is circumscribed by near-term marketing objectives rather than challenged by broad strategic goals like those described to Pake by Goldman and McColough. According to Goldman, "Nine out of ten research laboratories in the American industrial scheme operate from the top down. Orders come from the top, and the research director's role is to assign missions to each of the groups and tell them what they've got to do."

Both Goldman and Pake favor the inverse vector. "Bottom up," says Goldman, "is the only sensible research philosophy if you want to get the very good people. The ground rules ought to be as free and easy as possible. Tell them the overall goals, but then let them tell you what they have to do."

Pake agrees. "Little success," he notes, "is likely to come from showing researchers to a laboratory, describing in detail a desired technology or process not now existent, and commanding: 'Invent!' "

McColough's visionary language fit the Goldman-Pake research philosophy perfectly. Copiers aside, most front office technology—typewriters, rotary telephones, adding machines, dictaphones, pencils, pens, and paper—had not changed for decades. Since neither Xerox nor any company offered a system of interrelated products to manage information in the office, there were no near-term product or marketing objectives to influence Pake's center. Solving the mystery of an "architecture of information" *had* to depend on the ideas and insights of the researchers themselves.

The lone objection to the plan was made by Scientific Data Systems. To them, devoting resources to nonexistent products was wasteful, especially in light of McColough's dictate that SDS break into the commercial data processing field. To succeed against IBM, SDS would need all the resources it could muster. SDS pointed out that such advances in computing as the transistor and integrated circuit were made by components suppliers, not mainframe computer companies. According to Goldman, "The SDS people all said, 'Why spend money on something like that. You should give the money to us. We could make another mainframe computer product, get it out to the marketplace, and turn some profits.' "

SDS's position caught Goldman off guard. How could a company selling computers to scientists and engineers pooh-pooh basic research? In his formal proposal to McColough, Goldman described a research center with three separate laboratories, one of which would "reflect the long range requirements and desires of the SDS division and also focus on systems of potential corporate interest in which the computer is a key ingredient." But building another mainframe computer, even a bigger, faster, more powerful one, was not in the plan.

McColough sided with Goldman. Buoyed by top management's support, Goldman and Pake turned to finding a location for the center. Earlier, Goldman had rejected the possibility of combining it with the Xerox research facility in Webster, New York. In his opinion, Webster's laboratory manager was too weak, its scientists were too narrow, and its location in upstate New York was too remote to attract and keep the talent Pake needed. Goldman and Pake also considered El Segundo, California, the headquarters of SDS, but dismissed it because, despite McColough's decision, the computer division continued to protest long range research.

In the end, their list narrowed to New Haven and Palo Alto, with Goldman partial to the former, Pake the latter. Before hiring Pake, Goldman had recommended New Haven to McColough.· "If the new research center is too isolated from a Xerox environment and Xerox thinking," he'd written, "the chances of relevant coupling to Xerox's needs and practices will be severely diminished." In the same memo, he had added that "one area normally considered as an ideal research environment, Palo Alto, is eliminated only because of the absence of any nearby major Xerox facility."

But Pake put Palo Alto back in the contest. He knew the community well, having taught at Stanford University in the late 1950s. He pointed out that the number of semiconductor and other computer related enterprises then springing up in the Santa Clara Valley around Palo Alto almost certainly would grow, providing Xerox research with dependable vendors, experienced scientists, and an intellectually rich and relevant environment.

Goldman yielded; it was Pake's lab, after all, not his. And in June of 1970, the two physicists opened the doors of the Xerox Palo Alto Research Center, the acronym for which—"PARC"— was coined by the competitive Goldman to match the name of Eastman Kodak Park, a research facility in Rochester.

With the site issue settled, Pake could begin his computer education. He arranged a tour of the nation's foremost university departments of computer science. "I spoke to leading professors, asking their opinions on what the major research issues of the day were and who among the top people in the field might be attracted to PARC to fill significant research roles." As he listened, he learned that the most advanced work in computers was being funded by an arm of the Defense Department called the Advanced Research Projects Administration, or ARPA.

ARPA had, in fact, supported a Washington University computer research program that Pake had courted away from M.I.T. when he was provost. The director of that project recommended that Pake speak with Bob Taylor, the chief administrator of ARPA computer funding during the last half of the 1960s. Pake figured Taylor would be a good source to tap, especially for names. What George Pake could not have divined was that Bob Taylor had pledged his life to redefining the world of computers.

Taylor was born in Texas during the Depression, the only child of a Methodist minister. "Back then," he remarks, "people believed they were called to the ministry. So I grew up assuming that whatever you did as a vocation had to have that kind of dedication under it." His search for a worthy cause took him through a start-and-stop college career that surrounded a stint in the Navy and ended with a master's degree in psychology. Taylor still was looking when, in 1961, he joined the recently formed National Aeronautics and Space Administration as manager of a digital research budget. In Washington, he met a man named J.C.R. Licklider and learned about Licklider's campaign to advance a concept in computer science called "interactivity." It took little time before it occurred to Taylor that "This was it!"

J.C.R. Licklider and interactivity dominated a movement in the early 1960s to make computers operate in "real time." Automobiles, bicycles, blenders, lawn mowers, telephones, typewriters —they all functioned in real time because they responded instantaneously to people. But not, as fast as they were, computers.

Computers operated in a mode called batch processing. Programmers worked remotely, both in time and space, from the machines. After coding the instructions and data to be processed, the programmer had it keypunched on paper tape or, more typically, on specially designed IBM cards. Next he ran the tape or cards through a printer, proofread the printout for any keypunching errors, and, assuming no mistakes were found, submitted his input to official operators who had exclusive authority to run the expensive equipment. These officials scheduled a time for the job. It could be the same day; it could be later. When the appointed hour came, barring any folds, spindles, or mutilations, the cards raced through the computer, the instructions and data were processed, and the results printed out.

Changes in computer programming are commonplace. But with batch processing, people could figure out their next steps only after decoding the printout, an exercise taking hours, sometimes days, to complete. To try out the modifications, the programmer had to repeat the entire coding—keypunching—printing—proofing—submitting—scheduling—running—printing—decoding batch process. Read that again: coding—keypunching—printing—proofing—submitting—scheduling—running—printing—decoding. Painful.

The arrangement promoted bad feelings. By 1960, a number of computer experts were complaining, not because secretaries, executives, students, and parents were excluded from the digital world, but because they—the trained programmers, scientists, and engineers—could not interact with computers when and how they wanted.

J.C.R. Licklider, a psychology professor at M.I.T., was their chief spokesman. In a 1960 article entitled "Man-Computer Symbiosis," Licklider argued that the principal function of computers ought to be improving human thought. Yet batch processing machines operated before and after, not during, the thought process itself. While people thought, computers waited; while computers processed, people waited; while people thought again, computers waited.

"One of the main aims of man-computer symbiosis," Licklider wrote, "is to bring the computing machine effectively into the formulative parts of technical problems. The other main aim is closely related. It is to bring computing machines effectively into processes of thinking that must go on in 'real time,' time that moves too fast to permit using computers in conventional ways. Imagine trying, for example, to direct a battle with the aid of a computer on such a schedule as this. You formulate your problem today. Tomorrow you spend with a programmer. Next week the computer devotes 5 minutes to assembling your program and 47 seconds to calculating the answer to your problem. You get a sheet of paper 20 feet long, full of numbers that, instead of providing a final solution, only suggest a tactic that should be explored by simulation. Obviously, the battle would be over before the second step in its planning was begun. To think in interaction with a computer in the same way that you think with a colleague whose competence supplements your own will require much tighter coupling between man and machine than is suggested by the example and is possible today."

A few years after publishing "Man-Computer Symbiosis," Licklider found himself in a powerful position to promote interactivity. The Kennedy administration, convinced that normal government bureaucracy would strangle the research needed to beat the Russians in the space race, set up a new division of the Defense Department called the Advanced Research Projects Administration. ARPA had unprecedented freedom to select and fund research. And ARPA's director hired Licklider to manage the agency's computer arm, the Information Processing Techniques Office (IPTO).

Once in Washington, Licklider immediately promoted timesharing, an innovation many computerists counted on to remedy the pain of batch processing. The premise for timesharing was ingenious. Yes, computers were far too expensive to interact in real time with any single user. But computers also processed information much faster than human beings. Programmers didn't require *uninterrupted* access to a machine; they just needed interruptions measured in seconds and minutes instead of hours and days. If timesharing hardware and software could make a computer *switch back and forth* rapidly among many different programs, computers would appear to their slower human partners as though they were interacting with each of them alone. Instead of the waiting game played in batch processing, timesharing could put programmers *on-line* with computers.

Bob Taylor was at NASA when Licklider started ARPA's Information Processing Techniques Office. He became a follower of Licklider's and an advocate of interactivity. Although he did not have the technical training to conduct research himself, he closely studied the progress of timesharing and soon gained a sophisticated feel for the future of digital technology. When Licklider returned to the university, Taylor happily accepted an offer to become the associate director of IPTO under Licklider's successor, Ivan Sutherland. Then, in 1965, Sutherland left, and the Reverend Taylor's thirty-three-year-old son took charge of the world's largest governmental budget for advanced computer research. Bob Taylor had found his calling.

Taylor's great objective was to bury the conventional notion that computers could compute only numbers and data. As he put it, "I've never been particularly interested in the computer as an arithmetic engine. What really interests me is the computer as a medium for people to externalize their ideas, observe them, and communicate them."

He defined communication as "cooperative modeling," the process of sharing thoughts in order to identify differences, enhance creativity, and reach consensus. "Cooperative modeling" works best when people have pen and paper, chalk and blackboard, or some other means to capture and communicate what they are thinking. In the late 1960s, Taylor was convinced that future computer systems would surpass other methods of communication because they would have the graphic richness of pen and paper, the informative depth of libraries, and the instantaneous reach of telephones.

Telephones, for example, facilitate only talking, not drawing, writing, or painting. But at the time Taylor took charge of ARPA's Information Processing Techniques Office, telephones had one major advantage over computers—long distance communication. By contrast, people were forced to move information between computers the same way they moved a book—by carrying it. The hardware and software essential to electronic transmission, whether down the hall or across the country, did not exist.

After Taylor became director of IPTO, he funded several computer communications projects and eventually hired a man named Larry Roberts to coordinate them. Roberts, along with a few other computer scientists in England and the United States, had devised a technology called "message switching" to overcome the main obstacles to computer-to-computer communications. When he was certain that message switching was the right answer, Roberts engaged a private firm to build what became known (and still exists) as the "ARPAnet," the first nationwide computer communications network.

At IPTO, Taylor had wide latitude to back whatever research he wanted. "Our rule of thumb was to fund people who had a good chance of advancing the state of information processing technology by an order of magnitude." Immediate relevance to the Defense Department was the exception, not the rule. Nonetheless, on one occasion, Taylor was asked to improve the military's computer systems in Vietnam, an experience, he says, that led to his resignation from ARPA.

"At the time," Taylor recalls, "each of the armed services used a different computer system to manage and report the status of their materials and supplies in Vietnam. The Administration was concerned about the confusion and lack of control over purchasing and deployment, and President Johnson asked the Defense Department if there was anything that could be done to fix it. The Defense Department asked ARPA the same thing, and the head of ARPA turned to me for help.

"I went to Saigon, and eventually funded a study team to build a common inventory management system, and to design some local hardware facilities to process it. I made several trips over to Vietnam. By the time we were finished, they had a working system. But it also educated me about Vietnam, a civil war in which we had no business. I got discouraged. By '69 the ARPAnet had three nodes up and running. I had recruited Larry Roberts to set up and complete it, and I knew ARPAnet would work out with Larry as my successor. So I knew it was time to leave."

Taylor took a job at the University of Utah, where, in 1970, George Pake contacted him about getting advice on the Xerox research effort. They arranged for Taylor to fly to Palo Alto to talk with Pake and one of his associates, Bill Gunning. At the start of the meeting, Pake explained to Taylor that PARC would have three separate laboratories: the General Science Laboratory (GSL), the Systems Science Laboratory (SSL), and the Computer Science Laboratory (CSL).

In addition to directing PARC as a whole, Pake said he would manage the work of GSL, which was to conduct research in basic sciences like physics. Gunning was the manager of SSL with a charter covering "systems" in the broadest sense—mathematical, statistical, operations, engineering, and information. With respect to information systems, SSL's purpose appeared to overlap the intended focus of the Computer Science Laboratory to study computer systems in particular. CSL had no manager yet.

"I asked Pake what this new computer group was going to do," Taylor recalls. "He said the new lab would do research in support of the long range needs of SDS. When I told Pake I thought that was unfortunate, he asked, 'Why?' "

Pake's question sounded naïve to Taylor, who contemptuously thought of SDS as "ironmongers" and "not a systems company in any sense." He'd formed his low opinion years before Xerox purchased SDS. While at ARPA, Taylor had funded a Berkeley, California, effort called Project Genie that converted an SDS batch processing computer into a timesharing system. At the time, computer companies hadn't begun selling timesharing machines, and Taylor had known of several customers interested in owning the Project Genie system. Accordingly, he arranged to meet SDS's chairman Max Palevsky to propose that SDS go into the timesharing business. Palevsky, however, was apparently content with his company's existing product strategy, and his meeting with Taylor was a disaster.

"I started talking to Max," Taylor says, "about interactive computing, and timesharing. SDS had done quite well with batch mode computer systems for engineering and scientific applications, and Palevsky basically said that timesharing wasn't going to sell, and that he wasn't interested in it. I asked him if he had been to Project Genie, and seen their results, but it became clear he wasn't interested in timesharing. The argument got heated. I was really teed off at the obstinance of the guy. We couldn't even have a rationally based disagreement. So I all but threw him out of the office."

Taylor and others ultimately did persuade SDS to sell the system, called the SDS 940, but SDS never committed itself to the engineering, software, manufacturing, and marketing investments required to excel in timesharing. As a result, when the company brought out a successor to the 940 system, it bombed. In Taylor's words, "From the standpoint of someone who believed interactive computing was the wave of the future, SDS had blown it."

In trying to explain to Pake why supporting SDS with research would be a mistake, Taylor said, "I didn't think any of the peer scientists I knew were interested in problems that SDS was going to be interested in, and therefore, that of the people I knew, he wasn't going to be able to recruit any of the really top-notch computer scientists to come here and work under that kind of umbrella."

Pake asked him what CSL ought to be doing, if not supporting SDS. The answer sounded like a prescription for McColough's "architecture of information," and it came from a man knowing who and how to fill it: "I told him I thought Xerox was in a great position. They had a market presence in most offices in the world, at least in the large companies. They were using analog technology for their products, and there was an opportunity to apply digital technology to more functions that occur in offices than just copying. And there was even an opportunity to apply it to copying as well. It seemed to me that Xerox could emerge, over time, from being a copier company to being in office information systems. However, since they did not have the technology, that seemed to me what PARC ought to do."

Taylor left Palo Alto with mixed emotions. He doubted Pake's grasp of the technical challenge facing Xerox and was certain PARC would never get any good computer talent to work for SDS. Still, as he contemplated the millions of dollars Xerox had budgeted for long range digital research, Taylor couldn't help coveting a number of fantastic possibilities—if only he got the chance to run PARC's computer lab. But Pake hadn't asked him to Palo Alto for a job interview, only to give advice. And even if the meeting at times seemed like an interview, Taylor thought his bluntness about SDS had offended Pake. The chemistry just did not seem right between them.

Taylor's perceptions were partly right, partly wrong. In a pattern that would repeat itself over the next thirteen years, Taylor allowed his obsession for an interactive computing future to block out Pake's genuine interest in gathering first-rate resources at PARC. He construed Pake's imperfect knowledge of computers as an obstacle rather than an opportunity. Consequently, Taylor says he was surprised when, several weeks later, Pake offered him a job at PARC.

Chapter

5

George Pake hired Bob Taylor primarily to help him staff the Computer Science Laboratory at PARC. "Having been in charge of the ARPA research funds for information processing," Pake explains, "Taylor had traveled the country and knew where a lot of the bright people were. He knew the community extremely well. That was the important point." Pake's hope that, through Taylor, Xerox might reel in some of the best computer minds in the nation was realized.

Among the first members of the ARPA research community to hear about Bob Taylor's move to PARC was a colorful computer scientist named Alan Kay. Like many others in the field, Kay was both young and senior; at age thirty he was older than the world's first electronic digital computer by several years. Indeed, when Kay was growing up in the 1950s, "computer scientist" did not exist alongside of lawyer-doctor-teacher as a vocational aspiration. He had to find his own way.

Books and music dominated his childhood. Kay read before he was three and played jazz professionally as a teenager. He also scorned traditional education—although one of television's original "Quiz Kids," he nearly failed the eighth grade. After high school, Kay continued his jazz career, flirted with college, and then joined the Air Force, where he learned how to program computers.

In computers, as in books and music, Kay discovered a wonderful medium for self-expression. After completing his military service, he returned to college, studied mathematics, and, in 1966, was admitted to the recently formed University of Utah graduate program in computer science. He concentrated on interactive computing, regularly attending the annual ARPA graduate student conferences sponsored by Bob Taylor. By 1969, Kay had both his master's and doctorate from Utah and an appointment as associate professor in the school's computer science department.

In his doctoral thesis, Kay described an extraordinary programming language and computing machine called FLEX. FLEX defied all of the barriers to widespread interactive computing: price, required expertise, and functionality. It would be, Kay wrote, "an interactive tool which can aid in the visualization and realization of provocative notions. It must be simple enough so that one does not have to become a systems programmer (one who understands the arcane rites) to use it. It must be cheap enough to be owned (like a grand piano). It must do more than just be able to realize computable functions; it has to be able to form the *abstractions in which the user deals*. FLEX is an idea debugger and, as such, it is hoped that it is also an idea *media*."

Today FLEX sounds like a personal computer; in 1969, its specifications stretched far beyond the practical limits of digital technology. In that respect, Kay's ambition resembled the dream of Charles Babbage, the nineteenth century Englishman who tried unsuccessfully to build what many consider the precursor of the modern computer. Babbage had drawn his insight from a French invention that utilized punch cards to determine woof and warp patterns in an automated weaving loom. Convinced that similar digital means could "weave algebraic patterns," Babbage spent the better part of his life trying to perfect his "Analytical Engine."

Babbage's mind roamed far and wide. Among other things, he is credited with inventing cowcatchers and speedometers, figuring out how to use tree rings to analyze weather cycles, establishing the modern field of operations research, and improving the efficiency of the British postal service. Once, he offered to correct a piece of Alfred, Lord Tennyson's poetry.

The Analytical Engine, however, remains his most famous pursuit. With it, Babbage hoped to punch data and instructions onto cards, input them into a memory bank of registers he called the "store," process the calculations in a "mill," and print out the answers on an automated typesetter. Input, memory, processor, and output—all twentieth century computers, whether personal or otherwise, consist of these fundamental elements.

But after forty years of on again, off again effort, Babbage came up short; he could not effectively harness steam in support of mechanized computation. At the time of his death in 1871, his contemporaries considered him an ingenious failure. Alan Kay thought of him as an unconventional thinker quite comfortable at the far edges of imagination. And in a tribute to Babbage, Kay entitled his thesis about FLEX, "The Reactive Engine."

Bob Taylor admired Kay's originality and asked him to join

PARC. Kay was thrilled for Taylor when he heard about the Xerox research effort. "Utah was not the right ball park for Taylor," says Kay. "He needs a situation where you can have big successes and make big mistakes." Nevertheless, Kay wasn't ready to commit himself to PARC. He had just started a year as visiting lecturer at Stanford's Artificial Intelligence Laboratory and was considering a number of offers to pursue work on his "reactive engine." He did agree to hire on as a consultant.

In addition to Kay, Taylor set his sights on many other stars in the ARPA firmament. He persuaded Xerox to employ several of his University of Utah colleagues, and he approached scientists at Carnegie-Mellon, M.I.T., and other public and private institutions. But of all of his targets, Taylor most wanted to hire Butler Lampson.

At twenty-seven, Lampson was one of the handful of premier computer scientists in the United States. Born to foreign service parents, he had grown up in Turkey and Germany before moving back to the United States to complete high school. He got hooked on computers at Harvard.

"I studied physics at Harvard," says Lampson. "Toward the end of my studies I did quite a bit of programming for a physics professor who wanted to analyze spark-chamber photographs on a PDP-1. When I went to Berkeley to continue studying physics, a very interesting computer research project was going on, but it was well concealed. I found out about it from a friend at a computer conference I attended in San Francisco. He asked me how this project was doing. When I said I'd never heard of it, he told me which unmarked door to go through to find it."

The secret door led Lampson to Project Genie, the ARPA supported timesharing effort that later occasioned Bob Taylor's confrontation with Max Palevsky of SDS. Lampson joined the team, switched from physics to electrical engineering, and thereby initiated what Taylor described twenty years later as "the best track record for innovation in computer science of anyone in the world."

Those who have known, worked with, and learned from Butler Lampson describe him as though he were a work of advanced technology. He has "a very high data rate" according to one; to another, "he lives in a machine going twice as fast as the rest of the world." His mind operates much more rapidly than those of his not-by-any-means-unintelligent peer group. So does his voice. Admirers once invented their own informal measure for voice speed, hypothesizing that no human could speak faster than "1.0 lampsons."

At Project Genie, Lampson designed the operating system software that was essential to convert SDS's batch computer into a timesharing machine. Later, he joined other Project Genie alumni in setting up the Berkeley Computer Corporation, hoping to do what SDS had tried only grudgingly—make and sell timesharing systems.

Taylor regarded Lampson so highly that he suggested Xerox acquire Berkeley Computer Corporation to get Lampson on the research staff at PARC. However, a 1970–1971 downturn in the economy made that unnecessary. The recession hit the computer industry particularly hard, with cutbacks in government and institutional spending hurting most computer manufacturers. Xerox's billion dollar SDS subsidiary lost over $30 million before taxes in each of the two recession years. And there were even more dire consequences for start-up concerns like Berkeley Computer Corporation. Lampson and his partners needed more money to bring their timesharing computer to the marketplace but discovered that venture capital for digital projects had dried up. When Taylor called, BCC was in trouble. Most of its principal scientists and engineers knew they'd soon be looking for other jobs.

Lampson had to worry less about finding employment than about choosing the most attractive offer. Taylor painted him a bright picture. "Bob's pitch," Lampson recalls, "was that Xerox had a lot of resources, and it knew its basic business—stand alone copiers—did not have a long term future. In twenty years the whole office would have become entangled with electronics, and Xerox needed to figure out how to use electronics in the office. Peter McColough had said as much with his 'architecture of information' speech. The fact that Xerox was interested in computer applications for the front office, and not just the back office, also responded to my interest in making computers more useful to people."

In addition, Lampson welcomed the opportunity to work for Taylor. "Taylor is not a technical person," says Lampson. "Nonetheless, he has a remarkably high level of understanding of what is important about computers and what are some of the directions that will be mainstream ten or twenty years down the road." A PARC of Taylor's making could sustain Lampson's own wide ranging technical ambitions. "Bob basically told us that Xerox had a lot of money, they recognized they had a problem, they really wanted to solve the problem, and they believed they had a long time before the problem would become serious. As far as availability of resources, and the stability of it, this was a solid prospect."

Lampson hesitated only with respect to SDS. The El Segundo computer company had so bungled its timesharing opportunity that he doubted whether SDS would welcome, let alone capitalize on, ideas from a Taylor-Lampson computer laboratory. Worse, he feared that SDS might control PARC's budget or priorities.

Taylor told him exactly what he wanted to hear. "Xerox said it wanted us to support SDS, but that was just noise in the system. We believed this would go away from the very beginning because SDS had little to do with the office of the future."

Once Lampson accepted Taylor's offer, the two men turned their attention to selecting others at Berkeley Computer Corporation with enough talent for PARC's Computer Science Laboratory. Among those under consideration was Chuck Thacker, who, like Lampson, was just turning twenty-seven.

Thacker grew up in Los Angeles, the son of an electrical engineer, and he remembers doing "all the things one did in the late fifties—ham radios, et cetera—to prepare for a life in science and technology." He was also, in his words, a "wild kid." Following high school, he nearly flunked out of Cal Tech, then UCLA. By 1963, at the age of twenty, he found himself starting college over again at Berkeley. But a year later he got married, settled down, and began to work steadily toward the physics bachelor of science degree he received in 1967.

In 1968, Thacker took a job as a junior engineer at Project Genie, intending to remain only a short time before returning to graduate school for more work in physics. "I hadn't been real interested in computers, although I did what was necessary for physics. I wanted to do graduate work in particle accelerator design because particle accelerators were big, complicated machines doing exciting things. Of course during my time at Project Genie, I discovered that computers were also big, complicated machines doing exciting things."

Thacker decided to pursue graduate work in electronic engineering instead of physics. But, as he recounts, "I never did go to graduate school. When I changed directions to Double E, I realized all the good Double E profs, like Butler, were off to start BCC. So I joined them."

By the end of 1970, Thacker, like others at BCC, was subject to the fears and hopes triggered by the company's financial difficulties and the news of Lampson's decision to join Taylor at Xerox PARC. "Taylor and Lampson developed a hit list of people from BCC they wanted at PARC," Thacker says. "It sounded like a tremendously exciting place Taylor was talking about putting together. I had worked with these people at BCC for nearly three years, and they were, as a group, the smartest set of people I had ever been with. I was surprised and very excited when I learned I was on the list. To me it was like being accepted at a very good grad school. I leapt at the chance."

When a half dozen researchers including Lampson and Thacker moved from Berkeley Computer to PARC in January of 1971, Alan Kay changed his mind about joining Xerox. "Once Butler and the BCC guys came over to CSL," explained Kay, "it really started to get interesting. Carnegie-Mellon had invited me there to do the Dynabook [a later incarnation of FLEX], but in the spring I called them and said I was going to stay."

But when Kay told Taylor about his decision, Taylor had a surprise for him—instead of inviting Kay to join the others in CSL, Taylor asked him to enlist in the Systems Science Laboratory.

Despite Jack Goldman's original plan for PARC's Systems Science Laboratory to investigate systems in the most generic sense while the Computer Science Laboratory worked specifically on digital systems, the Systems Science Laboratory actually took shape as a second computer laboratory. SSL's manager Bill Gunning had done computer work for more than twenty years, and, like Taylor, he recruited computer scientists and engineers. For example, among the first to join Gunning was a group of computerists who resigned en masse from the nearby laboratory of Douglas C. Engelbart (like Licklider an early pioneer of interactivity).

Taylor applauded the change in SSL's charter; he had considered Goldman's scheme irrelevant to Xerox's office of the future ambitions. But he disliked Gunning's approach to organization. With Pake's approval, Gunning had set up SSL as a collection of unrelated project groups that, in Taylor's opinion, lacked the coherence and critical mass essential to significant advances in computer research.

Taylor wanted SSL to be an extension of CSL. In his plan, CSL would build an infrastructure of computer hardware and software while SSL identified and created user applications that operated on the CSL base. Taylor advised Kay to join SSL because he thought user oriented research suited Kay's originality and talent. Moreover, he explained to Kay, by "seeding" SSL with Kay's presence and influence, Taylor hoped over the long run to persuade PARC's management to coordinate the resources of both computer laboratories according to his own master plan.

The tactic made sense scientifically to Kay. It also appealed to his playful disposition. He'd be a charter member of Taylor's computer cabal that would reorganize PARC, then take on Xerox itself. What fun! Bill Gunning, who happily accepted someone of Kay's stature into his laboratory, says, "At the time I thought Taylor was trying to do me a favor. Only later did I realize it was not all brotherly love."

Taylor was excited. In Lampson, Thacker, Kay, the group from Engelbart's lab, and others, PARC had attracted more highly qualified talent in a year than most new research organizations assemble in three years. The national computer science community started to take note—something unusual was happening in Palo Alto. And Taylor knew that such impressions promised him even greater access to the best computer talent.

Furthermore, he was confident the team he had assembled could challenge the current limits of interactivity—by designing and implementing more powerful programming languages, building advanced systems in text and graphics, and constructing and enhancing computer communications networks. Taylor was prepared to take a bold step. When CSL discussed possibilities for their first major research effort, Taylor put forth an unorthodox proposal: Why not move beyond timesharing to a connected network of computers, each dedicated to a single user?

But in the spring of 1971, the idea of one computer for one person seemed nonsensical to the others. They politely rejected the suggestion. "We didn't understand what Taylor was talking about," says Lampson. "Besides, we had our minds set on a timesharing system."

Taylor didn't mind. As CSL set to work on its timesharing system, he knew he would get another chance. He was buoyed by the lab's future. The kind of opportunity to direct pathbreaking research he'd always dreamed about at ARPA was ready to move forward—if George Pake would only let him do it.

That was a troubling "if." Pake had hired Taylor to staff CSL, not to run it. According to Pake, Taylor lacked a critical qualification for research management: "Bob himself did not have a research track record." That Taylor had spent nearly a decade at NASA and ARPA selecting, sponsoring, and evaluating the most advanced interactive computer research in the United States evidently did not suggest to the former university provost an alternative credential. So when Taylor had arrived in Palo Alto expecting to be named manager of CSL, he'd been disappointed.

Pake intended Taylor to "head up a computer graphics research group where he could roll up his sleeves and really do some research. That would give him technical credibility as a real researcher." But Taylor wanted to guide research, not do it; Pake's formula, however appropriate to physics, misconstrued the special contribution Taylor could make to PARC.

In the end, Taylor concocted a perverse scheme to maintain control of CSL. He recommended to Pake that they hire a manager of CSL who could serve as a "Mr. Outside" while Taylor himself carried out the research coordination job of a "Mr. Inside." "I used the model of a university to describe it to George," says Taylor. "The chancellor is responsible for administration, fund raising, PR, et cetera, while the provost runs the faculty."

Pake agreed to the proposal despite the fact that it would leave Taylor with the very responsibilities Pake hadn't thought him technically qualified to undertake, namely managing research in CSL. The prospect of a *titled* manager with a proven record of research apparently was enough to keep Pake comfortable.

When Taylor told Lampson about the plan, the young computer scientist couldn't believe it. "The likelihood," Lampson said, "of finding someone where this scheme wouldn't fall apart was remote." Lampson remembers that the ensuing search for a lab manager was difficult because, in addition to the odd job description Taylor had contrived, "back then, computing was a new field and few people had had the experience of managing a research lab as opposed to a product development program. We surveyed the universities and a number of other labs. There weren't a large crop of candidates to choose from."

Finally, Taylor recommended they talk to an acquaintance of his named Jerry Elkind. He had first met Dr. Elkind while at NASA in the early sixties and had hired him later to consult on a number of different ARPA projects. They had had a good relationship, although it was a funder (Taylor) and recipient (Elkind), not as superior (Elkind) and subordinate (Taylor).

In 1971, Elkind had just left Bolt, Beranek and Newman, the computer consulting firm that built the ARPAnet, in the wake of a management dispute. Taylor got in touch with him. "I explained to Jerry that the next three years would be critical to CSL. We needed to hire three times as many people, and make progress on a variety of different fronts. I wanted to pay attention to the internal activity without the burden of the external responsibilities. Elkind and I privately agreed that since I had no corporate ambitions—I didn't want to go into a Xerox management development program—and since Elkind did, this platform would be ideal for him. By the time the next opportunity to advance for him came along, much of the early work in CSL would be complete, he could take the job, and I would step back in as manager of the lab."

He invited Elkind to meet the staff. To Lampson, Thacker, and others, the occasion was peculiar—they were, after all, interviewing the man Taylor proposed to be their boss. Nonetheless, according to Jim Mitchell, another leading computer scientist who had come over to CSL from Berkeley Computer Corporation, "Jerry gave a good interview. He came in, showed an interest in what we were doing, and asked good questions. The reason CSL was there was because of Taylor. I wouldn't have gone and worked for Elkind. But Bob knew him from ARPA, and thought he was okay. And the rest of us thought he'd be a good guy to hire."

Elkind's long record of academic and industrial research impressed Pake. In an explicitly positive reference to Elkind (and perhaps an implicitly negative swipe at Taylor), Pake later wrote, "A research manager who has not individually performed successful research is extremely unlikely to have a deep understanding of research or an appreciation for the basic ethic of science —and thus is quite unlikely to be a successful research manager."

Elkind remembers first hearing from Taylor about the post at CSL: "He called and told me Xerox was starting this new lab, and George Pake was the head of it. George was somebody Bob said he highly admired. Bob said he did not want to be the manager of CSL, and he thought it was something I'd be interested in." Elkind acknowledges talking to Taylor about a "Mr. Inside/Mr. Outside" arrangement. But the man who became CSL's official manager says, "It was not a model that I subscribed to. And remember I was being hired by George Pake."

With the employment of Elkind, PARC's management team

was set. Pake would direct PARC as a whole and the General Science Laboratory in particular. He reported to Jack Goldman at corporate headquarters. Bill Gunning, manager of the Systems Science Laboratory, and Jerry Elkind, manager of the Computer Science Laboratory, reported to Pake. Taylor was named associate manager of CSL. The organization chart notwithstanding, Bob Taylor reported only to himself.

Chapter

6

During the eighteen months it took PARC's Computer Science Laboratory to finish its timesharing system, Bob Taylor organized the lab according to his own carefully prepared design. At ARPA, he had studied the variety of ways project leaders managed research. "I would pick up things that I liked," he says, "and discard things that I didn't like. After three or four years of that I began to build a model of what I wanted in a research environment." In particular, Taylor concentrated on four aspects of how CSL would function: hiring, structure, communications, and tool building.

Taylor thinks choices of where to work, with whom, and on what, like decisions regarding marriage and children, deserve thoughtful deliberation. At CSL, he insisted on putting job seekers through a rigorous selection process to test the "quality of their nervous systems." Candidates presented a topic to, and fielded questions from, a labwide audience, then were interviewed separately by nearly every member of the lab. Later, Taylor asked CSL as a group to debate the strengths and weaknesses of applicants before any offers were extended.

Jim Mitchell viewed the process as an opportunity to probe the depth and breadth of aspiring researchers. "I would talk about what research they had done, and give them a problem that we were working on. I would also ask them, 'What would you like to know in five years that you don't know now?' We wanted people who would see a problem and be driven to solve it, even if it was outside their specialty."

Others tested working style. CSL looked for team players, not scientists who might isolate themselves from the group. A Taylor dictum holds that only a coordinated system of people can produce a coordinated system of hardware and software. As one lab member put it, "With systems oriented research, you need high powered people, but there must be cooperative development among them."

The process impressed the candidates. Patrick Baudelaire, a Frenchman who joined CSL in 1973, recalls, "I went through a full day of interviews, and then gave a talk. That was a very tough experience, giving a talk in front of top guys like the Lampsons, the Thackers, and Mitchell. I was a bit intimidated."

But for those, like Baudelaire, who received an offer, the hiring ordeal held out an extra benefit—the ongoing patronage of the scientists who supported them in hiring meetings. This was Taylor's intention. "Here they are voicing their approval, and that means if we make an offer to the candidate and he comes, there are already people in CSL who have built a commitment to his success because they spoke out for him. That's very important."

"We hired people with fire in their eyes," said one lab member, while another noted, "The people here all have track records and are used to dealing with lightning in both hands." Such glowing reports combined with generous Xerox funding to turn PARC into a mecca for gifted computer researchers. According to Alan Kay, "Taylor has an appreciation for talent and is an elitist. He would never hire someone who was just good. As he told me many times, 'You can't pile together enough good people to make a great one.' "

Kay, for whom numbers are but one class of metaphor, exclaimed, "Out of the one hundred best computer scientists in the country, seventy-six of them were at PARC!" He exaggerated. "Alan doesn't care that much whether what he says meets the narrow demands of technical accuracy," Butler Lampson later observed. "No matter what kind of wholehearted analysis you give to that statement, it's going to fall apart. This particular one is going to fall apart for the very primitive reason that we didn't even have seventy-six scientists. Still, it was generally recognized in the field that PARC in general and CSL in particular were by a significant margin the best computer science research establishment in the world."

After welcoming newcomers to CSL, Taylor encouraged them to review the lab's activities carefully before choosing a specific assignment. Baudelaire, for example, had many discussions with Taylor, Lampson, and others as a prelude to his work in computer graphics. Matching people to projects was critical because projects alone imparted structure to the laboratory.

Organizations often are described by the shape revealed when lines are drawn between groups of subordinates and the superiors to whom they report. The most common form, which characterized the other labs at PARC, is a pyramid—groups of employees report to superiors who in turn report to still fewer superiors until all lines merge in a single person with ultimate responsibility.

The Computer Sciences Laboratory was different. As Chuck Thacker describes it, "CSL was a flat organization. Every member of the lab reported directly to Taylor. Researchers were encouraged to move between projects as their talents and the needs of the projects dictated. The flat structure and the mobility it made possible encouraged members of the lab to become familiar with all activities. Additionally, it provided a continuous form of peer review. Projects which were exciting and challenging obtained more than financial or administrative support; they received help and participation from other CSL researchers. As a result, quality work flourished, less interesting work tended to wither."

A flat organization suited Taylor's view of large scale systems research. Advancing interactive computing depended upon breakthroughs in basic hardware design, operating systems, programming languages, hardware and software subsystems for communications, input and output devices, and user application programs. Cooperation was essential. In Taylor's opinion, a pyramid structure would have promoted organizational distractions, tempting researchers to worry more about titles and status than problem solving.

Furthermore, by making the entire lab—eventually numbering between forty and fifty people—report directly to him, Taylor positioned himself to manage labwide communications, a job he evidently was born to do. According to Lampson, "Taylor is very good at getting and running a collection of extremely intelligent and opinionated egomaniacs to work together reasonably well without fighting each other. Damned if I know how! I can't do it, but he does. Because of that, CSL was always able to get along without much organizational structure."

Taylor induced cross-fertilization of ideas and suggestions in part through a process he had originated during his years in Washington. While at ARPA, he typically monitored fifteen to twenty research projects across the country at any given time. To enrich them all, Taylor instituted an annual conference for project leaders. "The chief technical people at each of these places I was funding would come together for a multiday meeting which I chaired. At these meetings, I would ask each principal investigator to get up and give maybe an hour or more presentation of his work, what he thought its important promises and accomplishments were, what he thought its important problems were, and what he thought its important shortcomings were. Up front, I would invite the whole rest of the group—these are the senior principal investigators from about twenty different places, and they're not dummies—to criticize and evaluate and interact with what this guy was saying.

"Anyone could ask the speaker a question, and if somebody in the audience didn't agree with the speaker's answer, or they wanted to argue with the answer, they'd speak up, and an argument would ensue. They were very enlightening experiences, and very healthy meetings. And friendships got formed out of these meetings because people began to, in most cases, learn more about another fellow's work and his field, and respect it. Collaborations would begin. It had an enormous number of side benefits."

At CSL, Taylor established mandatory gatherings modeled on the ARPA conferences. Each week a different member of the lab reviewed the status of his or her research. To facilitate informality and openness, Taylor furnished the room with beanbag hassocks and let the speaker, much like a card dealer in Las Vegas, set the rules for conversation. The events, which became known as "Dealer" meetings, fostered camaraderie as well as progress.

"You've got to understand the essential need to do this kind of thing," stresses Taylor. "If you're going to use what somebody else is building, you better have some sense of what it's like because it's not going to work very well the first time or the second time or the third time. It was vitally important that, since everyone was going to use the system, they had to hear from the people that were designing its bits and pieces what those bits and pieces were like, and how they were going to fit together. And that would generate tons of questions. 'How am I going to do X, if you're building Y? How does Y that you're building fit with Z that he's building?' "

When arguments got heated, whether at Dealer meetings or in the halls or offices he constantly monitored, Taylor would engage the combatants in an effort to convert what he calls "Class 1 disagreements" into "Class 2 disagreements." He explains, "Class 1 disagreements are when neither party can describe to the other's satisfaction the other's point of view. Class 2 disagreements are when each party can describe to the other's satisfaction the other's point of view."

Most lab members applauded his performance as mediator.

Kay says of Taylor, "He was the most egotistical ego-free person in that he was a guy you wouldn't call shy, wouldn't call retiring, and yet he never, ever tried to turn the technical end of the discussion in a direction we didn't want to go." Instead, Taylor's overriding concern was directional—how best to advance the frontier of interactive and connected computing. His attitude kept it safe for others to put aside fears and egos and concentrate objectively on the problem at hand; in other words, to reach a "Class 2 disagreement," which then often produced a common technical understanding and approach.

"Most of the time what happens in this process," explained one CSL researcher, "is you'll end up agreeing because you share models with each other, and it's usually the case that one of you knows something the other one didn't. And by the time you get done, you all know the same set of things, and you end up concluding the same thing."

Taylor had a magical effect on the scientists—they cooperated and thrived in an environment they suspected could not exist without his leadership, yet had difficulty articulating how and what Taylor did to keep the enterprise together. Mike Schroeder, who joined PARC after Taylor's system was in full effect, gives a typical explanation for his boss's success: "Bob really thinks his most important job is managing the social part of research—fostering communication, knowing what people are doing, resolving differences when they come up, making sure that there aren't people who are festering resentments about X or Y or Z.

"I don't think you can do that if you have a structured place. The only problem is to make it work you need a really good manager who really understands how to do that. I don't know all the things he does to make that happen. It's a thousand little things, it's not one big thing. And I'm sure a lot of them are intentional. I suspect some of them aren't. They're intuitive on his part. I think one of the measures of how good he was was that you could never catch him doing it."

In this subtly orchestrated community, Taylor did strike one dominant note: "We use what we build." Tool building is not unique to computer science; physics, chemistry, biology, and other sciences depend on innovative tools to demonstrate the validity of fresh hypotheses. But computer investigations and the tools they yield differ from the classic sciences in one fundamental regard.

"Computer scientists," says Thacker, "don't have to worry about the world. They don't have to develop theories of the world and then build tools to test it. Rather, they just build tools to satisfy their own worlds. Ask a computer science graduate student what his or her thesis is and the best they can answer is that the program or machine they are working on will be a good thing to have."

Whereas demonstration tools are sufficient for biology, chemistry, or physics, new computer hardware and software must work repeatedly and in concert with other systems to have any value. As Jim Mitchell put it, CSL used each new tool "in anger" before concluding whether it was any good. Advances in the lab were not unlike new products. The best tools were incorporated into the daily work of many researchers; the less workable or interesting ones were forgotten.

"We used day in and day out what we built," insists Taylor. "This is totally different from a demo. In fact, if you stop at a demo, then there are all kinds of weaknesses that will accrue. Who knows whether or not what you can demo you can build upon next year? Some computer research has been characterized as people building 'toys' that are demonstrable, and they don't build them in such a way, they don't establish the design and the interface in such a way that one of their colleagues can six months later come along and design something new and put it on top of this thing. Instead, you have to start all over. If you build something and you just demonstrate it and go on to the next thing, there's an enormous amount of things that you haven't learned."

With CSL's timesharing system running in the fall of 1972, Taylor turned his researchers' attention to the next set of computing tools to be built and used. Once again he suggested they eclipse timesharing with a network of individual machines. The lab had ignored the proposal eighteen months earlier. This time, however, Taylor found a powerful ally in Butler Lampson, who had begun to think of timesharing as no more than a Faustian bargain forced on programmers by the economics of digital technology.

The engine of a computer is its central processor, and at the heart of every central processor beats a clock sending out the electronic pulses that power the machine's complex of switches. Each clock beat is called a cycle, and with each cycle, the computer's central processor executes a single, highly detailed task. Millions of such tasks are required to process computer programs. But since cycle times are measured in billionths of seconds, millions of steps take only moments to perform.

The impetus for timesharing had come from a startling insight: cycles could be shared with little inconvenience to users who, in any event, would gladly suffer small response time delays to avoid the long waits associated with batch processing. As an illustration, say that a computer's central processor executed 6 million cycles a second. If a single user's program called for 1.8 billion cycles, it would take five minutes to complete. By sharing the processor with four other programs requiring roughly equal numbers of cycles, all five could be processed together in twenty-five minutes. While twenty-five minutes was slower than five, it was much preferable to waiting hours or even days.

The scheme worked too well. As people like Licklider and Taylor had predicted, the quality and productivity of computer research jumped dramatically with the advent of interactivity. More and better systems were used to create still more and still better systems, a spiral of improvement that continued throughout the 1960s into the early 1970s. But with progress came difficulty.

Weaknesses cropped up from the very source that made timesharing possible—the pulsing clock cycles. As programmers produced new and more complex applications, the demand for cycles increased. Policies had to be written into computer operating systems to govern which uses and users would have priority, that is, be given access to the central processor's cycles, when the total demand for cycles exceeded the supply. Moreover, machine response times varied widely depending on the number and mix of programs being processed. Computing tasks requiring hours to process in periods of high cycle demand, for example afternoons when many programs were sharing the computer, took only minutes during the midnight shift. Finally, elaborate protection routines were installed to prevent programmers from interfering with each other's work or gaining access to unauthorized material.

"Timesharing had many of the same difficulties as trying to share a telephone party line," says Lampson. "It made the user uncomfortable." The worst problem was the lack of predictability. Not knowing whether a job would take minutes or hours forced users to manage their schedules around the computer instead of the reverse.

Some people overreacted. A dedicated minority of programmers —dreading the prospect of leaving a machine idle or wasting their allotment of precious cycles—took up residence near the computers, feeding off vending machines, and training themselves to avoid sleep for extended periods. Their unhealthy fixation, like the fluorescent pallor of their complexions, colored an entire generation's view about the sort of person who enjoyed computing.

To Lampson, the flaw in timesharing was its underlying premise. "The prevailing attitude," he noted, "was that machines are fast and people are slow; hence the merits of timesharing, which allows one fast machine to serve many of the slow people. And indeed timesharing, with response times measured in seconds, is an advance over a system which responds in hours. But this relationship holds only when the people are required to play on the machine's terms, seeing information presented slowly and inconveniently, with only the clumsiest control over its form and content. When the machine is required to play the game on the human's terms, presenting a pageful of attractively (or even legibly) formatted text, graphs, or pictures in the fraction of a second in which the human can pick out a significant pattern, it is the other way around: people are fast, and machines are slow."

"To play the game on the human's terms," however, dictated the one person, one computer solution Bob Taylor was recommending. That, Lampson says, "was considered somewhat of a crackpot idea at the time." In 1972, commercially available computers were still far too expensive for individual ownership or control. Advanced minicomputer systems cost $100,000, and mainframe prices reached even higher. Nevertheless, Lampson concluded that CSL might be able to make an inexpensive computer.

He pinned his optimism on the pace and direction of change in computer hardware, especially the electronic switches that conduct signals through a digital system. Just as the earth is more than 70 percent water, computers are dominated by switches. As Lampson well knew, switching technology had a history of rapid change; indeed, the first switching devices, called vacuum tubes, were technically obsolete even before the computers relying on them were ever sold.

The vacuum tube switch was a modified light bulb and, of course, got hot when it was turned on. Thousands of vacuum tubes were packed into UNIVACs and other commercial computers of the early fifties. Notwithstanding expensive air conditioning, the tubes burned out and shut down systems on a regular basis. Transistors, invented in 1947 although not incorporated into computers until the mid-1950s, were more reliable. Made from semiconductors like silicon, they could switch digital circuits on and off without producing crippling levels of heat.

Transistors improved computer dependability but did not change digital economics. Systems with any reasonable memory and speed required hundreds of thousands of discrete switches and other components to be wired together. By hand. The consequent labor and material costs were extremely high. In addition, theoretically achievable performance levels stayed beyond reach because people could solder together only so many electrical connections without making mistakes.

Such performance barriers crumbled under the impact of the next major hardware innovation. Within months of each other in late 1958 and early 1959, Jack Kilby of Texas Instruments and Robert Noyce of the Fairchild Semiconductor Company invented the integrated chip. By imprinting a conducting medium (the "wire") onto silicon, both men managed to etch complete electric circuits—switches, other components, and connections—on one piece of material. The expense and complexity of hand wiring disappeared. Manufacturing economies of scale then joined expanding circuit and component integration to drive chip capability up and chip cost down. In 1962, an integrated chip containing twelve complete circuits sold for thirty-two dollars; ten years later, a chip with a hundred times as much capacity cost a buck.

At first, manufacturers used integrated circuits primarily for computer processors. By contrast, computer memories relied on a technology called "core memory" that strung iron rings at intersections of a large wire mesh and applied magnetic forces to store computing data and instructions. Although bulky, core memory was both cheap and dependable. It was also doomed.

As chip efficiency continued to spiral, it was just a matter of time before an integrated circuit manufacturer took aim at the market for computer memory. Robert Noyce initiated that battle in 1968 by leaving Fairchild to found the Intel Corporation with Gordon Moore. Intel's first memory chips stored 256 bits of information, too little to be competitive. By 1972, though, Intel designers were working on a chip with sixteen times as many bits, easily enough to surpass core memory in cost and performance.

The progress at Intel inspired one of its engineers, Ted Hoff, to revisit the technology of computer processors. Integrated circuitry had made it possible to construct processors with hundreds of chips instead of *hundreds of thousands* of separate components. Hoff thought he could do better. In late 1971, he succeeded in connecting all the switches and components required for a very simple processor onto a single chip.

Hoff's invention was called the "microprocessor." Although it was far too primitive to drive a computer, it immediately affected the outlook for pocket calculators, a product line introduced by Texas Instruments six months earlier. The Texas Instruments calculators sold for $150 apiece, one-tenth the price of desktop calculating machines then popular in the office equipment market. With microprocessors, both the price and size of pocket calculators promised to drop by yet another order of magnitude.

Lampson was certain that continuing improvements in chip technology would affect computers as they had calculators. In a 1972 guest editorial for a professional journal, he predicted a major reduction in hardware costs over the next five to ten years, "making it possible to produce a system roughly comparable to [an IBM mainframe] 360/65 in computing power for a manufacturing cost of perhaps $500."

With such low cost hardware in mind, Lampson hazarded a "phantasmagoric" prediction for computing: "Millions of people will write non-trivial programs, and hundreds of thousands will try to sell them. Of course, the market will be much larger and very much more diverse than it is now, just as paper is more widespread and is used in many more ways than are adding machines. Almost everyone who uses a pencil will use a computer, and although most people will not do any serious programming, almost everyone will be a potential customer for serious programs of some kind. Furthermore, such a mass market will require mass distribution. Analogues of bookstores, newsstands and magazine subscriptions seem plausible, as well as the kind of mail-order and home improvement marketing patterns we have now."

Alan Kay loved that kind of talk. Kay had followed Taylor's advice to set up a research unit within SSL to pursue the themes articulated in Kay's thesis about FLEX, the "reactive engine." Once again the Babbagian vision included both a programming language and a machine. Kay called the language "Smalltalk," intending it to be used by nonexperts, especially children. And he named the proposed computer the "Dynabook."

As Kay described it, the Dynabook was to be a "dynamic media for creative thought." It bore practically no resemblance to what most people in 1972 considered a computer: "Imagine having your own self-contained knowledge manipulator in a portable package the size and shape of an ordinary notebook. Suppose it had enough power to outrace your senses of sight and hearing, enough capacity to store for later retrieval thousands of page-equivalents or reference materials, poems, letters, recipes, records, drawings, animations, musical scores, waveforms, dynamic simulations, and anything else you would like to remember and change."

According to Kay, he failed to win PARC management support for a Dynabook project in the spring of 1972. Consequently, several months later when CSL began discussing its next major program, Kay proposed they build him an "interim Dynabook." The suggestion fit Taylor's sense of the future, Lampson's view of digital economics, and Thacker's notions about how to put together such a machine. With these three in agreement, the rest of the lab followed. Taylor decided to call the project "Alto," and Lampson and Thacker set to work on a design.

That December, Lampson issued a labwide memorandum entitled "Why Alto." In it, he described the computer they hoped to invent. It would be nearly as powerful as the leading commercial minicomputer, include a remarkably rich display monitor, reside in a network of distributed machines, and, most important, be inexpensive enough for everyone to have his very own computer.

"Alto," "FLEX," "Dynabook," "interim Dynabook"—all referred to hypothetical computers unlike any the world had ever known. In explaining the primary purpose for the Alto project, Lampson also used a novel and more generic phrase: "personal computing." "If," he noted to his fellow lab members, "our theories about the utility of cheap, powerful personal computers are correct, we should be able to demonstrate them convincingly on Alto. If they are wrong, we can find out why."

Chapter

7

*I*n designing and building the Alto, Butler Lampson and Chuck Thacker had to master two conflicting objectives—how to make a system *cheaper and better* than minicomputers. Unless the cost of an Alto fell considerably below the price of a minicomputer, PARC would not have been attracted to the notion of replacing timesharing with an experiment in personal computing. Yet, as Lampson and Thacker conceived it, "personal" implied convenience in addition to economy. To them, a personal computer had to handle as easily as other common instruments of expression and communication—typewriters, blackboard pointers, pencils, pens, and paper. Only a state of the art system could approximate that kind of functionality, but only a stripped down computer would be affordable. Only an elegant solution would do both.

"Timesharing systems," according to Thacker, "had made computing more accessible and decreased its cost, but they had done little to increase the *quality* of man-machine interaction." Programmers drew charts and pictures with bulky characters like *1*'s and *x*'s rather than fine lines and points. Most people viewed their output on teletype machines instead of display terminals, and those lucky enough to have monitors suffered eye strain from low grade video performance. Documents looked very different on the user's display from when finally printed out; printouts themselves, on oversize paper with barely legible type, were no joy to read.

Lampson and Thacker had seen better "user interfaces," especially in the research of Douglas C. Engelbart, one of the patriarchs of interactive computing. In the 1950s, when many people feared computers might someday control or, worse, replace human beings, Engelbart originated a contrary view. Digital systems, he argued, should augment human intelligence, not automate it. He waged a lonely campaign for augmentation until 1964, when Bob Taylor, then at NASA, funded him to build his own research laboratory. Four years later, in a seminal event in the history of computing, Engelbart demonstrated an unprecedented variety of interactive technology. He introduced a national conference of computer scientists and engineers to, among other things, a hand-held input device called a "mouse," television monitors that could be divided into multiple "windows," and software with powerful outlining features to facilitate structured thinking and presentation.

Engelbart's mouse was an analog device housing large steel wheels and a series of buttons. The motion of its wheels controlled the cursor, the highlighted marker on a computer screen that indicates the current position of interest to the user. By rolling the mouse over a flat surface, people could move quickly through their work, pointing the cursor at target areas, and clicking the buttons to enter commands.

For the Alto, Lampson and Thacker hired an inventor to convert the mouse into a digital device, reduce its size, and simplify its handling and reliability. They also commissioned themselves to improve Engelbart's approach to television displays, hoping to engineer the Alto's screen to simulate the familiarity and flexibility of ink and paper.

Think for a moment about the infinite possibilities of these two simple tools. Ink renders characters of any size, shape, and style; it draws straight lines and curves; it produces textures and halftones. Ink can be positioned anywhere on paper with a high degree of resolution. Sheets of paper can be spread out and worked with concurrently, or bound together and reviewed a page at a time. Variation, amount, complexity, structure, relationship—the basic aspects of information are captured and communicated with ink and paper.

"Only one technique," Thacker once noted in a flurry of jargon, "is known for approximating all these properties in a computer-generated medium: a raster display in which the value of each picture element is independently stored as an element in a two-dimensional array called a bitmap."

This can be explained.

On average, Americans spend more than seven hours every day in front of raster displays. They call it television. A television monitor is, in effect, a grid of dots, or "picture elements," made by dividing the screen horizontally and vertically. Each picture element is like a microscopic light bulb. Images are formed when an electron beam scans back and forth across the screen, illuminating the picture elements with intensities that vary as a function of the originating television camera. "Raster" refers to the pattern of horizontal scanning.

Television is an analog technology. Nonetheless, the electron beam and picture elements provide a perfect digital application. A computer can turn the beam on or off; it can store each picture element's on or off status in memory. For example, this letter *A* might occupy a rectangle of four by six picture elements. If the electron beam lights up the correct picture elements, an *A* will appear against the background of the screen. By associating each picture element with a specific bit of computer memory and programming the appropriate bits to be "on" while the others are "off," the user both creates an *A* on the screen and reserves it in memory for future recall, as follows:

Computer Memory	Computer Screen
0110	11
1001	1 1
1001	1 1
1111	1111
1001	1 1
1001	1 1

Lampson and Thacker called this technique "bit mapping" because of the one-to-one correspondence between the bits in the computer's memory and the picture elements on the screen. How well they could capture the desired properties of ink—characters, lines, curves, textures, halftones, and positioning—depended upon the size of the picture elements. The smaller, the better. For example, two hundred picture elements per inch would produce video images of extraordinary richness.

That quality, however, came at a steep price. The Alto's screen re-created the standard 8½- by 11-inch piece of paper. (This was done by taking a TV screen, normally wider than it is tall, and turning it on its side.) Thus, the display area approximated 100 square inches. At two hundred picture elements per inch in each direction, the Alto would need nearly four million bits of memory for its bit map. In 1972, installed bits of memory cost just under one and a half cents apiece; a four-million-bit screen would have run more than $50,000, far too much for a personal computer.

Other display technologies required less memory. The most common was the calligraphic display. It too employed an electron beam and a fluorescent screen, but it operated the beam in a different manner from a raster television monitor. Instead of illuminating a grid of picture elements, a calligraphic electron beam painted patterns in continuous motions like brush strokes. The computer stored the location of the first and last points to be lit up; the electron beam completed the line. Thus, for any given stroke, a calligraphic display required only a handful of bits to govern where to start and where to stop.

But calligraphic displays had a major defect. They flickered. Screen images made by electron beams are not permanent. That's why the television screen goes blank when you switch it, and the electron beam, off. In fact, televised patterns must be illuminated at least thirty times a second to appear fixed; anything less produces a disturbing instability. When calligraphic technology portrayed a complex image like this page of text, the time required to trace each character prevented updating the screen often enough. Because raster technology controlled the computer image completely with switches (turning the beam on and off) instead of relying on brush strokes (drawing with the beam), it could re-light the screen much faster. Raster images appeared stable; calligraphic ones did not.

Consequently, only a bit mapped raster display, notwithstanding its voracious appetite for memory, could capture the richness of ink and paper while eliminating flicker. "Fortunately," Lampson and Thacker discovered, "surprisingly good images can be made with many fewer bits." They believed a grid of 500,000 picture elements instead of 4 million would "preserve the recognizable characteristics of paper and ink." Still, when finished, the Alto's bit map consumed nearly half of the computer's total memory. While Lampson, Thacker, and others could, and did, develop techniques to cut back on the display's demand for memory, the resources willingly dedicated to the Alto's user interface remained impressive.

The improved mouse and bit map display augured well for PARC—*if* Altos could be built inexpensively enough for everyone to have their own. Thacker accurately predicted the Alto's total memory would cost only $35 dollars in the early 1980s. But in 1972, it went for $7,000. He and Lampson had to find other ways to save money.

In one respect, the choice of a raster display helped because large scale television manufacturing made raster monitors cheap to purchase. Lampson and Thacker also economized by stripping the Alto's arithmetic functions to a bare minimum. And the abandonment of timesharing yielded up some savings since protecting users against one another became unnecessary. Finally, Lampson and Thacker knew PARC would assemble its own machines, eliminating the expense of labor, administrative overhead, and profit included in the price of another company's products.

All these measures combined, however, were insufficient to meet the Alto's cost objective. Minicomputer performance specified more hardware than the Alto budget could tolerate. Moreover, in light of the history of computer engineering, sophisticated facilities like the bit mapped display should have added, not reduced, the circuitry in the system.

Computers consist of four major parts: input, central processor, memory, and output. Data and instructions are transmitted from an input device such as a keyboard to memory. The central processor fetches the data and instructions from memory, and it executes the required computation. The central processor then dispatches the results to an output mechanism like a screen or a printer.

This scheme has an added wrinkle. The central processor itself comprises two subunits. Its "arithmetic and logic unit" manipulates the data to produce computing results; its "control unit" keeps order throughout the system, much as an air traffic controller directs takeoffs and landings to prevent collisions.

Control units in first generation computers were required to direct more traffic than is typical today. They did virtually all of the electronic processing necessary to operate each of the computer's other subsystems: arithmetic and logic, memory, input, and output. This slowed down processing.

Recall that the central processor carries out a discrete step with each separate clock beat, or cycle. More work means more steps; more steps mean more cycles; more cycles, or clock beats, mean more time to completion. By burdening the central processor with the jobs of input and output as well as arithmetic, logic, and memory, computing results took longer to obtain. Furthermore, to minimize the demand for cycles, input and output devices had to remain relatively primitive.

Engineers tackled this dilemma during the 1950s and 1960s

by adding processing circuitry directly to input and output accessories. Successive layers of hardware assumed more and more of the workload until, in the most advanced systems, input and output devices incorporated their own processors and memory, freeing the central processor's control unit of all responsibilities other than general coordination. Since the central processor could devote more cycles to memory, arithmetic, and logic, and less to input and output, computer systems ran faster. In addition, the added circuitry paved the way for more advanced input and output technology including keyboards, disk drives, and displays.

Of course the extra circuitry also cost a lot of money. Chuck Thacker realized a return to the concept of sharing a processor's cycles with input and output would reduce the parts bill for an Alto. The dilemma was how to cut back on hardware without sacrificing features like the bit map display that required access to powerful electronics—in other words, how to subtract circuitry while adding capability. A neat trick.

Thacker says, "The solution just came to me. It was an 'ah ha' experience."

His innovation, called "multitasking," effectively turned one processor into many. He wired the control unit of the Alto's central processor to take its instructions from up to sixteen different sources, or "tasks," instead of the usual one. Among these tasks were the bit map display, the mouse, the disk drive, the communications subsystem, and the user's program. The tasks were assigned priorities: if two or more of them signaled a request, the one with the highest rank took possession of the processor. When the display was in control, it was the display's processor; when the disk drive had precedence, it was the disk drive's processor; when the mouse took charge, it was the mouse's processor; and so on.

The instructions themselves controlled traffic. Each instruction contained information about its successor. Say the user's program was in control of the processor. As each instruction was processed, the ensuing instruction was fetched automatically from memory and signaled a request to continue using the processor. If this next instruction still had top priority, it too got processed, and the pattern was repeated. But when an instruction for the user's program ran into competition, for example, from the higher ranking bit map display, the user's instruction moved to an electronic warehouse while the display's instruction took hold of the processor. The user's instruction stayed in the warehouse until its request for the processor once again held the highest priority. At that point, the computation of the user's program continued exactly where it had left off.

Instructions for all sixteen tasks were subject to the same rules. If they had priority, they got processed; if not, they were maintained in the warehouse. As a result, the instructions for the display, disk drives, mouse, user's program, and other tasks were executed in the proper order regardless of when, and for how many consecutive cycles, they had control of the processor.

Multitasking provided more functionality for less cost. Priority control of the Alto's powerful central processor meant the computer's input and output facilities could perform sophisticated feats without their own circuitry. Total system hardware requirements dropped by a factor of ten. The parts bill for an Alto ran just over $10,000, about 60 percent less than spent on the components for a minicomputer.

Multitasking did slow down the Alto. The bit mapped display controlled the processor two-thirds of the time, leaving the rest of the system just one out of every three clock cycles to complete its work. Therefore, instructions and data took three times longer than normal to compute. The delays, however, were measured in microseconds. Furthermore, unlike timesharing, the speed of the Alto was thoroughly predictable. As one of PARC's researchers would later declare to the general applause of his colleagues, "The great thing about the Alto is that it doesn't run faster at night."

In November of 1972, with the Alto's design in hand, Thacker went to work on a prototype. He was joined by Ed McCreight and Larry Clark. Thacker says, "The hardware business is not like software. In software, you get immediate feedback. In hardware, there is a fairly long, unkind period when you have no idea if this pile of junk is going to work!"

By that measure, assembling the first Alto was exceedingly kind. "It worked just the way it was supposed to," recalls Thacker. "It was the most satisfying hardware system I had done, working essentially the first time. And that was because its design was so simple."

It took under four months to build the system. The first picture displayed on the new bit mapped screen was the Sesame Street Cookie Monster, which had been programmed as a test pattern by a member of Alan Kay's group. Says McCreight, "I hadn't really imagined what the bit map display would be like until I saw it running Alan's Cookie Monster. He had digitized two frames, and by switching back and forth, we got to see the Cookie Monster eating a cookie."

Thacker, too, was thrilled. "I remember checking out the display. It was late at night. There were only the three of us standing around and we were, of course, overjoyed. The display worked. You could see it! We all knew intellectually that this thing was going to be neat. But until it worked, we hadn't truly internalized what it would mean to be able to put pictures on the screen and change them on the fly. That made it all much more real. Later, people would walk by, and we'd just point, like the proud parents outside the maternity room in a hospital."

Chapter
8

"Whathat really captured the imagination of most computer scientists in the lab was the Alto," said one PARC engineer. "Two things about it were very different from before. One is that you had your own computer. And that means you're willing to use it for a much broader range of tasks because you don't sit there continually worrying about 'Gee, should I really be doing this or am I using up cycles that somebody else could be using to better advantage?' The second thing was the whole technology of the mouse and the bit map display. It was just a prod to your imagination. How could I exploit this wonderful new feature? What are the new things we can build out of this?"

There were many, many new things to build. The Alto may have been the world's first personal computer, but hardware alone does not a computing system make. Without software ranging from operating systems to programming languages to application packages, the Alto, in Chuck Thacker's words, "was no better than a hot rock—interesting but useless."

Thacker's team finished the first Alto in April of 1973. By the end of the year, PARC had ten Altos; by the following summer, the lab had forty. As the machines spread and the basic enabling software fell into place, dozens of projects were initiated. Of these, three particular innovations—in communications, printing, and word processing—illustrate how the Computer Science Laboratory, often aided by researchers from the Systems Science Laboratory, employed their Altos to advance the state of the computing art.

"In a few years, men will be able to communicate more effectively through a machine than face to face." When Bob Taylor had made that prediction in a 1968 paper coauthored with J.C.R. Licklider and Evan Herbert, computer-to-computer communications barely existed. Programmers sharing the same computer in a timesharing system could exchange information, but users of different computers could not. The difficulty, Taylor, Licklider, and Herbert had noted with disappointment, was that the nation's multibillion dollar telephone system left data communications out in the cold.

The telephone network operated in a pattern known as "circuit switching." As a phone call was dialed, telephone company operators and equipment made a series of connections from one node in the network to the next until a full circuit ran between caller and receiver. It took a second or two to complete all the parts of a circuit, but nobody much cared. People tended to talk on the phone for several minutes; a few seconds' wait was no bother. For computer communications, however, the set-up time was an eternity. Unlike telephone conversations, data exchanges lasted microseconds, not minutes. And a meaningful data message often required dozens, even hundreds, of separate transmissions. Interposing a second or two between each burst of digital code would have caused excruciating delays.

It also would have been prohibitively expensive. In order to amortize the heavy cost of circuit switching, the phone company charged its highest rates for the first minute of conversation even if the connection lasted a shorter time. Imagine the phone bill of a Boston programmer who incurred the full first minute charge for each one of the thousands of keystrokes needed to enter data and instructions into a California computer. The invoice would have extended for pages; its total would have exceeded the programmer's salary.

In the late 1960s, a handful of computer scientists developed an alternative to circuit switching, called message switching, which led to the ARPAnet, the first nationwide computer network. In message switching, information was routed through the ARPAnet like a baton in a relay race. Data traveling from A to E made the full trip in steps from A to B, B to C, C to D, and, finally, from D to E. This protocol was known as "store and forward." The ARPAnet computer at the first center waited for a clear line, then transmitted its message to the second center. Meanwhile, the first center's computer stored a copy of the message until the second center's computer acknowledged receipt. At that point, the second center's machine waited for a clear line, then forwarded the data on to the third. And so on, until the message reached its ultimate destination.

Since each of these computer-to-computer links happened in thousandths of a second, hundreds of digital dispatches could travel from origin to destination on the ARPAnet during the second or two it would have taken the telephone system's circuit switched network to even begin transmission. And because multiple node circuits were unnecessary, the bulk of the telephone system's expensive set-up charges were avoided.

The ARPAnet system worked well for long distance computer communications. But combining the Alto computers at PARC into an inexpensive local network posed a dilemma. Requiring a customized store and forward computer "partner" for each Alto in a PARC network would have destroyed the economics of personal computing. Unfortunately, without store and forward protocols, there was no way to prevent interference. Just as simultaneous telephone conversations on the same circuit are no good, two or more digital messages sent at the same time over the same wire collide, rendering their signals unrecognizable. That's why the telephone system has busy signals, and that's one reason the ARPAnet had store and forward computers.

Therein lay the challenge and the genius of PARC's short distance, or "local area network." With the help of Lampson and Thacker, Robert Metcalfe of CSL and David Boggs of SSL solved the reliability problem with a neat twist—they didn't insist on success. Their invention, called "Ethernet," plugged Altos into a cable strung throughout the building at PARC. Each Alto broadcast messages to the entire network but received just those dispatches carrying the correct address. Thus, unlike store and forward systems, the Ethernet permitted simultaneous transmissions and interference.

The lightning speed of a computer processor inspired Metcalfe and Boggs to tolerate failure. As long as the incidence of bollixed transmissions was kept to a minimum, they figured a blocked message now and then would not appreciably slow down overall communications. In their Ethernet system, if a transmitting Alto detected interference, it stopped broadcasting, waited a random number of microseconds, and tried again.

"The basic idea," says Butler Lampson, "is very, very simple. Imagine you're at a party and several people are standing around having a conversation. One person stops talking and somebody else wants to talk. Well, there's no guarantee that only one person wants to talk; perhaps several do. It's not uncommon for two people to start talking at once. But what typically happens? Usually they both stop, there's a bit of hesitation, and then one starts up again. That's essentially how the Ethernet works."

The Ethernet connected Altos to other Altos and to equipment shared by everyone in the laboratory. The most popular pooled resource was another PARC invention, the first xerographic laser printer. It combined the scientific legacy of Chester Carlson with the engineering wizardry of PARC's talented researchers. Xerography is a product of light and shadow. Put your hand up to a light, and the shadow of the hand appears on an opposite wall; put your hand on the glass of a Xerox copier, and the shadow of the hand appears on an electrostatically charged metal drum within the machine. The drum's charge is neutralized by light, perpetuated by darkness. Therefore, the metal surface remains charged only in that area of shadow corresponding to your hand. Black powder bearing an opposite charge is sprinkled over the drum. It sticks to the area of shadow and slides off the rest of the metal surface. A clean sheet of paper adheres to the powder, paper and powder are fused with heat, and a copy of your hand is set to roll out of the machine.

In the 1960s, a few engineers at Xerox's Webster, New York, research facility thought xerography might have applications beyond copying. Among them was Gary Starkweather, who demonstrated that lasers—powerful light sources—could create xerographic facsimile images. In 1969, Starkweather proposed to extend Carlson's process by inventing a laser printer. His boss said no. But his boss's boss, George White, believed lasers had great potential for Xerox, and he recommended that Starkweather transfer to PARC.

The computer scientists welcomed both Starkweather and his idea with enthusiasm. "They saw a common architecture in all of this," Starkweather remembers, "because they had been looking for something that could print in a bit map fashion."

If bits of computer memory could correspond to the picture elements of a television screen, they could also be mapped to dots created by a laser on a xerographic drum. In the printing application, the digital *1*'s and *0*'s control the path of the laser. If the laser illuminates a spot on the metal drum, its light neutralizes the electrostatic charge, the black powder slides off that tiny area of the drum, and the paper stays white. On the other hand, if the laser is prevented from reaching the drum, the spot stays dark, its electrostatic charge survives, the powder sticks, and the paper turns black.

The artistic method here is a hi-tech version of pointillism. Starkweather and the computer scientists conceived of the metal drum as a grid with five hundred dots per inch in each direction, providing more than twenty-three million dots for marking a standard 8½- by 11-inch page.

The laser had to shine on and off the metal drum with fantastic speed. To build his printer, Starkweather modified a Xerox 7000 Copier, which operated at the rate of one page per second. Subtracting the time required for paper to travel through the machine left the laser about two-thirds of a second to scan the twenty-three million dots on the drum. That meant the laser had to be turned on and off nearly forty million times a second.

Starkweather produced the necessary effect with a magician's touch. To the light and shadow trick of xerography, he added sound and mirrors. First, he designed a twenty-four sided polygon about the size of a doughnut. Each facet held a mirror to reflect the laser beam. By mounting the doughnut on a revolving shaft, Starkweather made it possible to scan the entire drum. And with the aid of sound energy, he figured out how to bend the laser on and off rapidly enough to mark the twenty-three million separate spots in the time allowed.

All of which called for a good deal of engineering creativity. Starkweather's most ingenious solution, however, was to a more difficult problem. To print clear and precise images, the revolving mirrors had to bounce laser beams against the drum with great accuracy. Think back to the bit mapped letter *A* discussed in the previous chapter. Let each *1* represent a dot created by the laser. If the laser did not scan the drum exactly as intended, the *1*'s would appear unaligned, leaving wobbly images on the final copy, as follows:

Computer Memory	Laser Printout
0110	11
1001	1 1
1001	1 1
1111	111 1
1001	1 1
1001	1 1

To prevent uneven pictures, Starkweather calculated that the position of any dot could not vary more than one thousandth of an inch from its "theoretical center," or target. If each mirror on the polygon were not cut to perfection, or if the bearings in the motor driving the spinning shaft did not operate exactly as specified, the laser's angle of reflection from the mirror would carry it beyond the required tolerance, producing a distorted picture.

Fabricating near perfect mirrors and bearings was possible but far too expensive. Starkweather devised a much simpler and cheaper approach. He chose to employ optical means to correct errant lasers instead of fabrication and mechanical means to prevent the irregularities. By interposing a special kind of lens between the rotating mirrors and the xerographic drum, he managed to concentrate the laser on the drum exactly where intended. Light that bounced off the spinning mirrors heading in the wrong path was caught by the lens, corrected, and directed to its intended target on the drum.

Starkweather named his machine "SLOT," for "Scanned Laser Output Terminal." To use an automobile analogy, SLOT was a fast and fancy set of wheels. But it required an engine to drive it, that is, to tell it *when* to bend the laser toward or away from the xerographic drum. That "engine" was a digital processor and memory called the "Research Character Generator" invented by Ron Rider of SSL under the guidance of Butler Lampson.

History's best known "character generator" is Johannes Gutenberg, who invented movable type in the fifteenth century for his famous Bible. Over the next five hundred years, craftsmen contrived a spectrum of typeface styles and sizes. Gothic, Greek, Helvetica, Times Roman, light, medium, bold, italic, serif, sans serif—these and other terms describe the typesetting choices available to printers.

Gutenberg poured an alloy of lead, tin, and antimony into molds to cast separate characters that could be set in any arrangement prescribed by a manuscript. Lampson and Rider shaped bit patterns for exactly the same purpose. With patterns of *1*'s and *0*'s, they could signal the laser to print any letter from a Times Roman italic *a* to a Helvetica boldface *z*. In theory, their Research Character Generator could have captured the entire heritage of the printing trade. But in practice, the number of memory chips required to store so much diversity exceeded their budget. Nonetheless, even a partial collection of type styles and sizes would provide PARC researchers with a rich and varied digital printing shop.

Rider recalls confronting an unusual problem at the beginning of his project. Xerox copiers run pages horizontally instead of vertically. Compare this with a typewriter. Pages are inserted vertically, and typing is done horizontally, one letter at a time in the same direction as reading. The Xerox 7000 Copier Gary Starkweather modified into the Scanned Laser Output Terminal had a different orientation. Pages went through the machine horizontally. As a result, the laser made its black and white dots vertically.

"This caused problems for building an image generator," explains Rider, "because you come across all lines at once." Look at the following passage taken from a sign Bob Taylor hung outside his PARC office (proving the biblical origin of binary computer logic):

> But let your communication be,
> Yea, yea;
> Nay, nay:
> For whatsoever is more than these
> Cometh of evil.
>
> —*Matthew, Chapter 5, Verse 37*

To print this verse, SLOT's laser scanned from top to bottom, not right to left. The first scan left a series of black and white dots representing a vertical slice of the letters *B, Y, N, F,* and *C.* The Research Character Generator retrieved the correct pattern of *1*'s and *0*'s from its memory for each letter, communicated the bits to the laser in the proper order, and kept track of the results so that, on the next pass of the laser, the machine could pull out the appropriate follow-on bits and send them to the laser. This cycle repeated until the page was complete. In this manner, images were assembled like multidecker sandwiches, one page length slice at a time.

Rider gleefully describes these digital logistics as a "massive sorting kind of disaster." With Lampson's help, he completed the character generator by laying out and wiring nearly twenty-five hundred integrated chips. When he finished, PARC's remote control print shop was in business. For a technology that had everything to do with visualization, PARC's computer people dreamed up the anatomically strange acronym of "EARS"—for the *E*thernet, the *A*lto, the *R*esearch Character Generator, and the *S*canned Laser Output Terminal.

Everyone at PARC—scientists, administrators, and secretaries—used EARS to print elegant documents. Before they could print, however, they had to compose. And the word processing package employed most often was a program called "Bravo," designed by Butler Lampson and another CSL researcher, Charles Simonyi.

Bravo introduced computer scientists to a fresh concept called "wysiwyg" (pronounced "whiz-ee-wig") for "what you see is what you get." In Bravo, the appearance and layout of a document on the Alto screen were identical to the hard copy printed by EARS. By contrast, software predating Bravo forced computer users to interleave text with specific formatting instructions that commanded a piece of software known as a "document compiler" to convert the input into a normal document. Consequently, what people saw on their screen—the desired words and numbers interrupted by the necessary formatting commands—was not what got printed out when they were finished.

"The document compiler," explains Lampson, "played the same role as a human typesetter. Instead of giving a manuscript to a typesetter, you gave instructions to the document compiler. Typesetters don't need explicit instructions for formatting because they carry the rules in their head. But a document compiler has to be told everything."

The document compiler routine of having to include command instructions in the body of a composition was disruptive to programmers and beyond the grasp of the uninitiated. Eliminating it required Lampson and Simonyi to program Bravo to perform as a document compiler each time the user entered a change of text. This was quite difficult.

A document compiler calculates all of its layout information at once, a sensible scheme when users complete their writing before the formatting program goes to work. But in Bravo, formatting calculations were to be processed during the composition session, not after it. Therefore, the effect of every textual insertion and deletion, every margin adjustment, every underline, every superscript and subscript—in short, of every change—had to be computed immediately.

Say we wished to add a word to the next sentence in this paragraph. A document compiler would recompute the layout of the entire chapter, taking perhaps as long as a minute or so to finish. If every correction or alteration of text in Bravo had caused such a lengthy delay, Lampson and Simonyi would have succeeded only in replacing one kind of interruption, the command insertions, with another—slow response times.

"The trick," says Lampson, "was to try to limit the propagation of changes as much as possible." They did this by raising digital walls. Bravo treated every line of text as though it were a separate document. When an insertion, deletion, or other change was made, the Bravo program, in effect, polled each line to find out which ones required alteration. When it recomputed, it did so only for the lines that mattered. As a result, the changes processed by Bravo appeared on the screen in a tiny fraction of a second. To the user, it looked instantaneous.

Bravo incorporated much of the new hardware and software at PARC. Text entries and changes were immediately visible on the Alto's bit map screen, a mouse could be used to point to selected portions of a document, windows were available to compare different sections of text, and results could be communicated over the Ethernet to other Altos as well as to EARS to get a printed copy that looked exactly like it was supposed to. Interactive computing had been extended to an entirely new frontier. The people at PARC who had Altos felt blessed—nowhere else in the world was there a computing system to match it.

Chapter

9

The first Xerox executive to seek an advantage from PARC's revolutionary technology was a man named, appropriately enough, Darwin Newton. Newton was the senior administrative editor of Ginn & Co., a Boston-based textbook publisher owned by Xerox. As such, his primary concern was productivity. In the early 1970s, newspaper, magazine, and book companies began experimenting with mainframes and minicomputers to expedite the publishing process, and Darwin Newton wanted PARC to help him improve efficiency at Ginn.

In 1974, Newton contacted Bill Gunning at PARC. After briefly serving as manager of the Systems Science Laboratory, Gunning had accepted an assignment from George Pake as technical liaison between PARC and the rest of Xerox. In response to Newton's inquiry, Gunning put the Ginn editor in touch with Bill English, the leader of an SSL project called "POLOS" for "PARC On-Line Office System." English, in turn, asked one of his researchers, Larry Tesler, if he would assist Ginn.

It was an ideal opportunity for Tesler. After graduating from Stanford in 1965, he had written software for computer-aided editing, formatting, and page layout. In addition, he'd nurtured an abiding interest in making computer tools more accessible to nonprogrammers. So the Ginn project appealed to both his interests and his inclination. And, as Tesler recounts it, the assignment also had a certain attraction to English and the rest of the POLOS team. "I didn't like the POLOS architecture at all," says Tesler, "and I complained about it a lot. I was disruptive. They were happy to move me to one side."

It soon became apparent, however, that adapting POLOS to Ginn's specifications, if possible at all, would be difficult for Tesler to do alone. To avoid diverting anyone else from the POLOS team, English proposed that Ginn hire its own computer person to help Tesler. English and Tesler wrote up a job description, had it posted throughout Xerox, and told Newton they would interview any worthwhile candidates.

In September, Newton introduced them to Tim Mott, a twenty-four-year-old Englishman who had come to the United States three years earlier with a computer science degree from the University of Manchester. Between 1972 and 1974, Mott had taught mathematics and computers at Oberlin College in Ohio, then had moved to Boston with the intention of working for a year before applying to business school.

"I went to the Boston office of Scientific Data Systems looking for a job in computer sales support," says Mott. "I was a long-haired freaky looking kid at the time, and they were skeptical. But they knew about Darwin's project and suggested I go talk to Ginn. I talked to Darwin, and a week later he invited me back to meet some of the people from PARC. Two weeks after that, I was in Palo Alto."

Mott's introduction to PARC was humbling. "I was totally at sea technically. There were so many new things going on that I had never seen before. And no documentation existed to help me teach myself. I felt I had been thrown in at the deep end."

After a month of intense self-education, Mott reached a conclusion that neither he nor Darwin Newton had anticipated—POLOS was far too complicated and incomplete to support the word processing and printing applications Newton wanted to try at Ginn.

The complexities of POLOS arose from its unique heritage, one dating back to 1945. That year, Vannevar Bush, who coordinated all federally funded scientific research during World War II, published an article entitled "As We May Think" in *The Atlantic Monthly*. In it, Bush warned that by relying on antiquated methods for storing, researching, and transmitting information, the postwar world risked losing control over the accumulated record of its own knowledge and history.

"The summation of human experience," he claimed, "is being expanded at a prodigious rate, and the means we use for threading through the consequent maze to the momentarily important item is the same as was used in the days of the square-rigged ships."

Bush speculated on a series of hypothetical information management technologies, the most intriguing of which he called "memex." "A memex," he wrote, "is a device in which an individual stores his books, records, and communications, and which is mechanized so that it may be consulted with exceeding speed and flexibility. It is an enlarged intimate supplement to his memory."

Memex users would manipulate keyboards, screens, microfilm, and photographic technology to build "trails" of pertinent information from any knowledge base, no matter how extensive or fast changing. As a result, Bush predicted, "wholly new forms of encyclopedias will appear, ready-made with a mesh of associative trails running through them, ready to be dropped into the memex and there amplified. The lawyer has at his touch the associated opinions and decisions of his whole experience. . . . The physician, puzzled by a patient's reactions, strikes the trail established in studying an earlier similar case, and runs rapidly through analogous case histories, with side references to the classics for the pertinent anatomy and histology. The chemist, struggling with the synthesis of an organic compound, has all the chemical literature before him."

When Douglas C. Engelbart, then a naval radar technician stationed in the Philippines, read Bush's *Atlantic Monthly* piece in 1945, he reacted to it with the same dedication of purpose fired in Bob Taylor many years later by J.C.R. Licklider's article "Man-Computer Symbiosis." Following the war, Engelbart earned college and graduate degrees in electrical engineering, and immediately began pushing his academic and industrial colleagues for the chance to develop the information tools Bush had envisioned. But throughout the 1950s, most people considered Engelbart's proposals mystical. Memex-style computing required interactivity; interactivity implied direct access to computers; direct access, in the days of batch processing, seemed out of the question for both technical and economic reasons.

Only the advent of timesharing made Engelbart's dream a possibility. He landed a job at the Stanford Research Institute and, while there, gained the support first of Bob Taylor at NASA, then Licklider and Taylor at ARPA for a laboratory dedicated to building interactive hardware and software on a timesharing computer base. He called the effort the "Augmented Human Intellect Research Center," although it became better known as the Augmentation Research Center, or ARC.

Engelbart sought to augment human intelligence through ordering the information on which people rely. His philosophy and leadership inspired ARC to invent hardware and software dominated by rules of hierarchy and structure. In the paper accompanying their famous 1968 demonstration of interactive computing tools, coauthors Engelbart and Bill English explained that ARC had "adopted some years ago the convention of organizing all information into explicit hierarchical structures, with provisions for arbitrary cross-referencing among the elements of the hierarchy.

"3c2b1 The principal manifestation of this hierarchical structure is the breaking up of text into arbitrary segments called 'statements,' each of which bears a number showing its serial location in the text and its 'level' in an 'outline' of the text."

The conference paper itself was presented as an example of Engelbart's text structuring. Every paragraph (including the one just quoted) started with an alphanumeric label in the manner of the classic outlining system learned by most high school students. Engelbart and English reported that, when made dynamic by a computer processor, their design facilitated a number of varied and well ordered perspectives on information. For example, users could check logic and completeness by requesting the screen to display "statements" having the same outline level of importance; they could quickly locate specific supporting material by selecting the appropriate alphanumeric heading; they could expand and tie together topics by creating a subheading at the most appropriate point in a given body of thought.

The impact on work and productivity at the Augmentation Research Center was pervasive:

> 3c4 The basic validity of the structured-text approach has been well established by our subsequent experience.
>
> 3c4a We have found that in both off-line and on-line computer aids, the conception, stipulation, and execution of significant manipulations are made much easier by the structuring conventions.
>
> 3c4b Also, in working on line at a CRT [cathode ray tube] console, not only is manipulation made much easier and more powerful by the structure, but a user's ability to get about very quickly within his data, and to have special "views" of it generated to suit his need, are significantly aided by the structure.
>
> 3c4c We have come to write all of our documentation, notes, reports, and proposals according to these conventions. . . . We have found it to be fairly universal that after an initial period of negative reaction in reading explicitly structured material, one comes to prefer it to material printed in the normal form.

Engelbart called the collection of hardware and software "NLS" for "oN-Line System." To computer scientists in the ARPA community, NLS represented the most impressive advance of inter-activity since the invention of timesharing, and it inspired many subsequent developments, including much of the work at PARC.

Engelbart, however, was apparently a querulous boss. In 1970, Bill English led a group of researchers from the Augmentation Research Center in Menlo Park, California, to the new Xerox PARC facility in Palo Alto. They brought with them two of Engelbart's deepest biases: faith in structuring and reliance on time-sharing. Both contributed to the failure of the POLOS office system project.

Unlike the decision of the Computer Science Laboratory to abandon timesharing, English's group in SSL sought to elaborate, even to multiply, it. They designed POLOS around a dozen separate timeshared computers, with each computer dedicated to a specific office function. For example, one computer would handle filing, one editing, one printing, and so on. Users were to sit at terminals with simultaneous access to all computers. It was an unbelievably complex scheme.

"English's group," says Tesler, "selected POLOS, in part, for conservative reasons. They didn't think personal computers would be economically viable. So they decided to build what they called a 'distributed system.' As it turned out, their approach was conservative economically but too aggressive technically."

The toughest job in a timesharing system is building the operating system, the software that enables the central processor to direct traffic. In both batch processing and personal computers, the operating system enables the central processor's control unit to keep order among input, output, memory, arithmetic, and logic. To this, timesharing adds the burden of avoiding collisions among multiple users. For example, preventing User A's input from disrupting User B's program or User C's output.

POLOS elevated this degree of difficulty by yet another order of magnitude. Its operating system would have to manage the logistics of *different computer operations* (input, output, memory, arithmetic, and logic), *different users* (Secretary A, Executive B, Clerk C), and *different office functions* (editing, filing, printing).

POLOS condemned its users to the same lack of predictability that plagued all timesharing systems. Furthermore, it continued to emphasize structured text editing. English's team was confident that memos, letters, proposals, and other documents coming out of a POLOS office would reflect a higher quality of logic and thought because of the system's outlining tools. All of which was fine in theory and acceptable to computer scientists comfortable with advanced systems. But it made no sense for Ginn because, as Tim Mott realized, most people do not comfortably compose in a hierarchically restricted fashion.

"Ginn needed fairly simple programs for word processing and page layout," says Mott. "The POLOS application was modeled after NLS which in turn was based on the Bush paper. They were really tools for organizing thought, not for editing and page design. While the word processing functions were there, there was also lots of other stuff that Ginn would not have needed and were too cumbersome. I didn't think the editors at Ginn would take the time required to learn. My model for this was a lady in her late fifties who had been in publishing all her life and still used a Royal typewriter.

"Also the POLOS hardware was too complicated to be moved out of the research lab. The hardware was wrong, the operating system and approach were wrong, and the applications were wrong. I was bummed out when I realized I had to write a letter to Darwin, almost a letter of resignation, saying 'I finally have a handle on what's going on here, and, believe me, it's not going to do you any good.' "

To Mott's relief, Tesler suggested they consider employing the Alto-Ethernet-EARS-Bravo system at Ginn. One of the first versions of Bravo had just been completed by Lampson, Simonyi, and a team from CSL. While this early edition of the program did not include the formatting and typeface capabilities needed for page layout, it did contain the basic word processing features sought by Darwin Newton for his editors. With English's permission, Tesler and Mott dropped POLOS and asked Lampson and Simonyi if they would agree to a series of modifications to make Bravo easier to learn and operate.

Tesler considered Bravo terrific with one exception—it reflected the habit among computer scientists of requiring users to memorize special instructions to enter what are called "modes" in order to manipulate the program. A mode is a means of putting the machine into a certain context to get it to execute a desired task. The shift key on a typewriter is a mode. Unless it is depressed, the typist cannot produce capital letters or any of the uppercase symbols represented on the number keys.

In Bravo, editing changes required a "command" mode. First,

the operator used his mouse to select a letter, word, or section of text to be edited. Then by pressing the "D" key, the Alto would delete the selection. Similarly, in the command mode, "I" would permit insertions of text, "R" would replace text, "U" would undo the effect of the previous command, "G" would get a document from memory, and "P" would put it back. If "D," "I," "R," "U," "G," or "P" were typed outside the command mode, they would merely appear as letters in the user's text.

Computer scientists like modes because they support flexibility in programs by allowing a variety of keystroke combinations to transmit a range of electronic meanings to the processor. For novices, however, modes can be treacherous. One leading commentator on computer anxiety writes, "There is a story, probably apocryphal, told about another text-editing program that has separate input and command modes. According to this story, a hapless user wanted to type the word 'edit' into his document. Unfortunately, the program was in command mode when he started typing—the 'e' selected everything currently in the document; the 'd' deleted everything that was selected; the 'i' caused the program to enter insert mode; and the 't' inserted the letter "t." The result: the entire document was replaced by the letter 't.' Sorry."

Mott agreed with Tesler that Ginn employees who, to a person, had little understanding and big fears of computing, were more likely to welcome word processing that was modeless. With the cooperation of Lampson and Simonyi, the two men went to work. For two months, they worked every day at their Alto in overlapping fourteen hour shifts to rewrite Bravo's code. They named their modeless program "Gypsy" after the costume worn by Mott's stepdaughter that Halloween.

When they finished, PARC had the first computer editing program easy enough to be learned in a few hours by people who had never touched a computer. As Tesler explains, "In Gypsy, there were no modes. 'I' meant 'I' and nothing else. If you wanted to insert text, all you had to do was position the mouse at the point in the text you wanted to change, click the button, and begin to type."

By February of 1975, Mott was back in Massachusetts installing the system for its initial test. "When it came time to begin instructing people about Gypsy," Mott remembers, "I went straight for the lady with the Royal typewriter, figuring if I could teach her, it would be clear sailing for the rest. After a few hours of coaching, she had learned enough to go off and use the system on her own. A few days later, she said the quality of her work had improved because she was always dealing with clean copy, and it was easy to make changes. She volunteered that she couldn't imagine having ever worked any differently."

The experiment at Ginn was a huge success. Darwin Newton estimated the system would save between 15 and 20 percent of the cost of editing Ginn books. While some editors balked at the new technology—"I'd rather be home with a tall drink than be at the office with a machine," one reported—most agreed with the assessments of Newton and the woman with whom Mott worked first. Indeed, the enthusiastic Ginn employees even proposed that PARC add more features to the program, including a computerized thesaurus.

Larry Tesler received a letter of commendation from Xerox and a large raise; Tim Mott, after spending the rest of 1975 and part of 1976 coordinating the introduction of the system at Ginn, was hired to work full time at PARC. They were deservedly proud of their contribution.

"Gypsy," Tesler points out, "was the first thing outsiders in the company understood. Ginn loved it. It was so easy to learn. They would hire temporary typists to come in at eight, they were trained on the system by nine, and typing full speed by ten. This was revolutionary in publishing. In a couple of years, they were using this word processing for over fifty percent of their books. Nowadays, so what? People use one hundred percent word processing. But this was 1975."

People throughout PARC shared Tesler's excitement. The creative effort behind Alto, Ethernet, EARS, Bravo, and Gypsy also had produced advances in programming languages, operating systems, drawing and painting programs, and communications. Of course some ideas, like POLOS, did not pan out. But as most researchers at PARC happily acknowledged, the POLOS project simply confirmed the willingness of Xerox management, and especially Goldman and Pake, to underwrite some failure as an inevitable cost of successful research.

Furthermore, the Ginn experiment coincided with a number of schemes in 1975 and 1976 that sought to transfer PARC's technology out of the laboratory. A Xerox division in Southern California requested permission to make and market a laser printer, a patent was applied for and received on the Ethernet, and headquarters approved the formation of the Systems Development Division (SDD) to engineer PARC inventions into products. By mid-1975, SDD had signed up a number of PARC's most illustrious stars, including Ron Rider, the designer of the Research Character Generator, Charles Simonyi (Bravo), Robert Metcalfe (Ethernet), and Chuck Thacker (Alto).

That spring, another CSL engineer, John Ellenby, got permission to redesign the Alto and set up a production line to manufacture the computers in small quantities instead of one at a time. A year later, Ellenby's project had gone so well that he was encouraged to submit a proposal on the Alto to a Xerox task force then deciding on new product strategies for the company. And by August of 1976, rumors were spreading at PARC that the task force had selected the Alto as Xerox's entry into the word processing market just then emerging in the United States.

Xerox's investment, inventiveness, and effort seemed ready to pay off with an "architecture of information" every bit as powerful and provocative as the one Peter McColough had predicted in his speech at the beginning of the decade. Thinking back to the accomplishments of PARC's first five years, Chuck Thacker says, "It was certainly from my own experience the largest continuous piece of creative output that I have seen anywhere. And it was like being right there at the Creation. A lot of people worked harder than I had ever seen, or have seen since, doing a thing that they all thought was worthwhile, and really thought would change the world."

Finance:
The
Rejection
of the
Alto

Chapter

10

*H*ighlighting the advances in computer technology being made at Xerox's Palo Alto Research Center, the June 30, 1975, edition of *Business Week* declared, "Office automation has emerged as a full-blown systems approach that will revolutionize how offices work." The article emphasized three predictions: the office systems market would be huge; only firms with courage, persistence, and enormous resources would succeed; the most likely winners would be IBM and Xerox.

That prognosis was logical. In the 1970s, offices remained the least automated part of the American economy. While investment in capital equipment per factory worker averaged more than $25,000 each year, the same measure for office workers was a mere $2,000, less than one-tenth as much. Business leaders and analysts alike expected the gap to narrow once the efficiency and productivity of new office systems were demonstrated. Furthermore, no companies in the world had the technology, marketing strength, and financial wherewithal to compete with IBM and Xerox; whenever the office automation market finally took off, America's two office equipment leaders were bound to reap most of the rewards.

In the *Business Week* scenario, therefore, only courage and persistence stood between market domination and IBM and Xerox. Those two qualities, however, are far more difficult to appraise than market demand, product specifications, sales capacities, or balance sheets. In 1975, notwithstanding *Business Week*'s rosy forecast and the outstanding achievements of the computer scientists at PARC, Xerox's commitment to the office of the future had drifted. Instead of looking and acting like an innovative company on the brink of another commercial crusade, Xerox more closely resembled a corporate behemoth under siege—attacked from without by antitrust lawsuits and economic recession, and afflicted from within by the utter failure of Peter McColough's Scientific Data Systems acquisition.

The company's antitrust woes had started in 1972, when the Federal Trade Commission accused Xerox of illegally monopolizing the plain paper copier market. According to the charges,

Xerox had manipulated the patent laws, discriminated in its pricing, forced customers to take uncompetitive products, announced bogus delivery dates for new models, and enforced its famous lease-only policy—all in a concerted scheme to fence out the competition. Moreover, the Commission alleged, Xerox had erected a worldwide cartel for the control and exploitation of the copier business through its ownership positions in Rank-Xerox of England and Fuji-Xerox of Japan.

The FTC's message was clear—Xerox had been *too successful.* In the three years since breaking the $1 billion revenue mark, company sales had more than doubled to $2.4 billion and annual profits had increased by 50 percent to a quarter of a billion dollars. Xerox, although the fifty-second largest corporation in America in terms of sales, was number seventeen in profits. Such asymmetry, groused the Commission, evidenced the misbegotten spoils of monopoly.

The Government demanded a dramatic reduction in Xerox's market power. It wanted the copier maker to abandon the lease-only policy, allow customers to contract with other vendors for the maintenance and supply of Xerox copiers, provide royalty-free licenses on all patents to all competitors, and divest itself of Rank-Xerox and Fuji-Xerox. The December 1972 announcement gave Xerox thirty days to comply or face a lawsuit. Xerox refused. The Commission went to court.

An indignant Peter McColough responded by questioning the patriotism of the Federal Trade Commission. Their position, he cried, "is almost impossible to understand without concluding that their strategy is not to attack one company but is in fact to attack the fundamental principles on which all companies in this country have grown, prospered, and, in point of fact, contributed in great measure to people all over the world."

By wrapping his company in the flag, however, McColough did not stanch the torrent of Xerox's legal difficulties. The FTC's action encouraged a flood of Xerox competitors to attempt in court what so far had eluded them in the market place. Company after company filed antitrust suits, and within a few years, Xerox's lawyers manned courtrooms throughout the country trying to protect their client against claims for hundreds of millions of dollars and injunctions seeking to strip away a variety of competitive advantages.

The spreading number of private lawsuits pressured Xerox's

strategists to try to end the FTC squabble without setting precedents adverse to the company's position in other litigation. That meant reaching an out of court settlement with the Commission, which in turn required agreeing to change some of Xerox's commercial practices. Forced to pick which of the corporation's many strengths to abandon, top management chose to forfeit Xerox's patent protection because, they believed, competitor access to the secrets of xerography was unlikely to diminish Xerox's strong market position. The company had too many other important advantages: Xerox's sales force had unparalleled entree to America's business offices; Xerox had more than two decades of plain paper copier manufacturing and servicing experience; Xerox alone offered a full product line covering all segments of the market; "Xerox" meant copying.

"Patents," McColough explained to *The New York Times,* "are not as important as they were when we were small and weak and had a big risk investment."

But while McColough was willing to negotiate on patents, he adamantly refused to deal away the relationship with Rank-Xerox and Fuji-Xerox, which, like so much else in the company's history, had sprung from Joe Wilson's ambition. According to John Dessauer, Wilson had begun as early as 1956 "to occupy himself with the international aspect of planning for the future. He had for some time maintained that to enjoy the full benefits of xerography the company would have to exploit its products throughout the world. This sounded like an exorbitant, even grandiose ambition. Once somebody remarked with an ironic laugh, 'There's no law against dreaming. Today Haloid Street, tomorrow the world.' "

As usual, Haloid's skeptics had not deterred Wilson. He courted dozens of European companies and eventually persuaded an English motion picture firm, the J. Arthur Rank Organisation, to invest with Haloid in a joint venture named Rank-Xerox Ltd. Haloid granted Rank-Xerox the exclusive right to market xerographic products throughout the world except North America. Then, in 1962, Rank-Xerox expanded Xerox's international family by combining with Fuji Photo Film of Japan to create yet another joint venture, Fuji-Xerox Ltd. Rank-Xerox licensed Fuji-Xerox as the sole agent for Xerox copiers and duplicators in the Far East.

Wilson's foresight paid huge dividends. Rank-Xerox and Fuji-Xerox, which contributed less than 10 percent of total Xerox profits in 1965, accounted for 25 percent of the company's bottom line by the end of the decade. By 1973, the year the FTC sought divestiture of the English and Japanese ventures, Rank-Xerox and Fuji-Xerox provided *45 percent* of Xerox's $300 million dollars in earnings.

In effect, the United States Government was insisting that one of the country's most prominent manufacturers cut itself in half and permit the offcast Rank-Xerox and Fuji-Xerox—two foreign concerns—to compete for revenues, profits, and jobs in America. The remedy was nonsense as a matter of public policy, and it might have mortally wounded Xerox. McColough and Xerox never budged on the issue.

When the FTC agreed to settle the case in November of 1974, two years of maneuvering appeared to vindicate Xerox's legal position and strategy. The deal required Xerox to release its patents, permit customers to buy toner from other suppliers, and adjust its pricing policies. But the company's equity in Rank-Xerox and Fuji-Xerox as well as its lease-only policy were left intact. Managers and shareholders were relieved.

The battle, however, was not finished. During the sixty-day review period mandated before any FTC settlement becomes final, the Commission faced a fire storm of criticism. Twenty-five Xerox competitors testified vehemently against the proposed arrangement, accusing the FTC of attempting to whitewash the litigation with a public relations hand slap. The Commissioners vacillated; in an unprecedented move, they reversed themselves, rejected the settlement, and forced Xerox back to the bargaining table for an agonizing six additional months. Not until July of 1975 did the two sides end the antitrust action. The final consent decree, which left Xerox in control of its international partners, so angered competitors that several of them—including SCM, IBM, and Van Dyk Research Corporation—continued to press private antitrust actions against Xerox well into the late 1970s.

The FTC's turnabout punctuated the adversity confronting Xerox in 1975. That year America's economy groaned, as a misguided policy of monetary expansion by the Federal Reserve, ineffective wage and price controls begun under the Nixon administration, international crop failures, and the first of the Middle East oil shocks combined to produce the worst inflation rate since the end of World War II and the most unsparing recession since the Depression.

In one respect, the general economic decline confirmed Xerox's fundamental strength—people made as many copies in bad times as they did in good. But while copy volume and Xerox revenues continued to climb during the recession, profits weakened. In 1974, Xerox's income fell below 10 percent of its sales for the first time in thirteen years. The bogey was rising costs and, in the opinion of some industry analysts, management's inability to control them.

Xerox misjudged the recession. Even though people continued to copy documents in record numbers, they did so on existing machines. Office managers virtually stopped leasing new copiers. As a result, Xerox installed a mere one percent more copiers than it removed in 1975, a net rate of addition previously typical of a good month. The change caught management off guard. Their decision-making systems and habits, formed during a decade of unmet demand, produced manufacturing and marketing plans that ignored the drop in orders. Unplaced inventory swelled, as did the cost to finance it.

Xerox's annual bill for employees and materials skyrocketed. In part, company executives could legitimately blame a general inflation rate that was beyond their control. Most of the pressure on Xerox's profits, however, came from the failure of management's layoff and other expense control programs to bring costs in line. The increases in interest, payroll, and materials robbed the company of an extraordinary amount of income. In 1972, the last year Xerox's profits had grown nearly as fast as its sales, the cost of interest, payroll, and materials had accounted for under 60 percent of revenues. In 1975, those same expenses absorbed close to 70 percent of every dollar Xerox received—a 10 percent difference that reduced the company's bottom line by more than *$400 million.*

Deteriorating economics forced Peter McColough to project a decline in 1975 earnings per share—the first fall in profits since the company had changed its name to Xerox in 1960. Wall Street noticed. Xerox stock, which had traded at an all-time high of $179 per share in 1972, plunged to $50 a share in early 1975. And that same winter, as McColough watched the stock plummet, the FTC reverse itself, and his competitors take Xerox to court, he still had not resolved the biggest blunder in the company's history—the catastrophe at Scientific Data Systems.

The press had long since dubbed SDS "McColough's Folly."

In the beginning, critics mainly attacked the exorbitant price McColough had gambled on the California computer concern. But as the years passed, and SDS racked up one whopping loss after another, Xerox's computer division increasingly loomed as a dark cloud over McColough's business judgment. Instead of price, the perennial issue centered on whether SDS had any value to Xerox whatsoever.

Max Palevsky thought not. The flamboyant former chairman of SDS, who had severed his relationship with Xerox soon after closing the $900 million sale, was reported to have commented, "We sold them a dead horse before it hit the ground."

Others disagreed, blaming Xerox for killing an otherwise profitable operation. "Xerox didn't do it right," opined Arthur Rock, the respected venture capitalist who had provided Palevsky with the money needed to start up SDS. "The only thing I can tell you is that when we sold SDS, it was a one-hundred-million-dollar business making ten million dollars after taxes. At the same time Digital Equipment did fifty million dollars and four million dollars after taxes. And we were direct competitors. Same business. I personally feel that Xerox just didn't do it right. Mismanagement, yes sir."

Prior to the Xerox deal, SDS had had a strong history of profitability. Like Digital Equipment Corporation and Control Data Corporation, SDS had prospered by avoiding IBM—in contrast to the strategies of larger companies that had tried without success to compete directly against IBM in mainframe commercial data processing. In the opinion of William Norris, the chairman of Control Data, the managers who tackled IBM misunderstood both computers and computer markets. "In big multidivisional companies like RCA, Sperry Rand, Honeywell or GE," Norris said, "top management is engrossed in many things and is not knowledgeable about the problems in the computer division. Top management in the conglomerates doesn't understand computers, and when the division is losing money, they won't take risks."

Xerox thought it was different. Peter McColough willingly took risks—he'd paid, after all, nearly a billion dollars for SDS. Furthermore, he acknowledged his ignorance about computers, implying that he would look to others with more experience to make computer business decisions. "I don't subscribe to the idea that a manager is a manager is a manager," admitted McColough. "I can walk into a laboratory and, without seeing any market research, smell whether a new copier is good or bad. But I don't have the same skill in computers because I wasn't brought up in that business."

But despite the gutsy price tag for SDS and McColough's humble management rhetoric, Xerox's maiden act as owner of SDS was to discard the California computer maker's proven strategy in favor of the discredited ambitions of companies like GE and RCA. Xerox charged head on against IBM.

"We evaluated the risks of being in the 'same arena with IBM,' " McColough explained later. "We viewed this as inevitable and felt that the market was so large and growing that we could become competitive. More specifically, we saw the trend toward communications and distributed computers in our favor."

In 1969, challenging IBM in commercial data processing was like taking on Xerox in copiers. IBM had the best-known name in computing; IBM's sales and service organization was unequaled; IBM's leasing policies and balance sheet represented overwhelming financial strengths. Moreover, according to a Justice Department antitrust complaint, IBM embroidered its competitive advantages with many of the same illegal practices later ascribed to Xerox by the FTC, including price discrimination, disparagement of competitors, and false product claims.

Notwithstanding any of that, however, IBM's most profound advantage derived from the nature of computing itself; only by understanding a phenomenon called "software lock-in" could an IBM competitor hope to shape a profitable strategy. Computer engineering requires choice. For example, systems designers at one manufacturer can decide to make the binary code "10001110" cause their central processor to add two numbers while their counterparts at another shop might choose the same signal for moving information to or from memory. Naturally, programmers applying one set of codes to the wrong machine make many mistakes.

The same pattern of choice and differentiation obtains in programming languages, application programs, and other software. Consequently, computer users must spend significant time, money, and effort to learn the operating rules of the systems they purchase—a painful education hurdle that discourages people from switching whimsically from one manufacturer to another. They get "locked in" to the software they already own, a reality that worked powerfully to the omnipresent IBM's benefit.

"Once an IBM customer had invested the thousands, or even

millions, of dollars needed to make a complex commercial application program work properly," wrote a government economist who helped prepare the Justice Department's case against IBM, "there was little chance he'd throw it away just to take advantage of the mere 10 to 15 percent savings in monthly rental that another computer vendor might offer. In fact, as IBM discovered, the lock-in effect took effect before a computer had even been delivered: the training of staff and the planning for the writing of application programs were often sufficient investments for the user to stick with IBM."

Put differently, once a customer's computer professionals had learned Spanish, they were loath to tackle Portuguese without some extraordinary rewards for their labor. Lower prices were not enough. In the opinion of an expert witness at the IBM antitrust trial, breaking through the barrier of IBM software lock-in would have required a "technological miracle."

PARC's personal distributed computing architecture might have been that miracle. But the Alto computer, laser printer, Ethernet communications system, Bravo and Gypsy word processing software, and other PARC advances were not fully operational in the laboratory until 1975. In 1969, by contrast, when McColough ordered SDS into commercial data processing, SDS lacked any clear technical or business advantages with which to challenge IBM's computer monopoly. Indeed, the single technology in which McColough thought SDS had a lead over IBM—timesharing—mainly served to illustrate the computer naïveté at Xerox corporate headquarters. SDS had entered timesharing reluctantly, had never made the engineering, manufacturing, and marketing changes required for success, and, consequently, never was the dominant player McColough imagined.

In effect, McColough and Xerox asked SDS to become number two in the computer industry by trying harder. And try they did. SDS developed new computers, peripherals, and software; they expanded their marketing, sales, and service organizations. In the beginning, everybody at the company talked and acted with the patience of a competitor in the race for the long haul. But when the 1970–1971 recession gutted SDS's traditional strengths in the scientific and government markets, causing the computer division to rack up a two-year loss of $71 million, Xerox management shifted course.

At the end of 1971, corporate headquarters rejected SDS's

long range plan and replaced the computer division's president with an ex-IBM executive. A few months later, the still dissatisfied copier maker eliminated the job of SDS president altogether by integrating the computer and copier divisions into a single, functionally arranged organization.

The chief of the new copier-computer combine immediately appointed a high level task force to reevaluate SDS's strategy. The study group worked for most of 1972. In the process, they provided Xerox for the first time with an objective assessment of SDS's strengths and weaknesses. Had a comparable effort preceded McColough's hasty acquisition of SDS, it is unlikely Xerox would have pursued its ill-considered attack on IBM, a strategy the task force criticized in its year-end 1972 recommendations. According to their report, Xerox's best hope to salvage SDS lay in scaling back its commercial data processing ambitions. Even then, the task force predicted, SDS would generate but a fraction of the revenues originally expected by McColough, and the computer operations' losses, though decreasing, would persist for at least five more years.

Thus, in 1973, four years after becoming part of Xerox, SDS once again pursued the "avoid IBM" strategy that had made the company successful during the 1960s. Regrettably, now that SDS had the right strategy, it had the wrong organization. In place of separate copier and computer arms, Xerox's 1972 reorganization had fashioned three functionally defined divisions. Engineering and manufacturing—for both copiers and computers—became known as the Information Technology Group. Marketing, sales, and service—for both copiers and computers—were called the Information Systems Group. And planning—for both copiers and computers—was done by the Business Development Group.

McColough, who had insisted he did not believe "a manager is a manager is a manager," asked all three functional groups to report to Ray Hay, a corporate executive vice president with copier background and copier training. Hay knew nothing about computers. Furthermore, the computer operations were far less significant than the copier business; Xerox copiers and duplicators produced more profits every six weeks than SDS computers lost in a year. Finally, Hay's office was in Rochester while SDS was in California. In the reorganized world of Xerox, therefore, business priorities and geography conspired with Hay's personal inclinations to effectively deprive SDS of a general manager.

There was no one at the helm—no decision maker with the exclusive, full-time responsibility and authority to set direction, coordinate activities, and resolve competing claims among the different groups building and selling computers. Xerox's functional setup produced a vacuum of leadership that, perhaps inevitably, was filled with copier thinking and copier actions, a result corporate headquarters initially considered both appropriate and helpful.

"The thought was," McColough explained, "that [SDS], being a very small company for its industry, would have better coverage in the marketplace and perhaps would do better in revenue if it were oriented somewhat closer to the rest of Xerox, and the sales offices were combined and different people, by and large, put in the same location, in the hope there would be some interplay or relationship between a much larger organization selling copiers and duplicators and computers, that they would work together to the benefit particularly of the computer operation. I think with that also went the expectation that by eliminating duplicate facilities, particularly in the marketing area, there would be some reduction of expenses and costs and therefore an improvement of profits."

It was a classic mistake. Like alchemists, McColough and his colleagues thought they might convert iron into gold by mixing the failing computer division with its much more successful copier counterpart. But computers and copiers are profoundly different. For all their mechanical and chemical complexity, copiers essentially are appliances intended to provide push button convenience. Computers, by contrast, rely on completely different technology and often demand as much ingenuity of their users as they do of their designers. The two products, quite plainly, have nothing in common.

"Folding SDS into the copier group made no sense," said one former Xerox executive. "Most copier salesmen wouldn't know a computer if they fell over it. Nor would the management of the Business Development Group or the Information Technology Group."

Instead of benefiting the computer business, Xerox's reorganization balkanized SDS and set it adrift. When SDS's chief of manufacturing had a problem, he turned to the Information Technology Group; when the leader of sales needed help, he looked to the Information Systems Group. The outcome was worse than management by committee. It was management by default.

"The effect was adverse," criticized F. Rigdon Currie, who managed SDS's national sales force prior to the 1972 restructuring. "Decisions became more difficult to be made. The three operating heads in California were not in agreement, were not meeting common objectives."

According to Currie, the Information Technology Group assigned the SDS manufacturing plant tasks unrelated to computers, the plant itself repeatedly failed to meet projected delivery schedules, and the splintered SDS lost control of its costs.

"We tracked what we characterized as 'unit manufacturing costs' of various computer system components and full systems," Currie later reported. "These costs are established once per year, generally. These costs appeared to us to rise faster than you would expect based on conventional forces of inflation.

"There was also another cost category called 'costs other than standard' which did not affect the unit manufacturing cost but did affect gross margins of the business. There were occasions when these 'costs other than standard' rose dramatically in a very short period of time without any prediction that they would rise."

The computer sales force, schooled by a world of rough and tumble competition, were stripped of some of their most important weapons, like price discounts, by the "proven" sales philosophy of the more genteel, monopoly-spoiled copier group. Without a leader to insist on functional coordination and to protect SDS's interests in the corporation, the unrealistic pressures from the copier side caused disorientation and despair.

"Morale in the field," lamented SDS marketing vice president Donald McKee in 1973, "is terrible."

When Xerox finally admitted error and reassigned a general manager to SDS at the end of 1974, it was too late. There had been five major strategic or organizational changes in five years and a sea full of red ink. Following the poor results of 1970 and 1971, SDS lost $47 million in 1972, $45 million in 1973, and $42 million in 1974. Since entering the computer business, Xerox had dumped $180 million.

Peter McColough had had enough. In the spring of 1975, while PARC celebrated advances in personal distributed computing, McColough appointed yet another computer task force, code-named Odyssey, and asked it to chart an end to Xerox's adventure in mainframe computers. Their findings were sobering. Xerox, the Odyssey team concluded, probably could not find a buyer for SDS—at any price. The most the company could hope for was to discontinue SDS's business, stop the operating losses, and try to sell whatever separate assets still had value.

Acting on their recommendations, McColough sent a long letter to members of the Xerox board, detailing the history of SDS and the current quandary over what to do about the division. He concluded with several facts in support of closing down the business. His list read like an obituary for six years of misman-agement:

1. The unit manufacturing and service costs of our product line are not competitive.
2. The computer lease base is becoming increasingly vulnerable and obsolete.
3. Replacement of the product line would involve hundreds of millions of dollars of expense, capital and cash.
4. The strategic relevance of this product line is less than that of other programs for which we also need funding.

At their July 1975 meeting, the board reviewed McColough's letter and the financial impact of Xerox's diversification into computers. Among other things, the board heard that, as a result of the division's poor performance and the ten million shares of stock issued to buy SDS, Xerox shareholders had earned $4.18 per share in 1974 instead of $5.15, a nearly 20-percent decline in performance. More damning yet, the total bill for "McColough's Folly," including the acquisition price, the operating losses, and the proposed write-off necessary to end the business, amounted to just under $1.3 billion. The board unanimously voted to end the nightmare.

"In retrospect," said a chastened Peter McColough at his press conference announcing the pullout, "the Scientific Data acquisition was a mistake."

Chapter

11

The SDS debacle rested squarely on the shoulders of a new management team at Xerox. Joe Wilson was dead. On November 22, 1971, the sixty-one-year-old businessman suffered a fatal heart attack. Much as the assassination of President John F. Kennedy on the same day eight years earlier had stunned Americans, Wilson's unexpected passing left the people of Xerox grieving over their loss and anxious about their future.

His message to Xerox employees always had been simple. "We aspire to be a leader throughout the world in graphic communications," Wilson said in a ten minute film shown since the early sixties to welcome newcomers to the company. "It is frightfully important for man to communicate with his fellow man. And this is the very heart of our business."

Viewers of the tape heard the plainspoken, optimistic executive back up his noble vision for Xerox with a list of guiding business principles—faith in people, concern for the customer, and economic power through innovation, marketing, patents, and worldwide presence. As the men and women of Xerox understood better than anyone else, it was Wilson's unique management of creativity, risk, and caution that produced one of the most successful companies in American history. With his death, Xerox passed suddenly, irreversibly into a different season.

In Wilson's place, Peter McColough became chairman and Archie McCardell, an ex-Ford Motor Company finance executive, moved up to president. Individually, McColough the salesman and McCardell the analyst possessed many of Wilson's best qualities: imagination, daring, rigor, and insight. As a team, however, the two men were destined to go awry, reinforcing each other's weaknesses as they steered their corporation toward diversification without direction and change without commitment.

No one at the company was more bereaved by Wilson's death than Peter McColough. Wilson had been McColough's business mentor and friend, helping to channel McColough's boundless enthusiasm into making Xerox a better corporation and the world a better place. Wilson had hired the Canadian, backed his aggressive sales force plan, promoted him when his marketing initiative began to pay off, and selected him as Wilson's successor to the company's top job. And when McColough had suffered a midlife crisis in the 1960s, Wilson was there to guide him through the struggle.

"When I was made president of the company in 1966," McColough recounted, "I went through about six months of getting congratulations. Instead of feeling elated about it, I was really rather depressed. Up until then I always felt I had the option if I wanted to do something else. I was interested in politics. I had the freedom, if I wanted to, to move into a government job. But then, after planning with Mr. Wilson the succession of the company, I realized I had taken on an obligation that no matter what I wanted to do, I couldn't leave."

Wilson advised McColough to expand his horizons. Xerox actively supported nonprofit causes both in Rochester and beyond, often incurring criticism from those who believed social and political policy were improper pursuits for a corporation. But Wilson disagreed; he encouraged McColough to accept the obligation, both as an individual and the head of a powerful corporation, to participate in matters of public concern.

"Under Mr. Wilson's influence," McColough acknowledged, "I realized that I really should try to play a broader role than just a businessman and try to play a role in society. I had an obligation to work for United Way, which I had never done before, to perhaps go on some nonprofit boards, which I hadn't done before. I got interested in politics. A lot of that had to do with Mr. Wilson's influence. He deeply believed that you really had an obligation in life if you were privileged, had a good education, making some money, to put something back for other people. Not just to take."

The late 1960s and early 1970s provided McColough plenty of opportunity to demonstrate his concern for others. One after another, America's most critical institutions—the rule of law, the Presidency, the judiciary, the armed services, the Democratic Party, the corporation, the university, the church, the family—came under attack or fell into disrepute. Xerox's energetic chief executive argued that corporations had a responsibility to help right many of the wrongs fueling the nation's unrest. And he did more than talk. Among other things, he changed the ethnic composition of Xerox's board of directors, set explicit objectives for minority hiring programs, doubled the rate of Xerox contributions to education and the arts, and paid for Xerox employees to teach basic skills to adults, counsel the elderly, advise minority businesses, and work with drug abuse programs and other community-based organizations.

When an angry woman at the 1970 annual meeting accused Xerox social action programs of abetting student uprisings instead of making money for stockholders, McColough admonished her shortsightedness. "This is the worst time in our country's history," he responded, "to show that corporations are only concerned about profit and have no concern for the problems of society. I think that would be suicidal."

McColough extended his activities beyond corporate policies and programs. He volunteered his own time and effort to the United Way, the University of Rochester board of trustees, the Council on Foreign Relations, the U.S./U.S.S.R. Trade and Economic Council, the Overseas Development Council, the International Executive Service Corps, the Business Committee for the Arts, the National Urban League, and the United Negro College Fund. In 1968 he was a Humphrey delegate at the Democratic convention in Chicago, in 1972 he co-chaired the national fund raising drive for Democratic congressional candidates, in 1973 he was named treasurer of the Democratic National Party, and in 1975 he chaired the committee exploring Senator Henry Jackson's presidential bid. Peter McColough was involved.

"I happen to like politics, probably as much as my business," he said in a 1975 interview with the *Harvard Business Review*. "I don't know if my political activity hurts Xerox. I don't think it does; but frankly, if it were damaging the company and the board of directors didn't like it, I would still do it but I would leave the company. I have some strong views on the necessity for political involvement; too many Americans leave the political process to too few people, or the wrong type. If you've been on the scene as long as I have, you will realize how few people in this country have any real voice in politics. And unless you work in it, you don't have any real voice and you don't have any impact. More people from business, more people from all walks of life, should be involved in the political process. This is the most important activity of all."

Critics moaned that McColough could afford to be liberal because of his company's monopoly power and profits. But their complaint missed the potential cost of his progressivism. Employees in all companies carefully monitor the words and actions of their top officers; no corporation, regardless of size or profitability, can easily sacrifice the presence and participation of its chief executive officer. When McColough became president of Xerox in 1968, he said he would maintain the company's momentum by changing Xerox from a one-product firm into a diversified, communications corporation, a goal he later elaborated to include the invention and exploitation of an "architecture of information." His ambition required a shift in his corporation's basic character as fundamental as the transformation of Haloid into Xerox; he, as much as anyone, knew that earlier change could not have succeeded without the full-time participation and guidance of Joe Wilson. Thus, by adding social programs and political activity to his personal schedule, Peter McColough risked communicating to his employees that his commitment to solving the country's problems outstripped his dedication to leading change and growth at Xerox.

The picture of McColough as a distracted leader intensified with Xerox's legal problems. In addition to his high profile in public affairs and his role as Xerox's ambassador to external constituencies, McColough assigned himself the task of directing Xerox's antitrust struggles. It was a heavy burden. According to the company's general counsel, the lawsuits pulled McColough away from Xerox between six and eight weeks every year during the mid-1970s.

Such extracorporate and legal agendas underscored the importance of McColough's choice of Archie McCardell to be president of Xerox. In a standard approach to the division of labor at the top, McColough set his primary responsibility as policy maker, McCardell's as policy enforcer.

"Between him and McCardell, Peter was the visionary," says one of their senior management colleagues. "He would also invariably bring good common sense to any discussion. He permitted Archie to make many decisions, although I'm sure Peter made some too. But he left it to Archie to communicate and implement the decisions. That's true of any company where you have a guy who's chairman and CEO and another guy who's president and COO. Peter felt that Archie should be running the company."

Archie McCardell had begun his business career in 1949 as a financial analyst for Ford. During his seventeen years at the car company, he learned the managerial uses of statistics introduced

at Ford by, among others, Robert McNamara. In that approach
to management, experience and gut feel were heavily supple-
mented (some have argued supplanted) by trend analysis and
financial controls. Decisions about car design, factory layouts, marketing programs, business plans, and ongoing performance were
made and monitored by the numbers. Managing without a good
set of historical figures, McCardell once said, would be as though
you "walked into a brand new airplane, somebody takes away all
of the instruments and tells you to fly it blind."

McCardell was no beady-eyed bean counter. Associates describe the midwestern-born executive as warm, affable, humorous,
brilliant—and enigmatic. His informality made him approacha-
ble; his habits of listening and laughing made him engaging. But
despite such bonhomie, he rarely changed his mind if the numbers
weren't right.

"Archie has a manner of interfacing one on one I wish to hell
I had," commented an executive who worked with McCardell at
both Ford and Xerox. "He may be dead set in his ways, but when
you come to him with a proposition, he'll listen and engage in
dialogue. When you leave without selling him on the situation,
you feel, 'Damn it all, he was so receptive and willing to listen, I
just couldn't muster up the proper argument to make the case.'"

His analytical talents had made McCardell a perfect candidate
to inject financial and administrative rigor into a monopoly gone
crazy. In 1966, when Peter McColough hired McCardell as group
vice president of finance and control, Xerox was in the sixth consecutive year of dizzying growth. That year sales increased by
more than three times the size of the Haloid company at its largest.
The next year Xerox grew by more than four Haloids, and the
year after by more than eight Haloids. Yet Xerox continued to
rely on Haloid finance methods and Haloid administration systems. They didn't work. Salesmen weren't getting paid, machines
weren't being delivered, company logistics in general were out of
kilter.

Once at Xerox, McCardell identified, categorized, and col-
lected the numbers he thought he needed to manage a company
of Xerox's size. In the process, he analyzed the basic business
economics behind Xerox's approach of selling copies instead of
copiers. Copiers were like money machines; with every copy made,
the customer deposited coins in Xerox's bank account. Therefore,
the earnings capacity of a machine was easy to calculate. The 914,

for example, produced seven copies per minute. In a perfect world, it would run all day without interruption and, at two cents per copy, generate about two hundred dollars of revenue every twenty-four hours. In practice, of course, the machines were not in constant use because of malfunctions or lulls in demand. But the revenue formula provided a valuable target against which to manage performance.

That perspective inspired the business strategy adopted at Xerox the year following McCardell's arrival. Under "Strategy Q," as it was called, Xerox grouped customers by the volume of their copying needs, then designed, built, and sold machines with copying speeds to match each segment. If a customer could keep a forty-copy-per-minute ("CPM") machine busy, then renting him a slower copier would sacrifice revenue; if his demand for copies would leave the forty-CPM copier idle, then Xerox could save money and forestall customer frustration by providing a less expensive and slower machine.

McCardell's performance earned him the nod over Ray Hay when Peter McColough decided to give up the job of president in 1971. Hay had a marketing background and, consequently, reinforced instead of complemented McColough's skills. McCardell's financial and analytical talents, on the other hand, promised a broader, deeper team at the top.

Leadership at Xerox, however, demanded more than a capacity for insight. Peter McColough's acquisitions and proclamations pointed toward a corporate transformation that both mystified and threatened his organization. Thousands of Xerox employees—from factory workers to salespeople to executives—had, at most, a vague notion about the need for, or content of, an "architecture of information." And at worst, they believed McColough's goal unnecessary or irrelevant. To instill conviction among the doubters and to provide direction to the doers would require constant explanation and hands-on experience; Xerox's top leaders had to *involve* their organization in the case for change. But in distancing himself from daily operations, then casting the number-crunching Archie McCardell as president, McColough seemed to do the opposite.

"Archie," declared one of his Xerox colleagues, "is a very, very, extremely bright individual. But he managed by the numbers. He wasn't a very good communicator. There would be meeting after meeting after meeting of whomever with him at which decisions would not be made with him *at the meeting*. Then shortly thereafter a decision would come out but with no explanation of why that decision was chosen and no communication of its implications to those affected by it. Archie would just confer with Peter and a decision would be made. His management style was not one that communicated much to the troops. It was not well understood why the company was doing what it was doing—whether good, bad, or indifferent. And that lack of understanding went to all levels."

McCardell's numbers sometimes blurred instead of clarified his judgment. For example, several former Xerox officials attribute the damaging 1972 decision to combine the copier and computer divisions to McCardell's apprehensions about financial reporting requirements. By consolidating its two operating divisions, Xerox avoided having to report SDS's poor results as a separate "line of business" in legally mandated disclosure statements. That made the company look better, these critics point out; but by depriving SDS of a general manager, the reorganization also hastened the deterioration of Xerox's billion dollar investment.

McCardell's numbers fixation and his cryptic style also conflicted with McColough's insatiable appetite for new and different challenges. Instead of managing Xerox in a relentless and well reasoned pursuit of an office products and information business, the McColough-McCardell combination too often sent incoherent and contradictory signals to their organization, a failure that extended to the most basic burden of any top management team—articulating a clear strategic direction for the company.

Problems with SDS and the FTC occupied most of McColough's and McCardell's first few years in office. But toward the end of 1973—three and a half years after McColough's "architecture of information" speech, and six months after Chuck Thacker completed the first Alto personal computer—McColough and McCardell agreed to reopen the question of Xerox's strategy. They decided, McCardell noted, to ask "some of our most imaginative people to look at Xerox with a wider perspective than we generally use."

They gathered together four men they expected to bring intelligence, company experience, technological breadth, and outspoken opinion to the task of recommending a corporate direction. Michael Hughes, whom they asked to chair the committee, was an Englishman recently transferred to corporate planning from the same function at Rank-Xerox. George White, the man responsible for laser scientist Gary Starkweather's move to PARC, had managed engineering development for both copier and non-copier products and, most recently, had joined Jack Goldman's staff. George Pake was on assignment at corporate headquarters after three years of managing PARC. And Jim Lyons, a copier division veteran, was directing a secret acquisition program for McCardell.

McColough and McCardell gave the Hughes group an extraordinary charter—identify a strategy by which Xerox could continue its record setting pace of growth while simultaneously absorbing the heavy investments required for copier product development and broader diversification. They asked the committee to exercise complete independence, imploring them to "look at Xerox without our customary blinders." Neither government regulation nor Xerox's current legal problems nor popular objections to conglomerates should constrain their thinking. The Hughes team was to analyze the company's existing businesses and to consider a virtually unlimited field of diversification possibilities including, among others, finance, health, energy, ecology, land development, and recreation. Not even the pursuit of an "architecture of information" was to be assumed as a necessary objective of Xerox's strategy.

They allocated the team an unlimited budget, encouraged them to hire as many consultants as needed, and assured them access to people at Xerox and other companies. To stress the importance of the project, the chairman and the president each promised to set aside one day a month for the duration of the project to review the committee's progress.

"After McColough and McCardell left the room," Hughes recalls, "we all looked at each other with out mouths agape and said, 'Shit! How are we going to do all of that?!?'."

The committee started by reviewing Xerox's copier business, and they soon reached some disturbing conclusions. Personnel, materials, and product development costs were rising beyond any reasonable proportion to revenues, making a sham of the administrative systems Archie McCardell had transplanted from Ford to Xerox in the late 1960s. By 1974, a nervous Hughes reported to McCardell, those systems provided only the appearance of control.

"Compared with the complete lack of controls that existed at

Xerox in the late sixties," Hughes says in recounting the committee's criticism, "the controls brought in by Archie were good. But they were the type of controls put on a company like Ford with model years, high fashion consciousness, low technology, and enormous numbers of blue collar workers. They didn't really fit Xerox which was a high technology company where product development was critical and the sales and service organizations dominated. Salesmen are the best beaters of systems in the world."

Inefficiencies were rampant. For example, although service costs then accounted for more than one-fifth of total company expenses, technicians corrected machine breakdowns on the first attempt only three out of four times, causing hundreds of thousands of unnecessary follow-up calls each year. Thirty percent of new machine installations were aborted because of failed coordination between the sales and service groups; nearly a third of total service visits might have been avoided if Xerox had done a better job of training customer operators in the proper care and handling of copiers.

Comparable problems existed in sales, engineering, development, finance—in short, throughout the company. The McCardell controls were overmatched by a Xerox culture immune to worrying about cost. After more than a decade of unprecedented profitability and monopoly privilege, budgets at Xerox, it seemed, were truly made to be broken.

"Xerox's vulnerabilities," wrote the committee, "basically accrue from the way we manage our costs and our marketing. [Our] challenge is not resources or technology over the next 3–5 years but management style, organization and discipline."

Furthermore, the Hughes team predicted the Xerox monopoly in copiers would soon end. FTC contentions to the contrary, competition was fast becoming a reality. IBM had established a respectable 10 percent share, the Japanese were exporting low cost machines to the United States, and Kodak was expected to introduce a copier at any time. More alarmingly, thousands of customers were primed to dump Xerox because of the copier giant's unrestrained pricing policies.

Recall that Xerox's pricing scheme guaranteed customers a certain number of copies in return for a minimum monthly billing. Thus, with the original 914 Copier, customers paid ninety-five dollars each month for the right to make two thousand copies before incurring an additional charge on a per copy basis. Over the years, as Xerox machines got bigger, faster, and more complicated, and as company development and operations grew more costly and unwieldy, the copier maker repeatedly raised minimum monthly rates to maintain profits. At times, Xerox also increased the number of guaranteed copies covered by the higher billings. But such gestures meant nothing to customers who made less than the monthly allotment of "free" copies. For them, the effects of Xerox's machinations were simple—higher copying prices and mounting frustration.

By 1974, nearly a third of Xerox copiers failed to reach minimum monthly copy usage, and 60 percent of customers who canceled their Xerox contracts cited higher prices as the reason. To the Hughes group, these signs indicated a spreading willingness, if not desire, among Xerox customers to look for copying alternatives. Once competition arrived in force, the committee warned, Xerox's prices would have to drop, and unless management had gained control over costs by then, falling prices would translate directly into lower profits.

According to Hughes, Archie McCardell listened attentively to the committee's criticisms and commented, "If this is true, then I am guilty of gross managerial neglect." On its face, his remark was conditional; "if" he said. True to form, McCardell gave no clear indication whether he accepted the analysis. But if he did, it was on an intellectual plane only; neither his management style nor his directives changed.

"Archie's idea of cutting costs," says Hughes, "wasn't exactly hands on. He would issue a budget and then sit back and expect others to carry it out. Then there would be eight hundred and thirty-seven reasons why the budget couldn't be met. People would tell Archie they'd have to cut one program or another, and either he or McColough, who hated to cut anything because he always felt every product might be the next 914, would say, 'Okay, don't worry about it.' "

McColough's and McCardell's uncoordinated objectives dominated the committee's acquisition work. McCardell wanted Xerox to expand into insurance, financial services, or some other industry that might cushion the huge amounts of capital required to develop copiers. The 914, for example, had cost $75 million to design and build; the 9200, a copier introduced in 1974, set Xerox back by more than $300 million. The finance man yearned for balance in the company's cash flow.

McColough had less sophisticated desires.

"Go find me another Xerox," he told the Hughes group. "It was great, and I want to do it again. Go out and find something we can really 'pop' with!"

The strategy committee devised its own shorthand—"zingers" and "stabilizers"—to identify opportunities that fit the goals and personalities of McColough and McCardell. "Stabilizers" had to provide the financial certainty and low risk longed for by McCardell. "Zingers" had to give McColough "pop," which a consultant to the committee described as follows: "recent growth must be good to sensational; future external trends must reinforce this opportunity; the businesses must relate in some constructive way to the current xerographic markets; and the investment level must be sufficiently high to make the venture meaningful." It was an impossible target.

"We decided," says Hughes, "to look only at companies growing at ten percent per year for the past ten years. There were none. So we reduced our sights to ten percent growth for five years. There were a handful, but they were companies like Exxon that we couldn't realistically consider acquiring. So we had to dilute the criteria again.

"The problem became clear. How can you find a company that can make Xerox take notice of it when Xerox itself was so large and had been growing at fifteen percent a year for so long? It can't be done. To grow Xerox through acquisition you'd have to find and buy a company just like Xerox and do it every five years without making a mistake. Acquisition just couldn't solve the problem of growth; it might contribute to it, but it was not the only answer."

Having concluded that a cost conscious copier business would provide more future profits than anyone had suspected while acquisitions were likely to yield less, the strategy committee turned its attention to business opportunities from research and innovation. They evaluated a range of technologies from videodisks to a national electronic mail system to computers. What they concluded supported McColough's original instincts—the biggest "zinger" of all would most likely be the office of the future. Furthermore, with the head start provided by PARC's technology and the company's recent entry into the typewriter word processing market, the group considered Xerox well positioned to stake a major claim.

Near the end of October 1974, after spending ten months and hundreds of thousands of dollars studying the great issues facing Xerox, the Hughes committee presented their report to Peter

McColough and Archie McCardell. They identified four alternative corporate strategies, each of which recognized the importance of making the copier enterprise more cost competitive. "The
profitable health of the copier duplicator business," the group
stressed, "is the single, most critical determinant in our future
growth and diversification plans."

The four plans differed with respect to the themes and objectives of diversification. In the first proposed alternative, Xerox
would continue its assault on IBM's data processing markets by
acquiring a life insurance company as a "stabilizer" and, given the
failure of SDS, buying yet another computer company as the "zinger" to mount the challenge.

The second strategy also pitted Xerox against IBM, but in the
office of the future instead of data processing. The company could
stabilize its cash flow by purchasing an information services company like Dun & Bradstreet. Meanwhile, through combining Xerox's resources with the likes of Texas Instruments and by bundling
copiers, word processing typewriters, and computers with PARC's
advances in microelectronics, software, and communications, the
Hughes committee believed Xerox could integrate most of its activities into a commercially successful "architecture of information."

The third plan avoided IBM altogether by moving into leisure
and entertainment industries; the fourth limited diversification to
financial services while emphasizing the pursuit of Xerox's traditional copying and duplicating technologies.

The committee assessed the four strategies against Xerox's
competitive strengths and weaknesses as well as general economic
expectations before presenting their final recommendation:

> The Strategy Committee unanimously concurs, after all ob-
> jective and subjective considerations:
>
> —that the IBM [office of the future] Head-on strategic theme
> be adopted in principle.
>
> —that actions be assigned towards its orderly implementation
> as outlined.
>
> We would be intensely proud to have been part of a Xerox
> which met this challenge.

Their choice laid out a commonsense path toward a prosperous Xerox future. By lowering its cost to make and repair copiers,

Xerox could prepare for, then survive, the competitive onslaught about to happen; by developing the office of the future as a business instead of a technology alone, the company could seize a unique opportunity for change and growth. The strategic thinking McColough and McCardell had requested was now articulated before them.

"When the presentation was finished," says a still bewildered Hughes, "McColough and McCardell left the room without saying anything. They came back a few minutes later and said to us, 'We have a problem. We're going into Manhattan tomorrow to borrow a large amount of money. If we tell you which of these recommendations we like or don't like, we feel we would be honor bound to tell our bankers.'

"And that was the end of it. A week or so later, a lawyer from the general counsel's office told us they would have to continue to defer a response to our recommendations pending the outcome of the antitrust litigation. He also asked for the only two copies of the slides and all of our working papers.

"We had, naturally, expected to play a major part in whatever specific strategy emerged from our work. But since they ignored it, there was really no place to go. It was very disillusioning. I don't think any of us was quite the same again."

Three years later, in a review of several attempts to choose a strategy under McColough and McCardell, Xerox's Corporate Business Planning department praised the Hughes group for accurately forecasting the major events in the copier and office markets. The summary concluded, however, that "there are no decisions or actions directly attributable to the Hughes committee recommendations." Among other implications, that meant innovative office systems from PARC's inventions had remained notional—fascinating for McCardell to discuss, fabulous for McColough to imagine, but fanciful for anybody else in the organization to expect as a clear direction from either man.

Chapter

12

A rchie McCardell had embarked upon the Hughes strategy effort by noting that, among Xerox's starkest weaknesses, were its failure to "manage the diverse technology needs of the future" and "to demonstrate the ability to market diverse products in the office." In other words, Xerox had yet to transcend the copier business. Peter McColough had not disagreed. Nor could he have, given the abysmal performance of Scientific Data Systems under Xerox management. But McCardell's late 1973 assessment went well beyond Xerox's problems with SDS—more than four years and a billion dollars after diversifying into computers, Xerox had failed to integrate digital capabilities into the mainstream of its organization. And none of the new endeavors stood more isolated than PARC.

"They are newcomers to the world of Xerox. Too new to know the traditions," wrote a company publicist about PARC's computer scientists for a 1971 edition of *Xerox World*. "Too new to know the lore of the 914, and the laboratory on Rochester's Hollenbeck Street, and the people who made Haloid into Xerox. Many of these newcomers have been part of Xerox for less than a year, most for less than two. Yet, talking among them, watching them work, one has the feeling that something akin to that Haloid energy is here in California."

Energy, enthusiasm, dedication—yes. But the organizational comparison of Xerox's two most significant scientific efforts ended there. Unlike Haloid's technicians of the 1950s, PARC's scientists were asked to research ideas, not develop products. The Haloid engineers had worked in the same town as other company employees; PARC sat a continent away from Rochester and Stamford. Most important, those who refined xerography for Haloid did so as partners with sales, manufacturing, and finance in Joe Wilson's all or nothing struggle for a viable office copier business. By contrast, the digital wizards in Palo Alto defined an "architecture of information" with neither active participation nor broad commitment from the business side of Xerox.

"PARC was floating around in free space," says George White.

"PARC was a head. But a head to which body? Who was going to pick up from whatever was done at PARC to do all of the rest of the hard work to make a business out of it?"

The answer, according to Jack Goldman's original 1969 scheme, was to have been SDS. Goldman's plan, however, reflected assumptions drawn from his own experience rather than from the history of Xerox's computer division. He had spent his career at Ford and Xerox, industrial mammoths that could afford to allocate significant resources to research and development. SDS was different. In 1969, it was less than one-tenth the size of Xerox and not yet a decade old. Its prosperity depended on existing—not future—technology. And it operated in an industry where its vendors, the hardware components suppliers, instead of itself or its competitors, underwrote long-term research advances. SDS lacked the capability to convert laboratory-proven inventions into products. Indeed, surfeited by their impressive early success, SDS's senior executives openly scorned research—surprising Goldman, for example, when they tried to scuttle his proposal for PARC.

Scientists more familiar with the computer industry expected such biases from SDS. Bob Taylor, Butler Lampson, and others from the ARPA research community had struggled to persuade a reluctant SDS to commercialize timesharing when that technology was the latest blossom of interactive computing. Many computer researchers bound for PARC had heard the story of Taylor's confrontation with SDS's chairman Max Palevsky over the future of timesharing. They also considered the timesharing systems SDS eventually produced mediocre, and they questioned the relevance of a mainframe computer manufacturer to the office of the future.

Thus, Goldman's dream that PARC and SDS would combine cheerfully to identify and exploit advanced computer concepts was at odds with reality. SDS belittled the very idea of PARC and lacked the capacity to develop inventions into products; many of PARC's computer scientists scoffed at SDS's talents and dreaded the prospect of working on behalf of the computer division. Far from the alliance Goldman expected, PARC and SDS antagonized each other from the outset.

Their mutual hostility erupted within a year of PARC's creation. In the spring of 1971, Bob Taylor's Computer Science Laboratory decided to build its own timesharing system instead of using an SDS "Sigma" computer to conduct research. The action infuriated SDS. How would potential customers react, asked SDS managers, to news that Xerox's own computer scientists had rejected the Sigma? How could Xerox afford such adverse publicity, they harped, in light of SDS's worsening financial position? The SDS men shouted foul; they demanded an explanation from PARC's director, George Pake.

Ever since Bob Taylor had warned him that supporting SDS would be a "mistake," Pake had known about the bad blood between many of his researchers and the management of Xerox's computer division. Pake's natural style was conciliatory; he wanted to cooperate with SDS. Nevertheless, an investigation into the matter satisfied him that the Computer Science Laboratory had sound reasons for rejecting a Sigma in favor of constructing their own "home built" timesharing system.

To proceed with its research, the Computer Science Laboratory required access to ARPA software previously developed on a Digital Equipment Corporation computer named the "PDP-10." The PDP-10, however, did compete directly against SDS's Sigma; for the Computer Science Laboratory to buy one clearly would have damaged SDS. By the same token, forcing a Sigma on the lab would have occasioned either years of effort to make the Sigma compatible with the PDP-10 so that it could run the required ARPA software or an even longer period to reinvent the software itself. Both outcomes would have wasted too much time and energy. The "home built" alternative, Pake concluded, was a thoughtful compromise, one that SDS did not appreciate.

"It is ironic," he wrote, "that a question has been raised by SDS over the way in which PARC scientists propose to use noncompetitive mini-computers—plus months of hard work—to get around any PDP-10 embarrassment for SDS. It is unthinkable to me that Xerox sets me the task of hiring creative, imaginative, top-rank researchers and then expects me to insist that they handcuff themselves with inappropriate equipment or that they fritter away their talents in make-work tasks that pointlessly tie SDS equipment into the research apparatus."

In his mind, the hue and cry over the "home built" decision had less to do with the best equipment for research than the willingness and ability of SDS to cooperate with PARC's charter. Instead of supporting PARC in a drive toward the information technologies of the future, SDS pressured Xerox headquarters to subordinate PARC's resources to the shorter-term needs of the computer operating division. To Pake, the current upset merely replayed the unacceptable objections posed by SDS ever since the inception of Jack Goldman's research proposal. He thought the bickering ought to stop so that PARC could get on with providing the technology Peter McColough expected to dominate Xerox in the 1980s.

That technology, Pake noted in his May 1971 memorandum to management, "is projected to be information systems we do not yet know how to build, that will include technologies we have yet to discover. For this, Xerox will require creative people exploring the frontiers of information science with the most effective tools available for the job."

Speaking of those scientists and their mission, Pake declared, "I will hire them for their competence and their judgment how best to do that research, and, until they prove my judgment wrong, I will do my best to provide them with the kind of first-rate technical support it is reasonable to expect in Xerox research laboratories. If that is the wrong way to build a first-rate corporate research center for Xerox, then I am the wrong man for the job."

Once Pake put his company badge on the line, SDS backed off and never again threatened PARC's budget or purpose. Nevertheless, the episode had continuing repercussions. In the midst of the controversy, Pake had argued that SDS desperately needed to organize a development function capable of turning PARC's inventions into products. Otherwise SDS—and Xerox—would remain critically disconnected from whatever PARC created. Unfortunately, however, Xerox waited several years before taking steps to overcome this serious flaw in its organization. And when, in 1975, the company finally did establish a development group for PARC, SDS had all but expired as an operation, leaving the new development group without any natural partners of its own in manufacturing, marketing, or sales.

The "home built" controversy also fanned the condescending attitude of many PARC researchers. When the Computer Science Laboratory completed its timesharing machine in the summer of 1972, one of the lab's resident wags christened the computer "MAXC." Literally, the acronym stood for "Multi-Access Xerox Computer." As any of PARC's denizens would volunteer with a smile, however, the *C* was silent. In a sarcastic swipe, PARC named the system SDS never wanted built after SDS's founder, Max Palevsky. A funny enough pun, but at SDS—deep into a third consecutive year of heavy red ink—no one laughed.

The "MAXC" insult typified a haughty, immature disposition prevalent among PARC's computer scientists. In part, their attitude reflected youth (their average age was less than thirty), background (for many, PARC represented the first job beyond academia), and inclination (they were scientists not managers). However, their arrogance also revealed the darker side of an exceptional group spirit fostered by Bob Taylor.

Only the most talented researchers survived Taylor's rigorous hiring system. Under the influence of his flat organization and insistence on constant communication, the elitism born of the selection process matured into a strong, commonly held world view. In office and hallway conversations, in group "Dealer" meetings, and, most important, in research, the pursuit of interactive computing mattered far more than title, position, or age. Taylor's organization produced spectacular scientific achievements. It was not, however, an environment in which to learn the subtleties of orthodox corporate behavior.

"The people in that laboratory," says George Pake, "did not interact with each other in what I would call a quiet way. They would sometimes be rather intemperate in their criticisms of each other's ideas. Out of all that, they had a high respect for each other's abilities."

In their meritocratic zeal, the young scientists too often employed the abrupt and argumentative style encouraged by Taylor inside the lab to deal with visitors from other parts of Xerox. Gloria Warner, who has worked at PARC since its founding, says the computer researchers routinely accused outsiders of having ignorant and addled minds. "Do you know," they liked to snicker, "that guy didn't even know what a 'byte' is?"

Ed McCreight, who assisted Chuck Thacker with the first Alto, admits to the charge of rudeness: "When we felt sometimes that someone wasn't worth talking to," he says, "we sometimes told them that."

With poor management, inadequate resources, mounting losses, and open rivalry destroying SDS as a manufacturing and distribution channel for PARC's inventiveness, such parochialism and intolerance were dangerous behavior for a research group bent on seeing their creations reach the marketplace—especially in a corporation dedicated to copiers and peopled by managers who, like most Americans of the 1970s, had yet to learn about bytes, bit maps, raster scanning, message switching, processors, object-oriented programming, or most of the other concepts common to the arcane world of PARC. The young men and women at PARC seemed to forget that they were the exception.

"PARC suffered from a whole lot of arrogance," remarks Bert Sutherland, one of a series of managers of PARC's Systems Science Laboratory. "If you didn't understand automatically, you were 'stupid.' It's hard to get a good hearing that way."

Stylistic differences common to society in the early 1970s also separated the research center from Xerox as a whole. A decade earlier, long hair, beards, beads, and sandals had surfaced among the baby boom generation as expressions of individuality as much as of rebellion. But after Watts and My Lai, after Chicago and Kent State, after the administrations of Johnson and Nixon, and after years of sex, drugs, and rock 'n' roll, demeanor in the 1970s signified political position instead of personality.

In fact, most of PARC's computer scientists dressed neatly, if casually. Nonetheless, in that predominantly academic and youthful setting on the perimeter of the San Francisco Bay, many of them bore all the trappings of the counterculture. "There were a few people within the computer work at PARC," Bob Taylor says defensively, "who wore long hair, didn't take baths, and didn't wear shoes. But there were very few of them."

There were no such people in the rest of Xerox. In December of 1972, PARC's contrasting demeanor made headlines. That month, when Xerox first learned about the Federal Trade Commission's antitrust action and SDS reeled under yet another major adjustment to its business strategy, PARC appeared in a *Rolling Stone* magazine article written by Stewart Brand, the publisher of the *Whole Earth Catalogue*. Brand was, in the words of his free-spirited friend Alan Kay, a "computer junkie." His piece in *Rolling Stone* told the history of a famous computer game called "Spacewar," which had originated with the beginnings of interactive computing. According to Brand's thesis, "Spacewar" evinced the determination of the nation's best young computer scientists to place digital technology in service of The People instead of The System. His article emphasized alternative life-styles as well as alternative computer futures, and it prominently featured, among a distinctly hairy crowd, Alan Kay, Bob Taylor, and a particularly hirsute PARC programmer named Peter Deutsch. The *Rolling Stone* article was entitled "Spacewar: Fanatic Life and Symbolic Death Among the Computer Bums."

"The article," recalls Bob Taylor, "had an offbeat aura appropriate to *Rolling Stone*, but not, according to some people, to a Fortune 500 company with lots of class and style like Xerox."

Like too many other incidents during PARC's early years, the "Computer Bums" piece burned, instead of built, bridges to the rest of Xerox. In assuming that Peter McColough's sponsorship automatically obligated the company to exploit their inventions, the PARC scientists demonstrated a naïveté to match their bad manners.

"To put it in perspective," said Tim Mott, "if you're on the West Coast and you are part of the computer science community, then PARC was a really big idea. You had a couple of hundred people with a multimillion dollar budget, and it's the best research center in the world and it's the most exciting technology around. It really looks like a big deal. However, that's a very, very small part of a company that's doing several billion dollars a year. It's absolutely true that there were a lot of people in the company who, at best, were skeptical and, at worst, had absolutely no interest whatsoever in what was going on at PARC."

Not everyone at PARC, of course, neglected the link between good corporate citizenship and commercial opportunity. Bill Gunning, PARC's technical liaison to other parts of Xerox, had worked in the computer field since the late 1940s and had more experience than most PARC people with the business side of industry. He tried hard to interest Xerox in PARC's output. Gunning, for example, was the first PARC manager contacted by Darwin Newton when the Ginn & Co. executive sought computer help for his editors. Although Gunning respected the creativity of Taylor's group, he bridled at their behavior.

"Taylor," says Gunning, "was extremely skillful at building an esprit in his group. However, it was very much a 'we-they' phenomenon. He said, 'We're going to move computer science forward.' And part of doing so was the idea that his group was better than everyone else. And they were better. But they were not skilled at communicating with the 'theys.' "

The PARC manager most admired by the broader Xerox community was George Pake. With his gentlemanly bearing and scholarly credentials, he maintained senior management's budgetary support for long-term research while smoothing over troublesome incidents like the *Rolling Stone* article. Pake, however, comprehended business economics and organization little more than most

PARC scientists. And he was a physicist instead of a computer scientist. Consequently, his effectiveness as a mediator between the alien worlds of Xerox managers and PARC's computer researchers was limited; not completely understanding either side, Pake could not make them understand each other.

Toward the end of 1973, for example, Pake took an assignment at headquarters that led to his participation in the Hughes strategy effort. His inclusion represented an ideal chance for PARC's director to proselytize on behalf of his estranged research center—not for the budgetary support already assured but for a commitment to the business implications of the office of the future technology being invented at PARC. Yet from the outset, other members of the Hughes team noticed that Pake had no commercial instincts at all.

"I don't think any of us," says Michael Hughes, "ever saw George as a businessman."

The former university provost had much to learn about markets, economics, organization, competition, and strategy. He spoke awkwardly about business, insisting that the Hughes group reach their conclusions by the "scientific method," a standard of inquiry more appropriate to physics than finance or marketing. When discussions turned to PARC's technologies, Pake emphasized the important work left to be accomplished in the laboratory instead of the commercial opportunities that might already exist.

"I felt rather pleased to be included in the Hughes committee," Pake explains. "The task force was supposed to think of daring new business strategies for Xerox. We talked a lot about many global things. And the others in the group—Hughes, White, Lyons—were all kind of iconoclasts. No one was afraid to speak out if the emperor had no clothes. Of the group, George White was probably the strongest proponent of the futures in PARC. But George can be given to excessive statement. So I would often have to bring the discussions back to earth."

Pake did not underestimate PARC's potential; to the contrary, he admired McColough's plan to use PARC as the catapult to Xerox's future. "There is absolutely no question," Pake commented in 1975, "that there will be a revolution in the office over the next 20 years."

That time frame, however, tipped off Pake's essential orientation. Like all good academic scientists, he knew that truth could not be hurried, that it would take decades to explore the role and function of novel information technology. Thus, in 1970, when Xerox had hired him, Pake had been impressed that Peter McColough "really seemed to understand that you don't get quick payoffs from research." In 1974, he felt the same way. But four years had passed, and PARC already had contributed much, including the Alto, toward McColough's stated objective. While payoffs from that research did not have to be "quick," they did have to proceed according to intervals paced by the clock of commerce rather than by maturing theory. "Timing," goes the business dictum, "is everything."

The key to PARC's Alto personal computer—the critical juncture at which the laboratory's invention and Xerox's market opportunity converged—had to do with Chuck Thacker's design innovation called "multitasking." With it, Thacker eliminated expensive processing circuitry by sharing the Alto's central processor among its various input and output devices like the bit-mapped screen, the mouse, and the laser printer. "Multitasking" made the economics of personal computing possible before 1975 by reducing the number of chips required in a machine.

But given the spiraling improvements in microprocessors and other chip technology, Thacker's ingenious scheme had passing value. Once high performance chips became cheap enough—an event Thacker, Lampson, and many others familiar with the computer industry expected to happen by the late 1970s—hardware cost would no longer stand in the way of inexpensive computers. Inventors would be able to employ as many chips as they wanted without running afoul of the economics of personal computing.

Therefore, it was just a matter of time before competitors could achieve through cheap hardware what Thacker had done with creative design. That made the competitive advantage of "multitasking" perishable. Xerox could have gained anywhere from a one- to five-year head start—had the company's business leaders acted quickly enough.

According to Hughes, Pake never explained this point to the rest of the group; he suspects Pake didn't understand it himself. Hughes might be correct. Thacker had completed the first Alto just six months prior to the formation of the strategy committee, hardly enough time for the physicist Pake to comprehend the full technical and business implications of the Alto.

It is also possible that Pake never had the right opportunity to figure out and articulate the implications of Thacker's achievement. Halfway through the Hughes committee's year-long effort, he suffered a stroke that sent him to the hospital for several months. When he recovered in 1975, Xerox gave him his choice of assignments: he could return to represent the promise of PARC at corporate headquarters, or he could go back to his job as manager of the research center. Pake, who had neither appetite nor aptitude for a mainstream corporate career, picked the research post. It was what he did best.

Chapter

13

*I*f George Pake's natural courtesy and business inexperience
caused him to push PARC's commercial opportunities too
meekly, Jack Goldman's love of battle and record of corporate
frustrations spurred him to push too hard. Goldman, says George
White, told a story on himself of a time when he'd been bragging
to Henry Ford II about the advanced fuel cells coming out of the
car company's research laboratory. According to the anecdote, the
auto magnate had cut the boasting Goldman short, remarking,
"Not much of your stuff gets on cars, does it Jack?" That biting
criticism haunted Goldman; he badly wanted to prove that Xerox,
unlike Ford, could follow bold discovery with more than bitter
disappointment.

Goldman blamed the auto maker's failure to commercialize
research on its financially trained and driven management. In his
opinion, provocative inventions at Ford could not survive the tyranny of corporate systems used to control cost, project volume,
and measure profit. He had left Ford for Xerox in 1968, in large
part, because the copier company's history and potential had appeared unshackled by quantitative constraints.

His first few years at Xerox justified his confidence—Mc-
Colough appointed him to the board of directors, acquired SDS,
authorized PARC, and announced the search for an "architecture
of information." Moreover, PARC gained stature and promise as
a research establishment much faster than anticipated. But Goldman's hopes for innovation and change began to unravel in 1972,
when, like a recurrent nightmare, the prospects of his laboratories
fell once again to the mercy of Ford-trained finance men.

To Goldman's enduring disappointment, his troubles began
with the appointment of his friend Archie McCardell to the company presidency. Initially, Goldman cautiously applauded Mc-
Cardell's promotion in the wake of Joe Wilson's death. He respected
McCardell's intelligence and imagination, and he shared with him
a fondness for wide-ranging conversation and low stakes poker.
Furthermore, McCardell was a staunch defender of PARC.

"McCardell," noted Goldman, "recognized right off how important it was for him to have capable technical resources, including research, and, as a result, he was one of the most supportive people in my efforts to try to get research really flowering, organized, and growing in the company. When push came to shove on the creation of the Palo Alto Research Center, McCardell was one of the most supportive guys."

But McCardell was a paradox; his intellectual curiosity sponsored creativity in research that his remote, numbers-dominated management style killed off. At the end of 1971, PARC was poised to provide Xerox with an unprecedented variety of new technologies. Three months later, McCardell announced the 1972 reorganization of Xerox, which collapsed the computer and copier businesses into three large functional groups and eliminated Goldman's authority to develop products from emerging inventions.

Prior to the reshuffling, Goldman had expected to transform PARC's research into products at SDS or, failing that, at a small technology company called Electro-Optical Systems owned by Xerox since the mid-1960s. Before McCardell restructured the company, EOS reported directly to Goldman, giving him control over project decisions. The new organization changed that. SDS and EOS were folded together with the copier division, and the authority for new product decisions—for copier and noncopier innovations alike—was assigned exclusively to the Information Technology Group (ITG). Still worse, for Goldman at least, McCardell named another Ford-schooled finance executive, Jim O'Neill, to head ITG.

Numbers bewitched O'Neill even more than McCardell. "Archie," says George White, "was attentive and flexible. He would at least listen to others, even if their analysis was more qualitative than quantitative. But O'Neill quit thinking with quantitative analysis."

The first casualty of O'Neill's ascendancy was Myron Tribus, a Goldman recruit who had preceded O'Neill as chief of engineering at Xerox. Prior to joining Xerox in 1970, Tribus had served as assistant secretary of commerce in the Nixon administration and, before that, as dean of engineering at Dartmouth. He had answered Goldman's call to Xerox because, having studied the nation's ailing economy while in Washington, he wanted to see firsthand why large U.S. corporations were stagnating.

What he discovered at Xerox shocked him. "It was an absolute disaster," says Tribus. "I had no idea it could be as bad as it was."

In his opinion, the Xerox engineering group suffered from a decade of unparalleled growth during which the company hired engineers willy-nilly, then threw them at projects without regard to qualification or standards of professionalism. Xerox engineers appeared to design and build products without fully comprehending their underlying technology, a habit that dated back to the 914 Copier.

"When the 914 came to the market," recalls Jack Crowley, a longtime advisor then executive of Xerox, "it was one of the engineering feats of all time. It was also probably the most overdesigned product in history because Joe Wilson was driven by the importance of bringing a product to market ASAP. The patents were running out. So the theory in the company was, 'Damn the costs! Make it work!' That instilled what we later called the 'Cadillac' mentality in the company. And it persisted, in engineering in particular."

Tribus hoped to establish technical standards and practices in order to eradicate what he perceived as rampant "sloppiness." His crusade did not make him popular.

"There was a euphoric state at Xerox," he recalls. "They had grown like crazy and they were spilling money everywhere, but still making unbelievable profits anyway. So if you got to Xerox and said, 'This is wrong and can be done better,' they'd say, 'Well, we must be doing something right!' "

Engineers grumbled that Tribus was too academic, too arrogant, and, in the ultimate refuge of the narrow-minded, too alien to xerography. He nevertheless made progress by forming engineering groups to document the technologies common to all copiers, changing the pattern and quality of technical reviews, and applying different reward systems to reinforce an ethic of careful engineering and design.

Jim O'Neill, however, had no use for Tribus. He much preferred the advice and counsel of Bob Sparacino, an engineer from General Motors who adopted O'Neill's view of managing. Eventually, O'Neill and Sparacino teamed up to force Tribus out.

"Myron Tribus," says Goldman, "was an absolutely brilliant engineer. But he wasn't a terribly good manager, and people were gunning for him from the start, especially O'Neill and Sparacino. Instead of finding a way to work with the guy, to take advantage of his brilliant talents, Sparacino played politics day and night to get rid of him."

"I was not used to the politics of industry," comments a bitter Tribus. "I was used to the politics of Washington, but at Xerox it was worse. In Washington, you knew your adversaries and accepted that they would work against you. At Xerox, you only found out who was not on your side after you noticed the knife in your back."

Whether or not Tribus was inferior to O'Neill or Sparacino as a manager, his demise marked a major drop in engineering productivity at Xerox. Tribus had railed against a system that produced copiers in haste and fixed them later; he believed too many Xerox engineers faked technical expertise. However unintentionally, O'Neill and Sparacino exacerbated the ailment Tribus had attempted, perhaps inartfully, to remedy.

As head of the Information Technology Group, O'Neill held the top engineering and manufacturing post at Xerox despite never having designed or built a copier or a computer or, while at Ford, an automobile. He understood financial systems. He knew how to control expenses, forecast volume, and measure profit. Evidently, O'Neill and his boss Archie McCardell considered such a background qualification enough to manage the engineering and manufacturing of copiers, duplicators, and computers—as though knowledge of finance were the universal code to make any art, any science, fully comprehensible.

Financial implications and promised delivery dates circumscribed the O'Neill agenda. According to Horace Becker, a respected veteran engineer of Haloid and Xerox, the finance people treated technical conundrums as inconveniences or, ignobly, signs of malingering. Engineers felt like mere "factors of production," fungible pawns to be tossed about on a spreadsheet and never trusted with confidence or technical liberty. Confronted with such arrogant presumption, many of them succumbed to the malaise of "faking it," to subordinating quality in copier technology and performance to concern for dates and numbers. While the theoretician Tribus may have undervalued the role of tinkering in good engineering, he at least did not mistake schedules for science.

"O'Neill's management theory," notes Jack Crowley, "was one of controls. His theory of controls came out of his experience at Ford. He really believed that if you sat on something hard enough and long enough, you could control the outcome."

To manage engineering at Xerox, O'Neill imported a system from Ford Motor Company called "phased program planning."

He and Sparacino divided development projects into hundreds of minute tasks, insisted upon dozens of review points, and subjected the entire process to committee, instead of individual, decision making. Programs grew ponderous in terms of people involved and time to completion. Initiative declined.

"For example," alleges Tribus, "we were having a great deal of difficulty with the toner for the 9200 Copier. Toner is the powder used to make the black marks on paper. One of the engineers got the idea that if, before you put the toner in the machine, you cut out the largest and smallest granules, what we called the 'bigs' and the 'fines,' the toner would last longer. Sparacino rejected the idea.

"So the guy went over to the pilot plant and asked them to save some extra toner each time they put it in the machine. After he had bootlegged enough, he cut out the 'bigs' and the 'fines,' put it in the 9200, and it ran two or three times as long. Once he announced it, the company went with his solution.

"Sparacino called him into his office and said, 'You got away with it this time. But you were lucky. Just be careful.'

"Instead of reward, there was punishment."

The specific example may be apocryphal, although Horace Becker jokes, "the possibility of that story being true is only about ninety percent—on a scale of one to nine. You just didn't work that way. It wasn't accepted."

O'Neill's financial background, belief in management by numbers, and concern for control made him virtually intolerant of risk—a perspective fundamentally opposed to novel technology and, therefore, to Jack Goldman. Goldman considered O'Neill an accountant dangerously miscast as an engineer; O'Neill, says George White, thought Goldman was "flaky."

"Jack was offended that the engineering organization would be put under a nontechnical manager," says George Pake. "This led to an interesting and predictable conflict because O'Neill had no technical instincts. O'Neill is an accountant and, by nature and training, is risk averse. But you can't do engineering without taking risks. And Jack is bold, aggressive, and, by nature, very much loved to take risks. As a result, research in Xerox became very risk oriented while development became just the opposite. Jack was not very temperate in his remarks on this to the rest of senior management. So you'd have to say that he helped to foster the feud. Once the feud developed, it was bad. And it got worse."

The opening skirmish between Goldman and O'Neill over the fruits of PARC's research concerned laser printing technology. Shortly after O'Neill gained control of new product decisions, Lawrence Livermore Laboratory, a nuclear science research center in California, expressed interest in buying the kind of laser printer invented at PARC by Gary Starkweather, Ron Rider, and Butler Lampson. Goldman was ecstatic. Starkweather had converted a Xerox 7000 Copier into the Scanned Laser Output Terminal, and Goldman knew that, since Xerox had introduced the 7000 Copiers several years earlier, hundreds of the machines were fully depreciated on Xerox's balance sheet. That made it possible, as Goldman hurriedly recommended to O'Neill, for Xerox to produce and sell the world's first laser printers at a cost lower than normally associated with breakthrough technology.

"If I started with a 7000," Goldman still argues, "that means to the company the cost is zero on the books. If I took that 7000 and put a laser head on it and put a processor with it, I can make a laser printer. If I had to go out and buy a new 7000, I would have had to add five or ten thousand dollars to the cost of the machine.

"But O'Neill took a look at this and said, 'No way!' He said he ran the risk of a hundred fifty thousand dollars based on service costs if he delivered on this, and he refused to allow it. McCardell was over both of us, and O'Neill was carping about the risk. The thing is that O'Neill didn't understand the risk. He was an accountant!"

What O'Neill did recognize, and Goldman neglected, was that the scanty Livermore proposal could not justify the investment required to start a laser printing business. Although clever, Goldman's idea left too many important collateral issues unresolved: How and where would Xerox manufacture the laser printers? Who would sell and service them? Who would buy them and why? According to several former Xerox people, the scheme was vintage Goldman—ingenious but unsound.

"Once something worked in the lab," noted George Pake, "Jack wanted to sell it. The idea to put out the 7000-based printer was a good one. Still, we would have had to put together a special manufacturing group to do this. And the other guys realized as well it would take a trained sales force and service force to do it."

"Jack," agrees Myron Tribus, "was inclined to pick up an idea that wasn't quite baked and champion it. He'd get up in public and say things that would just be wrong."

Goldman was not a detail person; his outstanding strength was enthusiasm for people and their ideas. He once saw a quotation that so perfectly captured his personal philosophy that he cut it out of the newspaper, circled it, and taped it to his wall. It read: "There are two ways of being creative. One can sing and dance. Or one can create an environment in which singers and dancers flourish." PARC epitomized that credo. With the help of George Pake and Bob Taylor, Jack Goldman had founded and staffed one of the world's most creative corporate research centers. But Goldman was not the impresario of Xerox's corporate headquarters. In Stamford, he had to play by house rules, and the house during the first half of the 1970s was controlled by McCardell, O'Neill, and Sparacino, all of whom considered Goldman's zeal as a promoter—unadorned by careful financial analysis and explanation—specious, even laughable.

Bob Potter, an O'Neill partisan, believes Goldman misread the basic economic purpose of Xerox. "The Xerox mission was not to build new corporations from the bottom up. Rather, it was to take new technology and ideas and put them into the multiplying machinery, the marketing and sales forces, that already existed. Jack Goldman always wanted start-ups. He thought Xerox was constipated, and the only way to get a product out was to force it out. To take a hammer and knock down the walls. His theory was a new product at all costs. But O'Neill saw the importance of using the existing corporation. To him, a product at all costs was not the answer. A product that made a lot of money was the answer."

Thus, the Goldman-O'Neill controversy swirled about a void. Goldman led with creativity and faith; O'Neill countered with predictability and logic. But neither man was an engineer. Neither man alone understood the combination of gut feel and careful practice required to develop successful products, whether xerographic or digital. Consequently, neither could persuade the other, based on a logic of common experience, about the problems in Rochester or the opportunities at PARC.

Engineering ignorance beset all the senior executives of Xerox. According to former executive vice president Jack Crowley, "Xerox was spending hundreds of millions of dollars a year on research, development, and engineering. Yet there was no one, literally, in top management who had ever run a product development program, who could say to the engineers that such and such should cost less or should be doable faster, and who would know, from their personal experience, that they were right. If Xerox had one single management weakness, it was that none of the powerful players from Peter on down, and that includes me, had a technical background or the technical support to permit them to challenge hard the judgments of the engineering group."

Crowley contends that other senior managers had hoped Goldman might provide the technical support they clearly needed, but he thinks Xerox's head of research simply lacked the right mix of skills to do the job. "Jack Goldman was a scientist, not an engineer. I have every reason to believe that he's quite a brilliant scientist. However, if you were to ask Jack about the cost or performance projections for some project, you got the 'two handed lawyer' response, or one response today and a different one tomorrow. So it reached a point where company management didn't look to Goldman for those judgments. That's not so unusual. I don't know of many research heads who, however talented, are well known for their business judgments."

Lacking the self-confidence garnered from personal engineering experience and mistrusting Goldman's business wisdom, McColough and McCardell chose to support the orderly, if onerous, system of "phased program planning." The influence of O'Neill and Sparacino expanded far beyond the reach of Goldman's bright ideas. Outside of research itself, Goldman was powerless, and other executives knew it.

"You know how a person is respected," says Michael Hughes, "by whether he does or doesn't get interrupted when he interrupts a meeting for a question. When McColough interrupted, everyone listened to his remark or question as well as the response. When McCardell interrupted, everyone but McColough would listen. But when Jack Goldman interrupted, often he couldn't even finish his question. People just felt free to ignore him. He did not have the respect of the group whose respect you needed in Xerox to get things done. He never did have that kind of clout. He should have had it, but he didn't."

More than a decade later, Goldman continues to feel the sting of peer rejection at Xerox. "When I came to Xerox," he says, "you might say I was number four in the company after Wilson,

McColough, and McCardell. I took Dessauer's place, and they viewed technology as being very important. Whenever there was a senior management group meeting, Peter's secretary would call all of us together. In the beginning, she called me third. Then it got so I was seventh. And as they pulled in O'Neill and others, I was called last. As the senior management group grew in number, I remained at the bottom of the list, no longer of importance."

Within a year of Joe Wilson's death, Goldman dropped like a kicked ball down the management ladder. He went from reporting directly to McColough to reporting to McCardell to reporting to Bill Souders, the head of the Business Planning Group. His demotions, however, did not stop him from battling for PARC.

In January of 1973, McCardell and O'Neill appointed Bob Potter, a manager with engineering as well as operating experience, to take over the Xerox group responsible for developing office products other than copiers. That division, originally established in Rochester in the mid-1960s, had produced a successful facsimile machine but otherwise had failed. Management believed the overwhelming emphasis on copiers in Rochester had kept noncopier activities underfunded and understaffed. As a result—and of central significance to Goldman—O'Neill and McCardell asked Potter to move his organization far away from upstate New York.

The issue was where. An outside firm commissioned by Xerox recommended two sites: the San Francisco Bay area and Dallas. Goldman lobbied for California for many reasons. First, since new office products would be digital, common sense dictated placing the development engineers near those Xerox employees who best understood computer technology. In addition, PARC sat in the middle of the Silicon Valley, the richest talent pool in the world for digital engineers and technicians. Dallas, by contrast, had neither advantage.

Moreover, by 1973, Goldman realized that SDS would not provide the outlet for PARC's inventions that he had initially expected. As George Pake had pointed out often, SDS lacked the requisite engineering skills to develop inventions into products. And mutual antagonism between PARC and SDS as well as SDS's continuing poor performance made cooperation unlikely. In short, PARC's isolation within Xerox exceeded what most corporate executives imagined; to Goldman as well as Pake, a Potter transfer to California could close that gap.

Goldman also hoped Xerox would demonstrate a willingness to invest more than money in PARC. He never complained about the company's largesse at budget time. But how PARC's well funded research would affect future products—in an organization as highly compartmentalized and risk averse as the Xerox of McCardell and O'Neill—remained uncertain and obscure. Xerox's top management could have commanded their engineers to develop PARC's inventions into products, or they could have induced a comparable result by providing the engineers the chance for daily communication and mutual involvement with the scientists of PARC. Locating Potter in California would have been consistent with either approach.

Nevertheless, O'Neill favored Dallas. According to Potter, an elaborate financial model of a factory in Texas versus one in California conclusively proved, on the basis of labor, transportation, taxes, and other cost indicators, that Dallas would save Xerox money.

Cost, however, tells but half of any commercial proposition. The other part—value delivered to customers—did not inform O'Neill's calculations, implying a frozen view of digital technology which in fact shook with change and possibility. Biennial leaps in integrated circuitry, a well established cycle by 1973, promised to continue. Indeed, efficient chips had already pushed computer science across an important threshold: for the first time in history, digital progress depended less on hardware innovation than software design. Therefore, making interactive computing products a reality for a broader market than scientists would require the combined genius of engineers and entrepreneurs, a distinctly qualitative variable.

But concerns for the needs and values of customers were apparently missing from O'Neill's financial model. "The bean counters," said George White, "don't have numbers for new technology."

When Goldman learned the results of O'Neill's factory analysis, he tried to head off a decision for Dallas by enlisting the support of his new boss Bill Souders. "That spring," Goldman recounts, "Souders and I were talking about Dallas. I told him, 'Bill, you've got to get in there and fight this Dallas thing. You're not "just some technical guy." They'll listen to you.' Souders took up the cudgel and fought the good fight. But one day he came into my office and said, 'Jack, we lost. Office Systems Division is going to be in Dallas.' "

"If you had to point to one clear fuck up," Goldman declared, "it was the whole effect of the Dallas decision on later development of digital technology at Xerox. Dallas turned out to grow a culture that was completely orthogonal to, and independent of, the digital world in general and PARC in particular."

Chapter

14

"*From the time I was a teenager," declares Bob Potter, "I've been in the business of making money from technically rich environments." His self-assurance augured well for Potter when he headed to Dallas in 1973 with the chance to breathe life into Xerox's noncopier office products business. He had the commitment from McCardell and O'Neill to invest whatever Dallas needed to succeed; he had a wealth of creative PARC concepts and technologies on which to build innovative competitive advantages. Potter, however, considered PARC's ideas and inventions too futuristic. Instead of embracing the company's most advanced digital research, he chose to lead Dallas, with McCardell's and O'Neill's blessing, down a safer, more predictable path—one that ended, sadly, in mediocrity.

Potter was a rarity at Xerox—a manager capable of both technical and business judgments. After earning his Ph.D. in optics from the University of Rochester in 1960, he had worked for five years at IBM's research laboratories before joining Xerox. Once there, he showed a strong interest in making research relevant to the bottom line, an emphasis he demonstrated in a variety of positions, including an assignment as the general manager of Xerox's subsidiary, Electro-Optical Systems. By 1973, the thirty-eight-year-old Potter had surfaced as one of the youngest of Xerox's senior managers.

"I was a powerful technical manager with general management experience," notes Potter in explaining why McCardell and O'Neill selected him to head the office systems group. "I had the kind of visibility that would put a whole lot of attention on that subject."

Among other things, McCardell and O'Neill asked Potter to develop Xerox products for the rapidly expanding word processing market, an industry that had begun modestly in 1964 with the introduction of IBM's Magnetic Tape Selectric Typewriter (MTST). The MTST operated like a player piano; keystrokes automatically followed a pattern encoded on magnetic tape unless the typist intervened. MTSTs reduced the drudgery, mistakes,

and expense of producing form letters, but, to the disappointment
of secretaries, the machines could not efficiently assist in making
extensive modifications to the spelling, punctuation, composition,
or structure of one-of-a-kind documents. That limitation frustrated typists who, having seen what MTSTs could do for repetitive chores, wanted more and better capability.

Manufacturers rushed to satisfy their demand. By the early
1970s, more than a dozen companies in addition to IBM claimed
to offer text editing machines with the best combination of features. New capabilities included diverse typefaces, television monitors, and communications as well as merging, scanning, and other
editing routines. Given the pace of development, observers believed no company, not even the market leader IBM, could yet
claim lasting dominance.

"The automatic typing and text editing industry," commented
Word Processing Management in 1973, "continues to be a fast changing one. Companies, jockeying for position in a market they still
perceive as fairly open, announce new equipment developments
or changes almost every week. With manufacturers, as with users,
no one philosophy of word processing marketing or technology
has yet emerged as the 'official' one. As a result, companies pursue
their own directions as suppliers to the growing word processing
market."

Unanticipated applications, changing technology, strong demand, and intense competition heated up the industry. IBM's
original forecast that, at most, 6,000 MTST-like machines would
ever sell was off by an order of magnitude. By 1973, customers
in the United States had purchased more than 100,000 word processing typewriters at prices ranging from $4,000 to $13,000 apiece.
Still, less than 4 percent of American "typing stations" housed the
new technology; millions of manual and electric typewriters remained to be replaced. The market, already significant at $200
million of annual sales, was projected to become huge—at least a
billion dollar business by 1980.

The opportunity for Xerox was self-evident: word processing
fit the company's "office of the future" ambitions; the size and
growth of the market promised plenty of room for sales and
profits; significant electronic engineering and computer capability
existed at PARC, SDS, EOS, and other subsidiaries; and, the
copier sales force could sell word processors to Xerox clients the
world over.

Equally obvious, to Potter and his engineers at least, was the technology with which to develop Xerox's first word processor. Nearly all existing text editing machines were nonprogrammable electromechanical devices that, like pocket calculators, depended entirely on hardware for function. Unlike computers, electromechanical devices could not be modified through software; designers added features to them by rewiring, not reprogramming. Despite such inflexibility, however, the electromechanical equipment had solid advantages over computers because of price, proven capability, and customer familiarity. For example, even the most expensive text editing machines, priced just above $13,000, cost customers a fraction as much as computers. Hence, Potter's team took it for granted that Xerox should stick with electromechanical technology rather than risking innovations in software and computers.

The researchers at PARC disagreed. "If it's a system and it's not programmable," Bob Taylor dogmatically asserted on behalf of the computer scientists, "then it's not worth doing."

The Palo Alto researchers considered electromechanical word processors primitive. Complex editing, formatting, and communicating options far exceeded the technical limits of such equipment, whereas a programmable computer could provide virtually unbounded word processing capability—a measure of adaptability, in the opinion of Taylor's lab, on which manufacturers would increasingly depend as they attempted to turn displays, communications, laser printers, expanded memory, and digital typesetting to better advantage.

Moreover, PARC's scientists already had lowered the computer cost barrier by the time Potter set up his engineering facility. In April of 1973, the same month O'Neill decided Potter would move to Dallas, Chuck Thacker's team completed the first Alto personal computer. Had the Dallas group tried to leapfrog its competition with programmable word processing computers instead of electromechanical equipment, they would have found much in the way of a head start at PARC. But to the people in Palo Alto, Potter appeared as inflexible on the subject of computers as the hardwired word processing technology he chose to pursue. And in their own abrasive style, the PARC team told him just what they thought.

"Potter came out and talked to us before setting up Dallas," remembers Bob Taylor with scorn. "He talked to us for an hour and a half about the technical program Dallas would pursue, and he didn't mention the word 'software' once! Xerox picked the wrong guy to head the office products division, put it in a place where systems talent was not overflowing, and didn't ask for joint planning. Potter was just another device guy."

Jim Mitchell echoes Taylor's reaction to Potter's initial PARC visit. "He gave us this presentation," says Mitchell, "and we just sat there aghast. We said 'You don't have the faintest idea this is not going to work. This is useless!' And he just basically said, 'Screw you guys. You don't understand anything, and I'm going to go off and do this.' It was the strongest 'not invented here' I'd ever heard in the world. He knew nothing about computers, and he wanted to know nothing about them."

Welcome to PARC, Bob Potter. Without warning or preparation, the freshly appointed Dallas chief found himself the object of a Bob Taylor "Dealer" meeting convened by scientists unfazed by business issues such as feasibility, price, cost, competitive position, and customer acceptance. McCardell and O'Neill expected Potter to market products within one year, not five to ten. However provocative, neither the Alto nor any of PARC's personal distributed computing concepts or technologies could satisfy that timetable in 1973. Thus, PARC's best chance to influence Potter's product plans more likely were to come with Dallas's second and subsequent efforts instead of its first.

Nevertheless, gaining influence in Dallas appeared to concern PARC as little as it had with SDS. Taylor's crowd considered the Dallas product strategy muddled and backward, failing to appreciate that, in 1973, few people grasped all the implications of the personal distributed computing system PARC had just then begun to invent. The scientists should have proselytized patiently. They should have practiced Bob Taylor's wise principle of modifying "Class 1" disagreements into the "Class 2" variety where both parties can describe to the other's satisfaction the other's point of view. Instead, they just bleated and belched, making it far too easy for Potter and Dallas to ignore their gifted insights.

"I went out there, and I sat in their beanbags," Potter says. "But I just couldn't get anything out of them. I even told them I was their savviest, best customer in the corporation. But they were only interested in their own thing. They thought they were four feet above everybody else. What the PARC people never understood was that they were supposed to help the less fortunate, less intelligent rest of the world."

To Potter, the California researchers, like too many scientists in the company, had their heads in the clouds. They were "computer-niks" who spoke about "liberating" secretaries and "push-button offices." "What PARC considered 'naïve,' " Potter acknowledges, "*was* naïve—with respect to *tomorrow's* products. They had so many concepts, they couldn't miss hitting with some of them. But you can't do that when you're running a business.

"We were trying to drive cost down and get a minimum product out. We were in the word processing business, not the personal computer business. So we couldn't very well fund something unless it was consistent with our business charter and made sense in a drive for profitability. I had to get through O'Neill and his financial ratios, to stand the test of return on investment, and of marketing and business plans. Not just gut feel. The pressure on me was to make money."

Still, nowhere is it written that the bottom line is immune to good ideas. Potter's sanctimonious retreat to Dallas made short shrift of his responsibility to tap Palo Alto's brilliant and creative engineers, notwithstanding their bad boy behavior. He, after all, ran Dallas; he had the confidence and support of McCardell and O'Neill. He should have employed his position as either weapon or inducement to gain PARC's support for better Xerox products, whether electromechanical or programmable. Under Potter, however, Dallas chose to compete rather than collaborate with PARC. His group repaid PARC's antagonism in kind, seeking to prove that Dallas's own solutions were "right." A wasteful, even silly, contest for technical prowess ensued. At one point, for example, researchers in Palo Alto heard that their Dallas counterparts had fashioned a hand-held input device like the mouse invented by Douglas Engelbart and improved at PARC. Dallas called its tool "the cat."

In late 1974, Potter and Xerox introduced the "800" word processing typewriter. The 800s operated twice as fast as arch rival IBM's machines and utilized an innovative printing mechanism manufactured by Diablo Systems, a company Xerox had acquired in 1972. The printing technology, known interchangeably as the "daisy wheel" or "print wheel," represented an advance over the "golf ball" device used in IBM typewriters and word processors, a point of some pride in Dallas.

"The print wheel," brags Potter, "was the most important introduction of technology to the office in the last decade by Xerox to have widespread impact on the business environment. And it had nothing to do with PARC!"

Reviewers were impressed, though not overwhelmed, by Xerox's new word processor.

"Featuring a speedy typing mechanism and an attractive price tag," wrote an editor of *Administrative Management,* "the Xerox 800 series will definitely be a hot contender in the text-editing market in 1975.

"Although somewhat basic (no present ability for communication and lacking a CRT option and photocomposition link-up) and 'green' (a brand new product with no in-the-field experience), the 800 is leaving all options open for further fine tuning. As is, the Xerox machines remain autonomous units just right for tackling basic editing and repetitive typing tasks."

Unfortunately for Potter and Xerox, the 800's missing features more than its speed or advanced printing element determined the product's market performance. Had the Dallas group introduced the 800 in 1972 or 1973, when they originally conceived it, they might have had a "hot contender"; by 1975, competitors' advanced display-based word processors with communications and other capabilities made the 800 too "basic."

"Within eighteen months," said one former Xerox salesman, "we had one of the oldest products on the market. It's tough when you have to look a customer in the eye and say, 'Yeah, I agree. There's really no reason you should buy this machine.' In my seven years at Xerox, I can think of no product more rejected by major accounts than the 800."

That Potter had produced, in his words, a "minimum product" did not surprise his senior colleagues in research and engineering. Jack Goldman, George Pake, and George White considered Potter hardworking and aggressive, yet unimaginative. In their minds, his selection to manage Dallas had had less to do with his talent as an engineer than the ease with which he handled McCardell's and O'Neill's insatiable appetite for numbers.

"Potter," says George Pake, "could talk to the businessmen in ways that they thought he understood their point of view. He was a glib, fast talking guy who was not very strong technically."

In addition to animosity, Dallas ignored PARC because Potter could not imagine a big market for advanced computer-based word processors. He could, and did, see the market only as it existed, not as it might become. "Moving to the office of the future," he once commented, "cannot be a social revolution. It has to be an evolution."

To George White, that perspective was born of an easy, and too narrow, fascination with numbers. "If you develop pedestrian equipment and then count up how many pedestrian places there are in the country, you can always identify a large enough number to get your money back, by which I mean general office typing. And you only have to postulate a modest penetration of all the typing stations in the United States and you have a big product forecast. That's the Bob Potter, Archie McCardell view on business development."

The 800 bore two critical cost burdens when compared to IBM word processors. First, Xerox's "daisy wheel" was more expensive to build than IBM's "golf ball," and second, IBM's much higher production quantities provided scale economies. Consequently, the profit margin on the 800 was squeezed; Dallas had to achieve its high volume sales forecast in order to avoid losing money. But the business plan postulated a higher share of the market than the unremarkable 800 could either gain or hold. The pressure, created by the finance staff's formulas, fell squarely on the sales force. Xerox, for example, set the monthly quota per salesperson at more than double the industry average.

"The bean counters want a certain return on investment, and they impose it in a plan that works from the top down," said a district sales manager. "They told us what we had to do instead of determining what we could actually sell."

Dallas sold thousands of 800s, but thousands were not enough. By 1976, Potter's group had yet to break even. To improve results, Dallas designed a prototype for the next Xerox text editor, the "850." Featuring a display screen plus improvements to the keyboard and printer, the 850 looked on paper like an effective entry against contemporary market competition. But so had the 800. This time managers from other parts of Xerox weren't sure the company should pursue Potter's product strategy without review or question.

Moreover, by 1976, Dallas no longer had sole authority to engineer and build office products. Xerox had converted certain manufacturing and other assets from the Scientific Data Systems write-off into a Printing Division located in El Segundo, California.

Led by an executive named Jack Lewis, the El Segundo group had persuaded Xerox to turn PARC's laser printing technology into a product. And under pressure from Jack Goldman and others, Xerox had established a small team in Palo Alto called the Systems Development Division (SDD) to engineer PARC's inventions into possible products.

Rather than accepting the 850 on its face, Xerox's planning department asked representatives from Dallas, the Printing Division, PARC, and SDD to recommend a strategy incorporating the best thinking then available to the company. The Display Word Processing Task Force, as the group became known, worked during the last half of 1976. Among other conclusions, they decided that Xerox should exploit the Ethernet communications technology as a common link among products being developed at their respective operations. They could not, however, agree as easily on a choice for Xerox's next word processing product.

According to Jerry Elkind, manager of PARC's Computer Science Laboratory and a member of the task force, the Dallas 850 word processor, though featuring a high quality display, remained unprogrammable. By comparison, the rich possibilities in the Alto's bit map display plus the computer's flexible support of communications, word processing, and printing encouraged several task force members to favor the Alto in terms of performance. Nevertheless, the task force assumed the Alto would cost far more to make than the 850. To find out, Elkind asked a PARC researcher named John Ellenby to put together a realistic estimate for the Alto.

"At the time," recalls Elkind, "Altos cost around fifteen thousand dollars to make. The manufacturing cost of the 850 was projected at around five to eight thousand dollars. The problem was that the Alto was produced in small lots by hand assembly and the 850's costs were based on large scale manufacturing. So I asked John to get a base component cost and compare it to the 850, and then to draw up a manufacturing plan."

John Ellenby earlier had spearheaded an effort to convert the research prototype Alto into a more reliable, less expensive machine known as the Alto II. His success convinced him of the existence of major opportunities to improve the reliability and cost of Altos. His report to the task force promised that by repackaging and reengineering the computer, "Alto IIIs" could be produced by the second quarter of 1978 at a lower cost than the 850. To back up his claims, Ellenby requested an independent team of Rochester engineers to review his analysis. They confirmed the Alto III plan.

That summer, the Display Word Processing Task Force made a preliminary recommendation that Xerox's next word processor be based on the Alto. When word of their decision spread through PARC, Jerry Elkind, John Ellenby, Bob Taylor, Butler Lampson, Chuck Thacker, Alan Kay—everyone—cheered. None of them, however, appreciated just how weightless study group recommendations could be at Xerox. A team sympathetic to Dallas double-checked Ellenby's analysis and claimed to find that the Alto III would take longer and cost more to develop than Ellenby predicted. In what must have seemed like a self-fulfilling prophecy, the 850's promoters concluded that the 850, not the Alto III, should go forward, and they had enough clout to prevent the Alto III recommendation from surviving to the Display Word Processing Task Force's final year-end report.

Jack Goldman learned of the Alto's reversal in August upon returning to the United States from a four-month sabbatical as technical advisor to the Government of Israel. He immediately flew to the West Coast to find out what had happened. Ever since the triumphant experiment with Altos and Gypsy word processing software at Ginn & Co., he had lobbied corporate headquarters to get an Alto-based product into the marketplace. After listening to Elkind explain the recent events of the task force, Goldman decided to try again. He approached his boss Bill Souders—not to kill the 850 in favor of an Alto III word processor, but to gain approval for a small entrepreneurial group who might introduce the Alto as a general purpose computer work station. Goldman pumped Souders to help him move Xerox's revolutionary technology out of the laboratory before it was no longer "revolutionary."

"I said, 'Let's establish a standard out in the world for a computer work station with bit map graphics.' And I wanted to do the same for the laser printer too. I wanted to alert the world of what we would be coming out with later."

But Souders rejected the proposal, choosing instead to listen to the O'Neill-Sparacino faction who pointed out that Xerox already had authorized the Systems Development Division to advance PARC inventions into products. To back the production of

Alto IIIs by yet another Xerox group, they argued, would only confuse the marketplace. Besides, they contended, an Alto computer work station business would not make money.

One former Xerox official who was opposed to Goldman summarized the case against the Alto. "There was a difference between having an available system work on something PARC did as opposed to going out to a totally different environment—a customer, a Mr. X—who's going to pay real money for it and is not going to be very happy when it breaks down and we say, 'Oh, sorry. We'll get to you, and we'll fix it.' "

He argued that the Alto would have been too costly. He assumed the machine's manufacturing bill would have fallen between $12,000 and $15,000, forcing Xerox to price Altos far higher than the most expensive word processor. Moreover, he correctly noted that Altos without printers would be useless, especially for word processing applications, and that purchasing the necessary Xerox laser printer would have added another $30,000 to the price of the full system.

"For the price that had to be paid," this official concluded, "the Alto would not live up to customer expectations. There were some people who would have bought anything, but it still wouldn't have been a successful business venture."

Several former PARC scientists shake their heads at such arguments. They note that between 1973, the year the Alto was invented, and 1976, when both Ellenby's and Goldman's proposals were rejected, integrated circuits advanced two full generations in performance and cost. Added to the benefits of production scale economies, the cheaper and better chips would have reduced Xerox's cost to manufacture Altos below the company's experience in 1973, 1974, and 1975. If Xerox had asked Butler Lampson, Chuck Thacker, and their colleagues to design a cost-reduced, market-ready computer system, the people who had invented the technology in the first place stood ready to provide it.

"If the Alto III had been approved," asserts Lampson, "we would have sat down and figured out how to build something that basically had the characteristics of the Alto, getting as much mileage as possible out of 1976–1977 technology which was quite a bit better than the 1972 technology. The main thing is that it would have been smaller and cheaper."

Lampson thinks that Xerox could have priced the Altos at $10,000 to $12,000, far lower than the O'Neill-Sparacino-Potter group assumed and well within the range of high end word processors. Customers still would have had to purchase a printer, but Xerox might have hurdled that obstacle in several ways. First, the Ethernet permitted one printer to serve more than one Alto; by selling multiple Alto work stations to a single customer, Xerox could have lowered the effective printing price per Alto. Second, the company could have grafted its laser printing technology onto slower, less costly copying machines. The 7000 Copier used for Gary Starkweather's printer was, by contrast, among the fastest, most expensive in the Xerox line. Third, Xerox might have offered an Alto system with a nonlaser printer—a less elegant yet less expensive way to meet customer needs. Fourth, and finally, the company might have lowered prices and sacrificed profits on its early laser printers as an investment to be recouped from the office market at a later time when, as everyone who understood digital science and economics expected, the cost of the technology dropped.

Such tactics often reveal themselves to businesspeople willing to bet on new technology. For example, a few months before Bill Souders killed Goldman's Alto appeal, Wang Laboratories, a Massachusetts technology company, introduced advanced computers to the word processing market. Wang had entered the industry two years earlier with a product that, like the 800, had failed to meet expectations. That disappointment persuaded Wang to abandon electromechanical devices in favor of computers. By 1976, the company had developed a prototype that established much higher standards of performance. But it also carried a price tag more than twice as high as the most expensive competitive product. Nevertheless, An Wang, the company's founder, decided to announce the product in June of 1976 at the annual word processing trade show in New York.

"We had to rush to get a prototype to the show," writes Wang in his autobiography, "and we had only three people capable of demonstrating the machine. But then something happened that showed that we had a revolutionary piece of equipment on our hands.

"We had a small booth on the main floor of the convention hall as well as a hospitality suite at the Hilton, where the show was held. Word spread like wildfire about the machine, and within moments of the first demonstration, people were lined up ten deep at the booth. The hospitality suite became so jammed that we had to issue invitations in order to control the crowds. Despite the fact that it was just a prototype, and not even fully working (the printers were not operational), people saw text editing done on a screen, and they thought it was magic.

"The basic equipment was so far superior to anything then available that even with a list price of thirty thousand dollars (for the hard disk version), one customer unflinchingly ordered a million dollars' worth of equipment on the basis of an advance look at the system."

Wang's machine, like his company, later became synonymous with word processing.

In 1976, however, Xerox chose not to introduce the Alto, either as a word processor or a more general computer work station. The decision emerged more from habit than reasoning; it was not Xerox's custom to fund entrepreneurial start-ups or several development groups seeking potentially overlapping markets. As Bill Souders explained subsequently, the copier giant had a more deliberate, albeit expensive, approach to marketing technology:

"The first policy consists of requiring immediate application to the full exploitation of those of our technologies that are already profitable. The second policy consists of *not* requiring immediate profitability where we are still developing or expanding technologies that we think are—or will be—crucial to our long-range future. We are going to have to continue to invest time and money in these technologies so that we can learn how to apply them more efficiently and economically and build the appropriate market position we intend them to serve. This is a costly procedure. There is no way to bypass it. In order to make big money, you must spend big money."

Xerox routinely spent hundreds of millions of dollars over several years to develop copiers before taking them to market. But that practice ignored the essential mystery of the Alto: How would people respond to computers they could program and use themselves? To have found out in 1976, either through Goldman's work station suggestion or Ellenby's Alto III word processor proposal, might have cost the company $10 million, maybe $25 million. Souders's logic in rejecting the Alto suggested either that such sums were not big enough for Xerox or that the company had nothing to learn from customers. Xerox managers simply did not understand how to think about a technology as different from copiers as digital computers.

In saying no to Goldman and, by implication, favoring the 850 over the Alto III, Souders made a critical decision, one that never reached the desk of Peter McColough. McColough's failure to intervene did not upset Bob Potter. He believed the issues surrounding the separate technological approaches of Dallas and PARC were details beneath the attention of Xerox's chief executive officer. But it is unimaginable that Joe Wilson would have abdicated to others any judgment about when to introduce profoundly new technology. Wilson had not done so with the Model A Copier, which failed, or with the 914 Copier, which succeeded. Yet McColough, who had funded PARC's creation of the Alto system, remained uninvolved while the management machinery of Xerox—the decision systems, the prevailing prejudices, the reigning executives—conspired to keep the company's great accomplishment a secret from the world.

Wilson had once proclaimed of Xerox, "We aspire to be a leader throughout the world in graphic communication." In 1970, McColough had expanded that dream. "Our fundamental thrust, our common denominator, has evolved toward establishing leadership in what we call the 'architecture of information.' " Both statements described leadership visions for Xerox. Both were simple, both noble. But neither could be found in the 1976 decisions about the 850 or the Alto. Those actions reflected a different vision, a vision of finance and control that tackled only what was already seen with technology already established through development, manufacturing, and marketing systems already in place. Such a world view could exploit leadership only when leadership already existed; it could suck value only from the already profitable. In the 1970s, it arguably could work at Xerox for copiers, but certainly not for word processors or computers. Under the influence of management by numbers alone, Xerox introduced equipment like the 800 and 850, which followed instead of led, while rejecting products like the Alto, which had every promise of leadership.

More dangerously, by keeping the Alto to itself, Xerox prevented Xerox from learning. An Alto computer in 1976 might not have been a financial success. So what? Neither was the Model A Copier of the early 1950s. Joe Wilson okayed the Model A because he had faith in xerography. When the Model A failed, he and Haloid took a beating. But he did not despair. He insisted that he and his colleagues learn from the mistake by discovering how to design a better office copier the next time. By failing to bring the Alto to market, Xerox lost much more than money or opportunity. They lost faith—in themselves, in their past, and in their future.

Marketing: The Reaffirmation of the Copier

Chapter

15

"*I*f we ever get to be afraid to stick our necks out, we'll be just another big corporation." Peter McColough had trumpeted those words in 1972 against the mounting criticism of Xerox's acquisition and management of Scientific Data Systems. It was a defiant statement, tersely evoking the business philosophy and spirit of Joe Wilson. At the time, Xerox had stood at the zenith of its twelve-year rise from obscurity, and notwithstanding the SDS blunder—indeed, because of it—McColough had insisted his was an enterprise determined to profit from mistakes as well as successes. Five years later, however, everything had changed; when McColough surveyed Xerox in 1977, he saw what he feared most—just another big corporation that neither encouraged experimentation nor tolerated error.

"I see a company which began with a culture of survival now more than a little encrusted with the culture of success," went one of McColough's speeches for Xerox ears only. "As we have grown, we have become an unwieldy bureaucracy, with a bureaucracy's tendency to bloat.

"As we have become more complex, it has become more and more difficult to either give or take responsibility. As it becomes more difficult to see whom to praise or blame, it becomes ever more difficult to determine the cost of product, the cost of operation, the cost of everything. And, as this happens, we are putting increasing burdens on ourselves in the competitive marketplace. And this leads to confusion and discontent."

At Xerox, a deluded obsession for controlling the variables of business had twisted caution into censorship. Objectivity, always vulnerable in large organizations, atrophied. Instead of measuring themselves against the needs of customers and the performance of competitors, Xerox's talented people competed among themselves in a race for personal aggrandizement.

"The premium is on political maneuvering," noted one of Xerox's consultants. "Most of the decisions are made around the issues of turf, career advancement, and those kinds of things."

Predictably, a technology as untested as PARC's personal distributed computing system scared away executives whose careers depended on managing certainty and who, after the abysmal failure of SDS, were afraid to gamble their Xerox futures on a computer business. Most corporate managers never even bothered to learn how to operate PARC's advanced systems, condemning themselves to perpetual apprehensions about computers that were as self-defeating as "math fear." The biases against the Alto should have startled McColough. Evidently, however, it took a far more perilous trend to grab his attention—specifically, the emergence of superior competition in the copier industry.

Xerox officials first began monitoring potential competitors in the 1960s. Through patent filings and other sources, they watched and waited as IBM and Kodak edged ever closer to product introductions. Xerox most feared IBM, and with good reason. Only the computer maker surpassed Xerox in the size and reach of its sales force. But IBM stumbled. Reliability and other problems plagued many of its copiers, and of its major product introductions between 1970 and 1977, only one, the Copier II, made the impact Xerox had anticipated. By 1977, IBM had placed between 80,000 and 90,000 Copier IIs around the world, accounting for about 10 percent of the market. Significant damage, but tolerable.

Kodak took much longer than IBM to enter the market. Xerox's crosstown rival invested a decade in improving copier technology before announcing its first product in late 1975 and following with a second machine six months later. Between them, the Kodak copiers won far less market share than IBM's Copier II. Nevertheless, Kodak hurt Xerox profoundly.

Kodak's machines produced better copies than Xerox's, introducing an entirely new phrase—"Kodak quality"—into the lexicon of the copier industry. "Kodak customers," concluded an internal Xerox report, "indicate general satisfaction with their units, stressing copy quality as the key feature."

Behind that laconic statement stood a startling fact, one the writer had difficulty admitting: Xerox no longer produced the best copier. In the opinion of many analysts, only the limited size of Kodak's sales force prevented a mass defection of Xerox customers; "If IBM had Kodak's machine," went the quip, "they would have handed Xerox its head on the platter."

The engineers at Kodak were not more talented than their Xerox counterparts, just less assuming. Xerox engineers cared about copy quality and worked to improve the crispness and consistency of Xerox images. But like too many other activities at Xerox, the yardstick that measured progress was calibrated entirely by Xerox's past, present, and future. Xerox did not look beyond Xerox for its standard of quality because Xerox copies by definition—by acclamation—were the best. Until Kodak.

Kodak's engineers were also better managed. Phased program planning, as implemented at Xerox by Jim O'Neill and Bob Sparacino, demanded perfection while discouraging risk. Engineers were expected to design against a set of marketing and financial objectives that were constantly in flux and that, at times, seemed beyond the ken of technical reality. When the consequent complexity threatened to overwhelm a program, Xerox hired more engineers. But more people succeeded only in making the company less effective by disrupting collaboration and by breeding the frightful disease called "not invented here."

"We became burdened with organizational weight," said Gary Starkweather, who had spent several years in Rochester before transferring to PARC. "We got too many people working on projects, and that led to reviews and reviews and reviews, and foils and foils and foils. And that meant we had to hire more and more people. The organizational layering began to get serious in the late 1960s. It began to be more important to get approval than to get something accomplished."

Supreme approval, of course, belonged to Jim O'Neill, a man who understood neither the science of xerography nor the discipline of engineering. His priorities, as the technical community quickly discovered, were governed by different criteria.

"You have to understand how hard product reviews were for the engineers," says Horace Becker. "If they would say there was such and such a problem that would cause the product introduction to slip for six months, the finance people would say, 'Well, since the life of the product is fixed, you have six months of revenues lost at the end.' They'd chop off the last six months— the best six months—and there goes the return on investment. O'Neill's response in that situation was to hold the engineers feet to the fire. He made them meet the date. But if you hold an engineer's feet to the fire, usually you only get burnt feet."

The engineers set less and less aggressive targets for themselves and held their tongues when finance or marketing executives did just the opposite. Conflicts were created, not resolved, and product development cycles stretched out, product costs rose, product improvements suffered. Xerox, creators of the first and second generations of copiers, read in shame the reviews hailing Kodak for producing "the first 'third generation' copier."

Kodak surprised Xerox with its quality, IBM with its mistakes. But at least Xerox paid attention to those rivals. Such was not the case with respect to the third major set of competitors who challenged Xerox in the 1970s. That group, consisting of Japanese manufacturers represented initially by American and European marketing firms, captured a large share of the worldwide copier market before Xerox cared enough to think they mattered at all.

The Japanese weren't new to copiers; for many years, they had manufactured small, slow copying machines that employed a greasy, chemical reproduction process similar to the technology displaced by xerography. But in July of 1975, the same month Peter McColough asked the Xerox board of directors to close down Scientific Data Systems and approve the consent decree settling Xerox's dispute with the Federal Trade Commission, a completely different Japanese-made copier was introduced at the annual National Office Machine Dealers Association convention in Minneapolis. That product, the Savin 750, changed the copier industry more than any machine since the 914.

The Savin 750 resulted from a multiyear international development effort led by an American named Paul Charlap. Charlap thought Xerox's monopoly was vulnerable, if for no other reason than Xerox's much evident bias against slow copiers that made between eight and twenty copies per minute. Xerox offered such equipment, but only in bulky, expensive, and unreliable form. With the help of a team of Americans, Australians, Germans, and Japanese, Charlap created a product to beat Xerox on all three counts.

The key to Charlap's accomplishment was liquid toner. Recall that xerography uses electrostatic charges to attract ink to those parts of an image to be copied. In the Xerox machines of the 1970s, that "ink" was dry powder; to fix it to the paper, the Xerox equipment first had to melt the powder, then cool it off. Liquid toner technology did not require such rapid extremes of heat and cold, thereby avoiding significant cost and reliability problems.

Savin and its Japanese manufacturing partner Ricoh parlayed the 750's advantages into a business bonanza. Every move they made turned Xerox's strategy upside down. Instead of employing a direct sales force, Savin/Ricoh distributed their machines through office equipment dealers. Instead of pitching service, Savin/Ricoh built machines that broke down one-third as often as Xerox's copiers and promoted dependability. Instead of designing customized components into their copiers, Savin/Ricoh used standardized parts wherever possible. And instead of leasing machines, Savin/Ricoh sold them.

Furthermore, Savin/Ricoh priced their equipment far below Xerox. The liquid toner technology, standardization of parts, and other Japanese manufacturing techniques gave Ricoh a 30- to 40-percent cost advantage over Xerox. Savin's introductory price for the 750 Copier was $5,000. By comparison, customers who wished to buy Xerox's most competitive product, the 3100, had to pay $12,000—until Xerox matched Savin's price in a desperate bid to keep the 3100 viable. The Savin 750 was an overnight success.

Savin/Ricoh and other Japanese competitors did borrow one tactic from Xerox: advertising spending. They matched Xerox dollar for dollar, and their ads hit hard. For example, one Savin ad depicted the "call key operator" button, used on a Xerox machine to signal a breakdown, as the "feature that works best." Such marketing campaigns, like the copiers they promoted, worked wonderfully. In 1976, customers around the world bought more than 100,000 Ricoh and other Japanese-made copiers, prompting Savin to assert boldly, "We are where Xerox used to be: No. 1."

That claim took slick advantage of the basic strategic difference between the Japanese and Xerox. The Japanese sold copiers; Xerox sold copies. By leasing instead of selling its machines, Xerox continued to earn money from customers long after the cost of the equipment was paid in full. Slow copiers were less attractive to Xerox because, making fewer copies, they earned less money. When the Japanese forced Xerox to cut prices and shift from leasing to selling the low end machines, the profit margins on those copiers shrunk even further. Therefore, from the financial point of view paramount at Xerox for most of the 1970s, the Japanese had assaulted the short end of the stick. True, Savin/Ricoh legitimately could claim to have sold thousands more copiers than Xerox in 1977. But the top managers of Xerox knew they had sold more copies—billions more.

Xerox's indifference to the low end of the market was such that company market share reports did not consistently include the Japanese until long after the introduction of the Savin 750. Pleas for better small copiers, whether from Xerox's Japanese partner, Fuji-Xerox, or from outside advisors, were rejected. One story seems typical. At the end of a full day of discussing the potential threat of the Japanese, Archie McCardell is reported to have laughed, simply laughed.

From a short-term financial perspective, McCardell's reaction may have been correct. Low end copier revenues and profits paled in comparison to the business Xerox enjoyed at the medium and high ranges of the market. But in terms of marketing and longer term financial considerations, Xerox picked a flawed low end strategy. As customers gained confidence in Japanese-made machines, the Japanese manufacturers secured a foothold in the offices of nearly every Xerox account. Given that position, a Japanese assault on what Xerox called its "heartland," the valuable medium-to-high volume market, seemed inevitable, prompting industry observers to describe the low end of the market, at least as it pertained to Xerox, in a sickening way—the "soft underbelly" of the giant.

Nevertheless, since Xerox sold copies instead of copiers, the McCardell team was far keener on high volume machines. Xerox's bread and butter—the majority of its revenues and profits—had always come from copiers generating thirty to seventy copies per minute. Those machines dotted hallways and offices throughout the world. They had not, however, made much of a dent in the most prodigious of all centers of copying activity—central reproduction departments. For every manager demanding ten copies of a fifteen page report, there existed a job order requesting a central reproduction department to duplicate a hundred copies of a two hundred page document. Such differences added up. If, as Xerox estimated for 1974, mid-range copiers in the United States produced thirty billion copies a year, then central reproduction departments made ten times as many. Three hundred billion copies. Each year.

Mesmerized by an astounding potential payoff, Xerox invested more than $300 million to design and build its 9200 Copier, an engineering marvel that made 120 copies a minute. When Xerox introduced the 9200 in 1974, the staggering cost of the project was compared to Boeing's 747, du Pont's nylon, IBM's 360 computer family, Ford's Edsel, and Polaroid's SX-70 camera. The machine was two years late, but Xerox's strategists weren't worried; their financial projections showed that once Xerox placed an average of a single 9200 in each of the nation's 100,000 central reproduction departments, company revenues would increase by $1 billion annually, of which $200 million would be profit.

But as much as the 9200 excited the finance people, it worried those in marketing. Central reproduction departments were small, in-house print shops staffed by skilled employees who knew the difference between high quality offset images and the comparatively low grade copies produced by Xerox machines. Such men and women credited their own talent and judgment in handling ink as integral to offset reproduction quality. The notion of pressing buttons to make copies offended their sense of pride and, worse, jeopardized their job security.

One consultant to Xerox sarcastically summed up the company's plan to market 9200s to central reproduction departments as follows: "XEROX having spent a decade going around the Central Reproduction Department manager, in an effort to sell Xerox copiers upstairs to the decentralized satellite areas, secretaries, art departments, accounting departments, anywhere but his area, thereupon earned a certain hostility from this man by virtue of having gone deviously around him to sell something to his company on which he at LEAST might have been consulted, combined with;

"his professional observation that xerography was a highly inferior process compared to offset printing (correctly observed), leading him in many cases to put down Xerox to his company motivated by a naturally possessive and very human tendency to want this duplicating work back into his protective custody,

"WHEREUPON, the Xerox sales force, in their infinite understanding of human nature, being trained sociologists, and schooled by someone at Xerox who had bothered to peer a full three inches into the future, proceeded not to try and win over this potential obstacle in their paths, but actually made a planned, concerted effort to ridicule this man openly, behind his back, referring to him as 'Charlie Printpants' down there, 'with the ink under his fingernails . . . he wouldn't understand Xerox,' etc. Actually, an official, programmed assault by Xerox, according to men I have questioned who were in the field at that time. Incredible as it seems, Xerox having by now not only walked around this man to make their sales, but *over* him as well, (XEROX itself being a company of trained sociologists and alert indeed to the sensitivities of human beings) decides that the thing to now do is to:

"Enter the offset printing field, and in that way be able to seize upon the wonderful friendship by now established with the very man they decide to sell these printing presses to. His name? . . . may we have the envelope please . . . well, well, it's good old 'CHARLIE PRINTPANTS'!!!"

The 9200 would be a tough sell.

"You want the problem in a nutshell?" a Xerox marketeer said at a pre-launch meeting on the 9200. "Here it is: We got a great new machine that the guy we're selling it to won't want to buy, sold to him by a salesman who doesn't really want to sell it."

Such concerns proved well founded. By the end of 1977, Xerox had placed only three thousand 9200s in central reproduction departments, far short of the target of fifty thousand units that could be extrapolated from company financial projections. Notwithstanding the abysmal results, however, the 9200 still promised to succeed—not as a substitute for offset, but as a faster, more powerful machine to service Xerox's mid-to-high volume market.

Ironically, the Xerox numbers-driven managers who ignored marketing common sense in their quest of central reproduction departments saved their dream product because of other, comparable mistakes of judgment. Under the regime of phased program planning, Xerox's engineering group failed throughout the 1970s to develop a new sixty- to seventy-copy-per-minute machine. That left the company peddling the 3600 and 7000 Copiers—1960s technology—against IBM and Kodak. The 9200 gave Xerox another, albeit expensive, option; when central reproduction departments balked at taking the machines, Xerox slashed prices and offered the 9200s to its more traditional customers.

By 1977, a total of fifteen thousand 9200s had been leased, and revised projections showed thirty-five thousand machines would be placed by 1980. Although that number of units remained short of the original goal, Xerox, as it had done so often in the past, had seriously underestimated the usage of its copy machines. When given the opportunity to make two copies each second instead of one, it turned out, people made more copies. Consequently, and notwithstanding its failure to capture the market for central reproduction departments, the 9200 remained on target for a billion dollars in revenue in 1980.

The serendipity of the 9200 aside, Xerox's market position was compromised by 1977. The company virtually had lost the low end of the industry to the Japanese; it confronted IBM and

Kodak in the mid-to-high end with outdated (the 3600 and 7000) or overcapable (the 9200) products. The picture, as painted by Xerox's planning department, was grim.

"A Review of Xerox Reprographic Business (1977):
—Rapid loss of market share.
—Copy volume & revenue growing but profit growth slowing or profit declining.
—True long term profit outlook masked by [selling off existing, depreciated copiers] in the short term.
—The Xerox lease base is being eroded by competitive products with superior performance & lower inherent costs.
—Xerox is in a defensive position, the leadership in product pricing & market growth is passing to the competitors (with exception of 9200).
—In no area does Xerox have both performance & cost advantage over the major competition; but most of Xerox's major competitors have both performance & cost advantages over the relevant Xerox products.
—In general, Xerox products are now over priced for the value offered.
The dilemma: price reductions are necessary but this may well stimulate competitive response which will lower the general price level.
—Xerox is in strategically reactive mode caused by weaknesses in product & cost structure, and desire to maintain short-term profit growth levels. The result is that Xerox is not participating fully in growth of market.
—A long-term strategy for Xerox to more fully participate in the market growth must be developed.
—The [Xerox Long Range Plan] is a *desired* outcome; rather than a *probable* outcome based upon an objective assessment of an achievable plan.
—Our strategic approach tends to be too introspective; our product planning & engineering too cautious.

For those executives at the company who preferred numbers to words, one figure stood out. Having controlled 95 percent of the copies made in the world in 1972, Xerox, according to its own analysis, accounted for 73 percent of the copies made in 1977. And outside sources put Xerox's portion closer to 65 percent.

Xerox remained large and prosperous in 1977. Company revenues were destined to break the $5 billion mark, profits would reach a record $400 million. There was no cause for panic. But the share loss figures bore a sobering message: in the five years of the McColough and McCardell administration, between one-fourth and one-third of the Xerox franchise had disappeared. The roots of the mighty Xerox money tree were more than a little diseased.

Peter McColough could not have been happy, either with himself or with Archie McCardell. A case could have been made for the removal of both men. But the board of directors maintained confidence in McColough, and McColough was not about to fire McCardell. It wasn't his style. Fate, however, intervened to give him a more gracious opportunity to pick a new president for Xerox.

In early 1977, International Harvester informed McCardell that he was a candidate to become the company's next chief executive officer. McCardell demurred. He liked the job he had and expected to move up to the chief executive's post at Xerox once McColough was ready.

But the Harvester executive recruiter wasn't as convinced of McCardell's prospects at Xerox. The previous November, Jimmy Carter had been elected President. Because of Peter McColough's high profile in Democratic Party politics, many people speculated that Carter would offer the Xerox chairman a Cabinet position. According to one source, Carter did ask McColough to be his secretary of commerce, but McColough declined. Thus, when the announcement of Cabinet appointments excluded McColough's name, Harvester's headhunter seized the opportunity to test Archie McCardell's level of job satisfaction once again.

"You know that McColough's going to be there a while now," prodded the recruiter. "It's McColough's company! It'll always be McColough's company. It will never be known as McCardell's company."

The recruiter reminded McCardell that Harvester actually was larger than Xerox. How many people, he mused, are asked to run one of America's twenty-five biggest corporations? McCardell agreed to meet Harvester's chairman Brooks McCormick, and an impressed McCormick eventually offered McCardell a multi-year compensation package worth more than $6 million. Still, McCardell might have stayed with Xerox—had McColough given him the right signal.

"McCardell," noted Jack Goldman from his vantage point as

a Xerox board member, "was willing to stay on at Xerox if C. Peter McColough, then CEO, would promise that eventually the CEO post would be his, but McColough balked at that."

With McCardell's departure, McColough hoped Xerox might change its ways—notwithstanding the billions of dollars of company revenues and hundreds of millions of dollars of profits. Those numbers were remarkable, but the organization needed more than numbers now. It needed to regain its spirit of accomplishment. Xerox had to learn how to win. So in choosing a successor to McCardell, McColough stayed away from numbers people like O'Neill. He wanted a salesman, someone like himself, someone who could motivate the 100,000 people of Xerox, someone who could inspire a magnificent resurgence.

He picked David Kearns.

Chapter

16

*I*n the late 1960s, when Joe Wilson and Peter McColough had decided their Haloid/Xerox colleagues were unequal to the task of managing a billion dollar corporation, they had courted more than a dozen men away from other Fortune 500 companies. David Kearns, for example, spent seventeen years with IBM before joining Xerox. The Wilson-McColough hiring program had brought much talent to Xerox. But it also had triggered a competition; Xerox watchers wondered who among the various alumni groups would win control of the company.

Two contingents gained the most prominence: Ford and IBM. The Ford managers, led by Archie McCardell and Jim O'Neill, practiced the careful finance and control theories introduced to the car company in the 1950s. The IBM delegation, on the other hand, were more inclined toward sales than statistics; most of them, Kearns included, rose through marketing. Thus with Kearns replacing Ford-alumnus McCardell in 1977, people expected a shift in the relative power of the two factions and in the marketing and finance philosophies they represented. Less obvious was how Kearns would convince Xerox's top managers, regardless of background and orientation, to work as a team.

"Xerox imported many managers at many different levels," says Jack Crowley, who himself joined Xerox in 1977 after a long career at the management consulting firm McKinsey & Company. "They all brought with them into the company their own widely different sets of value systems and management approaches and company backgrounds. There were guys from Ford, from GM, from GE, from IBM. From other companies too. To fuse those into a single set of values and systems was unbelievably difficult. All these guys were individually capable with proven records. But how do you get them to agree on 'the way we will do things around here'?"

That McCardell's departure had not stilled the confusion of voices became evident in November of 1977, when Xerox convened its first worldwide conference of managers in six years. The earlier affair, in 1971, had been staged to celebrate a monopoly

in full flower. This gathering had a more complicated purpose—
to boost morale by bearing witness to Xerox's financial strength
and glory while also talking straight about competitive weaknesses
and the need for corporate change.

Conference planners had started their work before McCardell
left for Harvester. At Peter McColough's request, they had recommended four days of meetings to discuss the critical themes of
change, competition, cost effectiveness, technology, people, and
the future. McColough was to lead off with a "Real World" speech,
commanding Xerox to take an honest look at itself in preparing
for change. On day two, Kearns, as chief of marketing, was to
discuss the company's competitive position in the copier industry.
The third day would center on a McCardell speech linking competitive strength to cost effectiveness. And on the fourth day, there
was to be a PARC demonstration of "the world of 1985," concluded by McColough's expression of confidence in the people of
Xerox to meet the challenges that lay ahead.

Kearn's August elevation complicated that schedule. It did not
seem appropriate for Kearns-qua-president to speak solely about
marketing; nor did the planners consider the speech on cost effectiveness, originally planned for McCardell, a sufficiently uplift-
ing topic with which to introduce Kearns as the new chief operating
officer to his two hundred fifty most senior executives. They knew
that unless Kearns was positioned properly, the potent signal of
change symbolized by his promotion would be diluted. They also
knew they had to carefully navigate Xerox's partisan cross
currents—how they matched speakers to topics would communicate as much to the audience as the words actually spoken.

Memos and meeting notes indicate much feeling and many
position shifts before a tentative decision was reached to have Jim
O'Neill discuss cost effectiveness while retaining Kearns as the
marketing speaker and enlarging his role by assigning him
McColough's session on people as well. That scheme, however,
was challenged immediately by Frank Marshall, Peter Mc-
Colough's long time speech writer and advisor.

"Kearns," wrote Marshall in a confidential memorandum to
the head of the conference, "is the chief operating officer of the
company and should not appear as if he is still running the marketing of our copiers and duplicators. In addition, if O'Neill were
to talk about cost effectiveness, it would appear as if that task were
his responsibility rather than Kearns's. The fact is that Kearns will

be responsible for implementing the policies and that should be made clear."

Marshall went on to argue that "O'Neill's concept of cost effectiveness is possibly at odds with other view points within the corporation. To assign him such a speech would [make it] appear that his views have prevailed."

And he concluded, "The two most important speeches in the conference are Peter's 'Real World' speech on Tuesday and Kearns's 'People' speech. For Kearns to carry the burden of copying before turning to the 'People' speech would in my opinion diminish the importance of the latter."

Marshall's logic persuaded the planners to modify the schedule once more. They dropped the separate talk on cost competitiveness, choosing instead to weave that theme into every speech, and they asked O'Neill to keynote the copier presentation. Kearns was thereby freed of all obligations other than giving an inspirational address about people.

The Xerox World Conference 1977 opened in Boca Raton, Florida, on Sunday, November 6. On Monday morning, participants and spouses attended a multimedia presentation of Xerox's entire product line. The exhibit, according to the manager in charge, was designed to build "confidence in the broad range of Xerox capabilities, [and] excitement about the significant new products we are introducing."

In other words, a show of strength. To underscore that message, McColough had insisted upon displaying several Xerox products not quite ready for the market. "He believes we must take some risks and live with them," noted one of the conference planners in recapping a meeting with McColough. "If we get resistance, it must be proven in writing that the [development] program would suffer a serious setback by having a product, such as the 9700, at Boca Raton."

Visitors saw more than three dozen copiers, duplicators, printers, word processors, communications devices, and other pieces of equipment. The latest version of the 9200 duplicator, known as the 9400, was on display, as were several machines still bearing project code names instead of numbers. Of them all, however, the most remarkable in terms of business and technical heritage, was the 9700 laser xerographic computer printer.

The 9700 was the acme of Xerox's investment in PARC, a pure marriage of digital and xerographic technologies that had

followed a timely, if bumpy, path to the marketplace. Gary Starkweather had first demonstrated that a laser could print xerographic images when he invented the "Scanned Laser Output
Terminal" at PARC in 1971. A year later, Ron Rider and Butler
Lampson had designed and built the "Research Character Generator," a digital processor to control the printing done by Starkweather's laser. Once combined, their technology had provided
PARC with the world's most advanced electronic printing capability; nonetheless, early proposals to exploit the invention, such
as Jack Goldman's Livermore plan, had encountered opposition.

Many voices spoke against laser printing. Some said lasers,
hardly more than a decade old by the early seventies, were dangerous death rays to be kept out of Xerox products. Others pushed
alternative printing technologies under development by company
engineers in New York. And still others argued that the market
for such a printer, if extant at all, was too small to justify the
required investment.

Over the years, Lampson, Rider, and Starkweather each spent
time on task forces and project teams explaining and promoting
their technology. With important contributions from a series of
compatriots, they demonstrated the safety of lasers and repeatedly
proved the superiority of laser xerographic printing over competing technologies. Furthermore, they insisted throughout the
period that an attractive market did exist, even if most of the
businesspeople at Xerox couldn't see it.

"It sounds arrogant," says Starkweather, "but we really saw
what laser printing could do for the market. The reason no market
existed before was that no capability had existed. But we believed
no rational world could reject it."

Despite such conviction, however, the engineers and scientists
advocating laser xerographic printing would not have prevailed
had it not been for Jack Lewis, an executive who ran Xerox's
Printing Division. Lewis championed the PARC invention and
provided the funds for its development throughout the battle over
which printing technology Xerox would market. His position involved some risk; at least twice, says George Pake, Lewis had direct
orders to kill the 9700.

Nevertheless, after IBM introduced the first high speed laser
printer in 1975, Xerox okayed the PARC inspired product. Lewis
assembled a specialized sales force to market the laser printing
system, and by the fall of 1977, had a product ready for display

at Boca Raton. For his efforts, Lewis earned kudos from others at Xerox; the conference planners, for example, referred to him as "the make it happen man." More important, once in the hands of Lewis's sales force, the 9700 became one of Xerox's fastest growing products.

The laser printer was by far the most advanced product at Boca, an indirect reminder that Xerox's all-important copier line had not kept pace with its competition. Indeed, the machine most crucial to Xerox's prosperity—a replacement for the seventy-copy-per-minute 7000 Copier to compete with Kodak and IBM—was not on display. Instead, those attending Boca learned that the development project called "Moses," which was to have produced the much needed copier, had been killed on the eve of the conference.

Moses was the nadir of Xerox's product planning system. Originally conceived in 1972, the project stalled repeatedly while marketing and finance people debated its features and economics. None of them, however, were attentive to early warnings from Jack Goldman and Horace Becker that researchers had yet to solve serious technical problems in the proposed machine. By 1977, those and other obstacles remained—despite efforts to overcome them by a thousand people at a five-year cost of at least $90 million. Meanwhile, both IBM and Kodak had introduced copiers with superior features and lower manufacturing costs than promised in the Moses blueprints. The search at Xerox for a perfect replacement of the 7000 Copier had produced instead a perfect mess.

"We became convinced," Jim O'Neill announced to the conference, "that the large development costs yet to be spent on this product were not warranted and might better be directed to give greater assurance of the success of our many other products now under development."

The absence of Moses provided a dreary context to Peter McColough's "Real World" speech on Tuesday morning. "We have been met by strong, intelligent and well-financed competition," McColough told his audience. "We are being out-marketed, out-engineered, outwitted in major segments of our market. We have found it shocking. We simply have not been prepared for this.

"I think we should all agree at the outset of this talk that things will never again be the same for Xerox as when we had the markets essentially to ourselves, almost fully protected by our patents. That was a time when our exuberant growth was almost our sole problem; when we could take our own time to develop and introduce new products; when the premium our products commanded forgave almost any high cost factor we could introduce into the enterprise.

"Now I have no intention of inducing panic among the management of Xerox. But there is no doubt that we—and I include myself—have already waited too long to face some of these issues publicly. I know that many of you, and certainly I, have been wrestling with them privately. Many of us have made tentative efforts, hoping to alert the bureaucracy which we created and of which we are a part, to the danger, with the hope that this company would turn itself around. That hasn't worked.

"We are now faced with the urgent need for change within this company!"

Xerox's chief executive proceeded to describe the company's strengths and weaknesses, both in the copier/duplicator business and the newer, less formed office information markets. But it was McColough's blunt opening salvo that rang in people's ears when he concluded his remarks and handed the platform over to Jim O'Neill to address the conference's most critical subject: what Xerox planned to do about its eroding position in the copier industry.

O'Neill took the stage with an obvious handicap—in the eyes of many, though certainly not all, he had come to symbolize Xerox's troubles. Xerox had not faltered because of the failure of the sales force to sell. Rather, the company had designed too many second-rate copiers that were too expensive to manufacture, a fact bitterly underscored by the fate of Moses.

"We had nothing but refried beans in the marketplace," the head of the U.S. sales division was quoted as saying. "I was out there with a rusty bayonet and an empty rifle."

As everyone at Boca well knew, both the engineers who designed the copiers and the manufacturers who made them had been O'Neill's responsibility for many years. His words were subject to a special scrutiny. Given the speaker and topic, O'Neill's detractors were listening for contradictions, and they weren't disappointed.

His assessment of the competitive situation was straightforward enough. Xerox was trying with outdated copiers to hold mid-volume share against superior products; Xerox had failed to appreciate or participate in the rapid expansion of the low end;

Xerox stood vulnerable to a Japanese move up market; Xerox was less cost effective than each of its major competitors.

But when O'Neill turned to prescriptions, his critics heard only a rehash of what they considered a discredited management style. He waffled in his remarks about phased program planning even though other speakers, including McColough, had criticized that system directly. He seemed to imply that Xerox might settle for second best when he said, "We will not always have an overall lead in all market segments." He accused sales, service, and distribution of excessive spending habits. In short, O'Neill appeared to point his finger at everyone except himself.

Moreover, as Frank Marshall had warned, many executives questioned the efficacy of O'Neill's approach to cost effectiveness. O'Neill equated expense reduction with improving efficiency by limiting head count, getting people to work harder, and cutting wasted material. Some thought that approach too narrow. For example, by manufacturing with standardized parts, the Japanese avoided the high costs Xerox incurred when it asked vendors to create special tooling for limited production runs of customized components. Resolving such a dilemma had nothing to do with efficiency; it required fundamental design choices that were the proper province of engineers, not accountants.

If O'Neill understood this, his management system did not convey the insight. Phased program planning and other techniques tended to compartmentalize activities, then set rules and limits on behavior. The constant objective was to find the policies, information, and systems that could generate the numbers O'Neill needed to manage. People—as a category—were not to be trusted; they were to be measured and controlled.

"He was going to control expenses," complained Horace Becker, "rather than let people go out and see how they were spending their money and figuring out how to do it better, for example by improving the interfaces between manufacturing and engineering. And making a better product that cost less to service."

In contrast to O'Neill, David Kearns had more confidence in people than in numbers. His Wednesday speech at Boca was a plea for openness, delegation, and honesty. Kearns did not attack O'Neill or Kearns's predecessor McCardell; that would have been out of character and out of place. Nevertheless, Kearns's remarks painted a dark picture of the joyless atmosphere wrought by the management philosophy of those two men.

"We have believed," Kearns said, "that because we are an 'open' company, we have established a rapport with our employees. I am now convinced that this is not true."

Management surveys as well as personal observation suggested to Kearns that Xerox's employees were not receiving the information they wanted or needed. Starved of communication from above, they more often than not concluded that their superiors trusted no one. Remarkably, they openly questioned whether the company had the leadership capacity to set a direction and follow it.

"It's been said," Kearns recounted, "that our decision-making is cumbersome and slow. That sometimes decisions are outdated before they're made. That they're ambiguous or equivocal, the very process is indecisive.

"So be it. I'm not about to defend the process or specific decisions. In too many ways on too many occasions, these criticisms have contained truth. To whatever degree they are accurate in any situation, we have to change. And fast."

Controls intended to prevent mistaken assumptions had instead suppressed the truth. "We must have, in this company, absolute honesty about our business among ourselves. Honesty in the literal sense of truth and accuracy and disclosure—and honesty in the sense of absolute realism, the willingness to face and deal with the facts as they are.

"Nobody in this company," announced the new Xerox president, "has a license to shoot the messenger who brings bad news."

Kearns did not offer any quick fixes. For the company to get well, he implied, the bad habits of its people must first be cured. His was a different approach from O'Neill's, and notwithstanding Kearns's recent promotion, managers at Xerox continued to consider the two men as rivals for company control. Each had many adherents and many critics. O'Neill's admirers credited him with Xerox's fivefold expansion over the previous six years; his detractors considered him a "slave to numbers." Some hoped Kearns's humanism would prevail; others thought him too softheaded to make the tough choices ahead.

Still, compared with the candor of Kearns, O'Neill's prominent role and proffered solutions—at a conference billed as a frank discussion about change—looked and sounded too much like business as usual. And, despite its wizardry and contrary purpose, so did the demonstration of PARC's technology on the fourth day of Boca.

On Thursday morning, Xerox's executives gathered in the Great Hall of the Boca Raton Hotel for "Futures Day." There they saw—nearly all of them for the first time—the fruits of Xerox's seven year investment in the Palo Alto Research Center. They were shown the workings of the keyboard, mouse, processor, screen, and printer of the Alto system, and they watched as Alto operators employed Bravo word processing and other programs to produce invitations to a hands-on session in the hotel's Granada Rooms that afternoon. Some of PARC's most advanced software was demonstrated, including a system for handling interoffice communications, a program for drawing graphs and organization charts, and an innovative solution to the challenge of typing documents in Japanese, a language with four written forms. The entire show, said George Pake, was "a really spectacular tour de force."

Afterward, McColough took the podium to sum up his views of the Boca Raton conference. He reiterated that cost leadership, shorter product development cycles, more effective planning, and less bureaucratic administration were the criteria for Xerox's success. Then, against the backdrop of PARC's accomplishments, he reminded the audience of his 1970 call for the "architecture of information."

"Seven years later," McColough declared, "I don't think I would retreat an inch from that statement. 'The architecture of information' is still the basic purpose of Xerox, except that it's no longer just a concept."

McColough's reaffirmation of the "architecture of information" had stirred controversy in the planning sessions prior to Boca. "It's a catch phrase that wore out" went one objection; "its use is hackneyed and passe," went another. But McColough had insisted. He hoped PARC's revolutionary technology would inspire confidence among Xerox's managers that their company truly could produce the office of the future.

Juxtaposed, however, against the first three days of Boca— and the previous seven years of company history—PARC's dazzling display served only to symbolize the missing balance between McColough's words and actions. His 1970 vision had implied two major hurdles for Xerox. One, to invent technology, had come to pass. But the other, transforming Xerox from a copier maker into an office information systems company, had yet to begin.

"It will not be technology alone that renews our corporate

vitality and direction," advised a memorandum submitted to corporate headquarters earlier that year, "but a fundamental organizational commitment from the top down that we will become a systems and service company through and through. No radical new technologies are needed; everything is at hand. It is our organization itself that must be made ready."

Xerox executives should have, but hadn't, used the 1970s to learn as much as possible about how to develop, make, sell, and finance office systems to the customers who needed them. Instead, they bought and mismanaged a computer company without relevance to the office of the future, and despite consistently funding long term research, they demonstrated a systemic lack of interest in PARC's work—and, therefore, in making their organization something other than a copier company.

The deep biases against computers found expression throughout the corporation. Xerox product development cycles consumed five to eight years; new generations of computer technology appeared every twenty-four months. Management authority for computer-based office products resided first with the copier organization, then in Dallas, a city and a division both geographically and technically a long distance from PARC. Xerox's powerful sales force, practiced in marketing push-button appliances, had neither the experience nor inclination to sell complex systems of hardware and software. Even PARC's use of the word "computer" had not penetrated much of Xerox. To the vast majority of people in Rochester and Stamford, computers were not the interactive communication tools conceived by Bob Taylor's researchers but, rather, arithmetic data processing machines operated by back office technicians.

"Futures Day" did initiate a long overdue educational process. But it arrived quite late. Changing the fundamental character of Xerox from a copier to an office products organization would require many years—a daunting reality in 1977 because, as McColough and the other senior executives explained so pointedly at Boca, Xerox sorely needed a second and comparably difficult transformation just to regain the strength of its copier past. To expect the organization at one and the same time to learn how to win as a copier company while becoming something other than a copier company strained credibility.

Nevertheless, in a flight from reality, McColough summed up the World Conference by announcing, "We are for the first time faced with the delicate and subtle task of dedicating our very large resources to two major purposes, rather than one."

To kick off "Futures Day," the conference's directors had shown a short film extolling the glory of Xerox's past and the promise of its future. In it, full screen photographs of the company's two patron saints, Chester Carlson and Joe Wilson, were followed by the famous lines of Robert Frost:

Two roads diverged in a wood and I
I took the one less traveled by,
And that has made all the difference.

If ever Peter McColough should have picked a single path for Xerox, it was in 1977. Instead, he staged David Kearns and Jim O'Neill as a team who could lead together, and he layered the "architecture of information" over the more pressing challenge of turning around the copier business. Each combination was an impossible dream; each pair, like the roads in Frost's wood, diverged.

For whatever reasons—the loss of Joe Wilson's sure hand, the fatigue of litigation, the concern for national politics, the natural limits of a salesman—Peter McColough had become a manager of gestures. He lacked the will to back bold initiatives with hands-on perseverance. At Boca, he was like a man who, upon waking to find his house afire, screams for his family to put out the blaze while he runs to the bedroom window to admire the rising sun.

Chapter

17

The 1977 "Futures Day" marked the high point of John Ellenby's career with Xerox. Three years before, he had come to PARC from a dual position as computer science teacher at Edinburgh University and design consultant to a European computer maker. His path to the digital world was unplanned: a decision to avoid science as a career followed by a degree in accounting followed by graduate work at the London School of Economics followed by a computational nightmare of a thesis followed by—revelation! Computers could calculate in weeks what would have taken Ph.D. candidate Ellenby years to do by hand.

Once in Palo Alto, however, Ellenby's business training and background shaped his activities as much as his interest in research. By 1974, Altos already had demonstrated the possibilities of advanced interactive computing; yet, few of the systems had been built. Until each PARC researcher had his own machine, personal computing would remain more hypothesis than reality. Therefore Jerry Elkind, who hired Ellenby, encouraged the Englishman to propose a manufacturing program to meet internal demand.

"I did a survey of likely needs for the Alto as a development and demonstration tool," noted Ellenby, "and came up with a fair volume of machines that would be required assuming we could address some of the producibility, reliability, and maintainability issues. In June '75 I submitted a proposal scoping the redesign and proposing the Alto II. I also proposed that a group should be formed that would provide a tightly integrated design, engineering, and manufacturing capability to work closely with research on the production of advanced systems."

His timing was fortunate. Xerox executives, having decided in July of 1975 to shut down Scientific Data Systems, were eager to retain as many of the best of SDS's four thousand employees as justified. Ellenby's request was approved. That autumn he organized a team of SDS veterans into a "Special Programs Group," who began shipping Alto IIs to Xerox recipients the following summer. Eventually, the Special Programs Group made and de-

livered hundreds of Altos along with specially designed and manufactured laser printers called "Dovers." The initial step of shifting
PARC's inventions beyond the laboratory had been taken.

"Technology transfer was really working here," glows Ellenby.
"That was my job. I was hired to do that."

His first setback at Xerox did not happen until 1976, when
his proposal to design and manufacture an "Alto III" product
was shelved despite winning favor from the interdivisional Display
Word Processing Task Force. He watched with dismay as the
Office Systems Division in Dallas pursued the 850 word processor,
a machine Ellenby considered inferior to and, prevailing company
opinion aside, more costly than the Alto III.

Adding to his frustration was an objection he heard credited
to Bob Sparacino that producing an Alto III would interfere with
the plans of the Systems Development Division, a group established by Xerox in 1975 to develop PARC technology into products. SDD was going nowhere. Bob Potter's Dallas division had
yet to evince any interest in manufacturing what SDD developed,
and in any event, SDD's engineers worked within the scheme of
phased program planning, a system far too cumbersome to satisfy
Ellenby. From all indications, the high officials of Xerox did not
appear to grasp their extraordinary opportunity with the Alto.

Thus when Peter McColough personally asked Ellenby to manage "Futures Day" at the 1977 World Conference, the request
fired the thirty-six-year-old engineer's imagination.

"McColough," recalls Ellenby, "told me he wanted to show all
the Xerox managers a new information architecture had been
created, and that Xerox was going to deliver products based upon
it. He said he wanted it to be extremely real."

Ellenby took McColough at his word. He promised Xerox's
chief executive an ambitious show, including the demonstration
of several still incomplete hardware and software systems, then
put together sixty-five Xerox researchers, engineers, technicians,
and administrators to help him do it. The men and women labored
through summer into autumn; many of them compared the pace
and atmosphere to the final phases of a product introduction. By
the end of October, when they staged a dry run of the production
for McColough in Hollywood, the "Futures Day" team believed
much more was at stake than a one-time education program for
corporate executives.

"We were into the day as a crusade," declares Tim Mott. "We became maniacs about doing the right thing, getting out the right, most accurate message. Namely, this stuff is real, and this is what you can do with it, and we should GET-IT-OUT-OF-THE-LAB!!"

Their enthusiasm, already pitched high, intensified after McColough, upon seeing the October preview, asked them to expand the scope of their show. Nothing was going to stop this group. And nothing did. In Boca Raton, they worked nonstop between the afternoon of the conference's third day through the evening of the fourth to unpack, install, test, rehearse, and go live with a morning show plus manage an afternoon "walk-in" session where Xerox managers operated the systems themselves.

To the audience, "Futures Day" appeared spectacular nd seamless, but only because Ellenby's group struggled to prevent the inevitable snags from ruining their production. Of the many obstacles, the most threatening involved air conditioning.

"We had a consulting firm from New York City set up all the communications, power lines, and logistical support," says Chuck Geschke, a researcher who had been shifted from PARC's Computer Science Lab to Ellenby's project. "They were a theatrical group—if things get hot, just put more make-up on the actors. But it doesn't work like that for computers, which, if they get too hot, won't function.

"The 'walk-through' was supposed to be a real hands-on simulation of what the office of the future was going to be like. Florida is hot and humid, and the room was just too hot. We were working twenty-four hours a day and couldn't solve the problem. Finally Ellenby, Richard Bock [another "Futures Day" team member], and I got together to discuss it and asked, 'What the hell are we going to do?'

"Then Ellenby, to his credit, said, 'You know when I fly into Miami, my airplane stays cool even after we get on the ground. They have these huge trucks that drive up, stick a hose into the belly of the plane, and provide air conditioning to keep the plane cool.'

"So Bock, a prototypical Navy chief petty officer, went to Eastern Airlines and asked to get one of the trucks. The people at Eastern said they'd be happy to help, but that the trucks had no license plates. How was he going to get them to Boca? So Bock went to the Florida highway patrol and got them to provide an escort for the truck for the entire trip from the airport to the hotel.

"Once the truck got to Boca, the only way to get the hose into the building was through a duct near the kitchen, then take the hose down the corridor from the kitchen to the demonstration room. However, there was a tree in the way of the kitchen duct.

"So Bock cut it down!

"The room temperature got down to sixty degrees immediately."

An error free day, of course, was not the primary purpose of Ellenby's crew; they longed to make PARC's technology "real" to the rest of Xerox. Everything the "Futures Day" team did—every system provided, every decision made, every word scripted—focused on that goal. Even their crash project humor reflected the obsession. For example, at one point, Ellenby and his fellow Briton Michael Hughes, who was the corporate official responsible for "Futures Day," disagreed with their American colleagues over who among the world's great English-speaking peoples had originated the phrase "suspension of disbelief." A wager was made, research was done, and, a few weeks before "Futures Day," the answer was duly transmitted to the victorious Englishmen via electronic mail:

" 'It was agreed that my endeavors,' wrote Samuel Coleridge in explaining the inspiration for his poetry, 'should be directed to persons and characters supernatural, or at least romantic; yet so as to transfer from our inward nature a human interest and a semblance of truth sufficient to procure for these shadows of imagination that willing suspension of disbelief for the moment, which constitutes poetic faith.' "

The critical test of "Futures Day," put similarly if less elegantly than by Coleridge, was this: Did the Xerox managers relate to what they saw? Was there anything within their nature, whether manufacturing, finance, or marketing—or more basically entrepreneurial—that encouraged commercial faith in the technology created by PARC and magnificently displayed before them?

Ellenby thought yes. Following the PARC demonstration, he heard Peter McColough praise the show while condemning the excessive caution of phased program planning. "We must," the chief executive declared, "simplify new product cycles in research and development."

"I thought to myself," remembers Ellenby, " 'This is it!' And I gave the thumbs up to a number of people backstage with me. That night we had a wild celebration at the Blue Bayou in Boca

Raton. Everyone was exhausted and burned out. But we believed we had succeeded."

There were, however, some disturbing, contrary signs. Chuck Geschke had spent that afternoon assisting Xerox managers and their spouses as they operated the personal distributed computing systems during the "walk-in" session. His observations clashed with the promise of McColough's rhetoric.

"The reactions we saw in the wives," Geschke explains, "were what we had hoped to see in the men. What was remarkable was that almost to a couple, the man would stand back and be very skeptical and reserved, and the wives, many of whom had been secretaries, got enthralled by moving around the mouse, seeing the graphics on the screen, and using the color printer. The men had no background, really, to grasp the significance of it. I would look out and see bright enthusiasm in the eyes of the women, and the men just asking, in a standoffish way, 'Oh, can it do that?' "

Nonetheless, on "Futures Day" itself, Geschke chose to join Ellenby in believing Peter McColough. Like other naïve PARC engineers and researchers, he thought if the chairman and chief executive officer of the corporation declared an end to Xerox's defective product development cycle, then Altos surely would reach the market. Even Michael Hughes, a fifteen-year Xerox veteran and the once-frustrated leader of the 1974 strategy committee, allowed the frenzy surrounding the PARC show to sweep cynicism aside. That Thursday, when McColough asked for advice on next steps, Hughes earnestly replied, "Launch the Alto by the next shareholders meeting!" McColough smiled.

For John Ellenby, euphoria soon gave way to depression. Shortly after the World Conference, he confidently asked personnel what he should do with the team he had assembled, expecting to discuss a major assignment. Instead he was told, "Send them back to their jobs." The energy created by "Futures Day"—the organization, the talent, the experience, the desire to make Altos "real," to make them happen—would have no managed afterlife at Xerox. The sizeable bonus McColough subsequently awarded Ellenby bore a bittersweet message: the company's appreciation, it appeared, was limited to his *past* accomplishments.

Two months elapsed before a more skeptical Ellenby heard about the only concrete action to follow the Boca Raton demonstration. He was not impressed.

Jack Goldman had taken advantage of "Futures Day" to renew

his call for an Alto market probe. As usual, the response from Xerox's line managers was cool; they reminded Goldman that the Systems Development Division, reporting to O'Neill's and Spar- acino's Information Technology Group, had the authority to cre- ate products from PARC's technology. Goldman argued, gave ground, and argued some more. If Xerox would not test the viability of an Alto business venture, he suggested, at least the company ought to try to learn whether and how potential Xerox customers might use personal distributed computing. Put that way, his recommendation had a certain appeal—when executives who had attended or heard about "Futures Day" asked what had happened to the office of the future, top management could say they were pursuing a careful product development path that in- cluded market tests. Xerox would be showing the flag.

Accordingly, in January of 1978, the company set up the Advanced Systems Division (ASD) under the direction of Jerry Elkind. ASD had an awkward charter. First, in an incomprehen- sible move bearing no relation to the Alto, PARC, or the products being engineered by the Systems Development Division, Xerox assigned Elkind the task of managing a group of ex-Scientific Data Systems engineers who continued to provide customized com- puter services on behalf of Xerox. Second, and more relevant, Elkind's ASD was instructed to "develop markets by establishing early market presence with pre-products."

Elkind invited Ellenby and other "Futures Day" veterans to join ASD. For them, it was Hobson's choice: the Advanced Systems Division could place Altos in the hands of customers right away, but had no authority to make products or operate a business; the Systems Development Division, their only alternative within the company, had the charter to develop products for a Xerox office enterprise, but, as one Alto advocate put it, "not in my lifetime."

Patrick Baudelaire, the Computer Science Laboratory re- searcher who had created "Draw," PARC's most popular graphics software program, explained why he, Ellenby, and others reluc- tantly decided to give ASD a chance: "Altos were spreading within Xerox in large numbers by then and the Draw package was one of the standard packages that people were using. It became ob- vious to me that the next step was commercialization. I considered SDD. But SDD looked like a big machine, on the heavy side from the viewpoint of organization. It had too many people, and it was spread over two places. ASD was different. We could do something immediate, starting with existing technology, whereas SDD had bigger plans calling for building a whole new machine."

As anticipated, Jerry Elkind's ASD contacted a number of institutions about systems trials. The response was encouraging; banks, think tanks, government agencies, and oil, aerospace and auto companies, among others, expressed interest in the Alto technology. In fact, Elkind complained that Xerox could not manufacture enough Altos and Dover printers to meet the demand. As a consequence, ASD concentrated its most important efforts on four test sites: the White House, the U.S. House of Representatives, and the Atlantic Richfield Company, plus the Santa Clara offices of Xerox's copier sales force.

The Santa Clara experiment was a holdover from PARC activities predating the formation of ASD. During the spring of 1977, six months before "Futures Day," the chief of copier sales in the United States, Shelby Carter, had visited PARC and, upon seeing the Alto, had exclaimed, "I can sell that!" Subsequent meetings between PARC researchers and sales managers concluded that, notwithstanding Carter's confidence, it would be a good idea for copier salespeople to use personal distributed computing systems before trying to sell them. They selected Santa Clara to test their idea, but because of the World Conference and other interruptions, the project did not begin until the spring of 1978. It then was assigned to ASD and managed by Tim Mott under John Ellenby's direction.

By summer, Shelby Carter's enthusiasm over the Santa Clara trial both excited and upset Mott, Baudelaire, and Ellenby. More than ever before, they believed in the commercial prospects of the Alto; more than ever before, they chafed at the Xerox bit. Phased program planning as well as more rejections by Dallas mired down the progress of the Systems Development Division. Moreover, ASD's engineers were convinced that the Systems Development Division's proposed computer system, known as the "Star," was far too ambitious. Finally, and most important, by mid-1978, the market was sending a warning—relatively inexpensive, albeit limited in function, "personal computers" from a number of companies, most notably Apple Corporation, were gaining in popularity.

"The personal computers," said Ellenby, "certainly told us that there were going to be lower cost work stations required and that there was going to be a fairly large population of users who were not going to be interested in doing full-blown document preparation jobs that Systems Development Division in particular was targeting."

Nevertheless, their attempts to persuade Jerry Elkind and his superiors to authorize an Alto product failed. Tensions between Elkind and Ellenby mounted; ASD, the disgruntled men were told repeatedly, would not venture beyond its charter to test "preproducts."

Ellenby was stranded with but one hope: "I had a powerful friend in Shelby Carter." Earlier, the sales executive had suggested that ASD expand the Santa Clara experiment to sales offices throughout the country as a prelude to launching Xerox office systems. The idea made sense to Ellenby; until copier salespeople understood computer hardware and software, they'd find them difficult to sell.

Solid logic. But in 1978, Shelby Carter's copier salespeople had no authority to market systems products. That job belonged to the Office Systems Division sales force. And the Office Systems Division, to which Jerry Elkind's ASD then reported, had time and again rebuffed Ellenby's product ambitions.

Ellenby decided to act anyway—his "powerful friend" Shelby Carter had the ear of Xerox's president David Kearns. So with help from Mott and Baudelaire, he put together a "Capability Investment Proposal" that included a manufacturing and marketing plan for the Alto founded on Carter's notion of broadening the Santa Clara trial. After the plan was finished, its existence was leaked to Carter—Ellenby says by accident; others say by "accident."

"At that point," explains Tim Mott, "we had each had endless conversations with others about how to get new products more rapidly through the company, and we still weren't getting anywhere. So why not go to the top? The alternative to not putting this in front of Kearns was just not acceptable."

Inadvertently or not, Kearns learned about the "ASD proposal" and called Dave Culbertson, the head of the Office Systems Division, to ask for a copy. Culbertson, through whom any ASD plan normally would flow, had never heard of it.

Culbertson contacted Jim Campbell, to whom Jerry Elkind reported. Campbell had never heard of the plan either.

Campbell got in touch with Elkind, who said he too had never seen it.

Elkind called Ellenby onto the carpet.

"Culbertson," winces Ellenby, "bounced all over Campbell, who bounced all over Elkind, who bounced all over me. And very fast too. It's called the shit rolls down hill, gathering speed and quantity."

Ellenby regrouped. On November 8, 1978, two days before the first anniversary of "Futures Day," he submitted copies of the "Capability Investment Proposal" to Kearns, Culbertson, and Campbell. He insists he did not have to send one to Elkind because, Elkind's recollection to the contrary, an earlier copy already had been delivered to the head of ASD. He made one final pitch for the Alto in his cover letter accompanying the proposal.

"SDD's timetable had slipped," Ellenby recalls. "Meanwhile, through the efforts of ASD and others, there were over fifteen hundred Altos in use both within and outside of Xerox. While the systems installed in non-Xerox sites were covered by nondisclosure agreements, most of the inherent advantages to the Alto came from the ideas behind the user interface. So anyone who *saw* the product would know what needed to be accomplished to copy it. Now that was not trivial, but talented computer engineers could, and later did, copy many of the user interface features of the Alto. So to me, it seemed only a matter of time before customers would ask for more machines. The question I raised in the cover letter was whether that demand would be met by Xerox—or the competition."

A few weeks later, Kearns thanked Ellenby for the proposal, then delegated the task of investigating its merit to Robert Wenrik, a member of the corporate staff. Although Wenrik spoke with Ellenby, Mott, and Baudelaire, he spent most of his time testing the attractiveness of the "Capability Investment Proposal" with people in the Systems Development Division and officials of the Office Systems Division. Neither group thought much more of Ellenby's plan than, in light of how the proposal had reached Kearns, they did of Ellenby himself.

In the end, nearly six years after its invention, the Alto's fate rested on David Kearn's decision. Ellenby, though sobered by the rift he had caused, remained hopeful. Kearns said he believed in betting on people; Kearns had expressed excitement about the plan before submitting it to Wenrik; Kearns knew that Ellenby would gather the same team who had engineered "Futures Day" to implement the proposal.

Ellenby got his answer in late January 1979. "John," wrote

Robert Wenrik, "this memo summarizes my findings regarding the Capability Investment Proposal. I have reviewed your proposal in some detail with a number of people in order to present an objective position that considered alternative solutions along with arguments for each alternative.

"We have concluded that Xerox will not adopt the proposal you have prescribed; however, we appreciate the thought you have given to the many issues covered in your proposal. Some of the challenges which you clearly identified are being pursued through normal management channels and should be resolved over the next few weeks. Your proposal assisted us in dealing with the problem more expeditiously than we normally might have. I am confident that you will continue your support to the challenges we face in Jerry Elkind's probe activity.

"On behalf of Dave Kearns, I want to convey our appreciation for the thought and effort you put into your proposal."

Chapter

18

*T*he cry for change made at the World Conference in Boca Raton led nowhere; Xerox in 1978 and 1979 was just a worn out copy of Xerox in 1977, 1976, 1975, 1974, and 1973. Management continued to announce new diversification adventures—a scheme to offer long distance communications; the acquisition of Western Union—without following through on previous programs. SCM's $1.6 billion antitrust suit took fourteen months to try, and although Xerox escaped without damages, the fear of liability made an already risk averse company paranoid. Kearns rejected John Ellenby's Alto proposal while Xerox provided money but neither manufacturing nor marketing direction to the Systems Development Division. Delays plagued the "third generation" of copiers; manufacturing costs remained too high; cynicism spread. The politics of blame festered and flared.

In the spring of 1978, less than six months after "Futures Day" had demonstrated the possibilities of Jack Goldman's research philosophy, both Goldman and his organization came under fire. Jim O'Neill and Bob Sparacino, disparaging an independent research function, demanded tighter integration among research, development, and manufacturing. They wanted Kearns to bust up Goldman's group and to assign most of the pieces to their direct control.

They raised a reasonable issue. Ever since Archie McCardell's 1972 reorganization, research had grown further and further apart from development. The company's long term science and technology activities at PARC, at Webster, and at the newest research center in Toronto, mirrored the freewheeling "bottom up" principles of Goldman and Pake while product development was directed "top down" by O'Neill and Sparacino. Too many possibilities fell into the gap. For example, in light of its investment in PARC, Xerox should have but didn't pioneer digital control of copiers. Kodak did, and its use of microprocessors helped earn the "third generation" label for Kodak machines.

O'Neill and Sparacino accused Goldman of not pulling his oar on the copier side; Goldman questioned their commitment to the office of the future. Both sides had merit, and an open discussion of how research could better coordinate with development was overdue. But O'Neill and Sparacino weren't interested in debates. They wanted a decision. And they had the power to get one.

"In May of 1978," Goldman recalls, "we had the annual meeting in San Francisco. The day before, we had all the directors over to PARC and made a presentation. It was very impressive. The guys did a magnificent job. Other directors made a point of telling me how surprised and impressed they were at the scope and the power of what had been accomplished—and was still emerging—at PARC.

"After the board meeting, my wife and I flew back East with Dave Kearns and his wife. As we were saying good-bye, Kearns told me he had something he wanted to discuss with me the next morning when I got to work. So on Monday, I went to Dave's office, and that's when he told me he wanted to reorganize the research function at Xerox.

" 'Jack, I think we want to make a change in the reporting relationships of research. We don't believe research is working closely enough with the operating divisions. Therefore, research is no longer going to be a corporate function.'

"Whereupon I hit the ceiling. I was outraged that this man who was my junior on the board of directors and knew little about the principles and functions of good research had so cavalierly decided to take a step which would jeopardize all we had accomplished over the past nine years.

" 'First of all, David Kearns,' I screamed at him, 'you are trying to make a decision about the technical organization of this company without even consulting me, the senior technical officer. Second, your proposal makes no intellectual sense whatsoever in terms of how to organize research and technology in this corporation. This is unimaginable! You cannot wipe out research in Xerox! I won't let you do it!'

"I went straight into McColough's office, banged my fist on Peter's desk, and told him directly I'd have no part of this.

" 'Peter, I just heard something which I suspect you know about because I believe the organizational announcements have already been printed. There's no way I'll let you go through with this. I'm not going to stand by and watch Xerox kill research. If you make this move, I'm resigning effective today. And I'll go to work for a competitor who, as you know, has been after me for a long time.'

"McColough listened to me and eventually calmed me down a bit. After talking it over, and increasingly sensing that the move was at least in part directed at me personally, I decided I'd be willing to step aside, but not at the expense of an independent research group. I told Peter that if he wanted to get me out of the picture and needed a sacrificial lamb for that son of a bitch O'Neill and to let Kearns save some face, then I would step aside. But I would not let him wipe out research!"

In addition to the ad hominem tone of the proposed reorganization, Goldman heard a replay of objections to PARC posed years before by Scientific Data Systems. "The operations guys," he says, "had persuaded Kearns to give them control over the dollars being spent on research, arguing that they would make better use of it."

George Pake had the same reaction. The next morning, after Goldman told him of the plan, Pake blanched. Putting the research budget at Sparacino's disposal, he thought, could only mean less research, more development. And given Xerox's track record, it did not portend better, less costly, or more timely products.

To avoid the reshuffling, Goldman asked Pake to volunteer for the top research job on the condition that the function retain its existing corporate reporting line. The two men approached McColough with their plan, several meetings followed, and, a few days later, the organization announcements were recast. Goldman became "chief scientist" of the corporation, Pake was named vice president of research, and research itself continued as a corporate function. Sparacino apparently remained adamant in defeat.

"I had a stormy meeting with Sparacino," remembers George Pake. "He was telling me I was crazy to take the job, that it couldn't last. The thinly veiled threat was that if I took the job of heading up research, he'd get me. He seemed to be impugning the dedication and hard work of people in research. When I said they worked very hard and long hours and not for money either but because they loved it, Sparacino said, 'People shouldn't work because they love it. They should work because it hurts.' "

Whether cause or effect, pain did afflict Sparacino's copier development organization near the end of the decade. He ordered his engineers to shorten Xerox's new product cycle, but did not abandon the discredited system of phased program planning. Instead, he stepped up the pace. Machines reached the market faster, though neither more cheaply nor more reliably. In 1979, for example, Xerox brought out the 8200 Copier to replace the outdated 7000 series. Although not "third generation" (Xerox tabbed the 8200 one of its "two and a half" generation of copiers), the 8200 provided the sales force a seventy-copy-per-minute machine with which to compete against IBM and Kodak.

Nevertheless, the contradiction between faster development and better development compromised Xerox's reputation. None of the new copiers was outstanding; one, the 3300, simply did not work. Six months after introducing it, Xerox received so many complaints about the 3300 that management had to suspend production and ask the proud Xerox sales force to offer their customers a choice between taking another model copier on favorable terms or getting a full refund. In its 1980 Annual Report, Xerox euphemistically described the 3300 as an "uncharacteristic mistake"; others were less charitable, using words like "low point," "disaster," "botched," and "severely tarnished."

Performance deteriorated so badly that at one point Peter McColough told the engineers they were jeopardizing the future of the company. For evidence, he needed only to point to Xerox's continuing and rapid loss of market share—from 65 percent in 1977 to 54 percent in 1978 to 49 percent in 1979 to 46 percent in 1980.

Although company profits jumped in each of those years, analysts and company executives alike knew that beneath the rosy income figures lay a thorny reality—to prop up current earnings, Xerox was selling its future. Historically, Xerox earned high profit margins by leasing instead of selling copiers; long after the machines were paid in full, the rent checks kept coming. Meanwhile, the company depreciated the machines to zero on the books. Thus, every leased copier constituted both a valuable revenue promise and a hidden asset.

In the late 1970s, however, as copier rental rates and market share both plummeted, Xerox began selling more copiers than ever before. Since Xerox's sale price exceeded the total amount of first year rent, sales of new copiers inflated short term results. In addition, sales of old copiers generated high accounting profits because of the depreciation already taken on such equipment. But sales of any machines, whether new or old, masked the loss of long term revenues. For the copiers in question, there would be no money forthcoming the following year, or the year after that, or the year after that. Or ever again. Competitive sins had caught up with Xerox's most cherished financial strength: the company that had innovated the sale of copies instead of copiers was reversing course.

The decision to exchange its historic advantage for relief from near term profit pressure made sense; Xerox needed time to straighten itself out. But the gambit had a short fuse. Unless the copier maker found a way to develop high quality, low cost, competitive copiers that it could lease instead of sell, performance soon would topple as earnings bolstered by sales gave way to results robbed of lease income. Time was running out, a fact Xerox executives evidently understood without believing.

According to Eddie Miller, a management consultant who advised Xerox at the time, "You had a group of managers who had never lived through tough times before. They basically came from Xerox, Ford, and IBM. Xerox was a monopoly for so long. And because it was a lease business, you always had that stream of cash coming in. And you could always sell off your lease base in the fourth quarter to make your numbers.

"Thus when the Xerox people finally did begin to recognize their problem, it was only an intellectual recognition. It wasn't visceral. They didn't really *feel* there was a problem because they really didn't *feel* any pain.

"Finally, there were so many bright guys at Xerox, especially in the corporate staff, that there was always someone who could shoot down an idea and do it with solid, insightful arguments. There was a saying around the company that the staff felt they had the 'right of infinite appeal.' The staff just felt that they had the right, if not the obligation, to critique everything that was said or suggested."

On its face, therefore, David Kearns's August 1980 declaration—"We are determined to change significantly the way we have been doing business!"—was unpersuasive. His protestation came *three years* after Peter McColough told the executives in Boca Raton, "We are now faced with the urgent need for change within this company!" As much as any other indicator—weak products, negative politics, loss of market share, shifting from lease to sale—the very identity of language showed how hopelessly Xerox had stagnated since Kearns had become president in 1977.

Many people believed Kearns was now part of the problem instead of the solution. Detractors whispered that he was too nice, that he wasn't bright enough, that he couldn't make a tough decision and stick to it, that the last person to whisper in his ear won. His actions, like the flip-flop on how to organize research, often seemed to confirm such complaints. He'd been a popular executive when McColough had named him to replace Archie McCardell; many people had had high expectations. But as one executive is reported to have commented, "Nothing happened. Kearns became another Peter McColough."

Kearns, however, was remarkably unlike McColough in one crucial regard—he was determined to change Xerox. In the beginning of his presidency, according to one of his close advisors, he simply had not known in which direction to move. Consequently, his speeches and actions lacked consistency and undermined confidence among those who saw a will-o'-the-wisp. Not until 1980 did Kearns discover both the strength and the direction to make a difference.

"In 1979, morale was really getting low," says Eddie Miller. "There were already people taking wagers on Kearns not lasting the course. And a little bit of pain was beginning to show up because it was getting harder and harder to manage the numbers by selling off the lease base.

"We kept talking to David periodically about how he really had to change the company. Then sometime in early 1980, he called us in for a frank discussion about change and asked us to go around and talk to a wide variety of people and to feed back to him what we found out.

"We were excited about the assignment because for the first time we had finally been asked by Kearns to tell him anything we found out, anything we wanted to.

"It was, however, a frustrating exercise because we learned nothing new. The reality was that top management had to get serious about changing the entire culture of the company by getting rid of people, changing other people who stayed, changing systems and processes. Changing everything.

"We said, 'David, we feel unhappy about this exercise. We can't tell you anything new. You know everything we're going to tell you, and so does everyone else in this company. People have known what's wrong for a long time, and, frankly, they are disappointed.'

"I think the one insight we could tell him was that there was no brilliant new answer out there. It was not a question of being brilliant about what to do; it was a question of doing it.

"We told him to capture the hearts and minds of his best guys, his movers and shakers, and convince them he was serious. He had to find his opinion makers and set them loose."

Among the many issues about which Kearns needed to gain confidence, three stood out: the nature of cost effectiveness, the feasibility of change, and the responsibility for making it happen.

Xerox executives had debated for years the best way to think about the cost of a copier. Some argued in favor of "life cost," the sum of original manufacturing cost plus the cost to service a machine as long as it was in use. The prevailing philosophy, however, treated manufacturing and service costs separately. Like so much else, that approach came to Xerox from Ford where, during the fifties and sixties, financially oriented leaders had supplanted product performance with product cost as the car company's most important goal. In Detroit, any reduction in the quantity or quality of materials, or in the cost or volume of labor—no matter how small—would yield huge savings given the millions of cars produced each year. But unfortunately, the zeal to drive down manufacturing costs caused Ford to make products that broke down too often, and critics believed the same self-defeating spiral bedeviled Xerox.

"They would be very concerned about getting modest amounts of savings because in automobiles, modest savings added up to big dollars," Michael Hughes said of McCardell, O'Neill, and Sparacino. "If you saved a penny, you were a hero. However, if the result of saving that penny is that every time you do a repair job on the copier, you spend a penny, it's dumb economics."

Executives like Hughes argued that Xerox should reduce overall "life cost" by spending more to build a better copier that would need less service later. Still, in light of the truck loads of cash being dumped daily on engineering and development at Xerox, the suggestion that the company increase its investment in that area —even for a logically attractive result like lower "life cost"—was suspect. Moreover, as the parties for and against "life cost" argued, the actual cost gap between Xerox and its competition widened. By 1980, the Japanese were *selling* copiers in the United States at a price below what it cost Xerox to *make* comparable models.

More money was not going to cut the cost of a Xerox copier.

But more responsibility, properly placed, could—and already had done so at Xerox's Japanese affiliate Fuji-Xerox. In the mid-1970s, after Rochester had bogged down in the morass of phased program planning and had postponed or canceled a series of proposed copiers, Fuji-Xerox had decided, against the express wishes of Xerox, to develop their own machines. Furthermore, they had predicted they could reduce the time and cost of the American product cycle by 50 percent. Although their initial effort fell short of that goal, subsequent copiers surpassed it. By 1980, Fuji-Xerox's engineers had established a new standard of performance within the Xerox family.

Fuji-Xerox excelled by, among other things, entrusting a fewer number of engineers with greater technical freedom and authority. To be sure, financial and marketing considerations contributed to product concepts. But once such proposals were made, engineers familiar with both design and manufacturing were left alone to figure out the most appropriate set of product specifications. As a result, the project engineers spent their time solving problems against a fixed target instead of endlessly adjusting their blueprints to meet the latest whims of accountants, salesmen, or corporate executives.

The low cost and high quality of Fuji-Xerox's copiers impressed Kearns and others, including Jim O'Neill. During one product review in Japan, for example, O'Neill was surprised when he asked the five engineers in the room how many other people had worked on their project.

" 'We did,' the five said.

" 'How long did it take you?' O'Neill asked.

" 'Six months,' they said.

" 'I'm not even going to ask you my third question,' O'Neill said. 'The cost is insignificant.' "

Kearns took heart from Fuji-Xerox. He was convinced that Xerox too could design better copiers faster by truly delegating that task to the people responsible—the engineers—then holding them accountable to the standards set by the marketplace. And he believed the same commonsense rule could improve productivity throughout the company. Xerox could lower its manufacturing costs by truly delegating that task to the people responsible—manufacturing— then holding them accountable to the standards set by the marketplace; Xerox could sell and service its copiers better and less expensively by truly delegating those tasks to the people responsible—marketing, sales, and service—then holding them accountable to the standards set by the marketplace.

Like most appealing ideas, the formula sounded simple. Yet for twenty years Xerox had measured itself more by its own standards than those of customers or competitors; company employees had a lot to learn. Notions of true delegation and accountability were alien. The thousand person corporate staff—none of whom designed, built, sold, or serviced copiers—routinely invoked the "right of infinite appeal," thereby denying instead of delegating authority. Some systems, like phased program planning, required so many sign-offs from so many people that no one could be held accountable for anything; others, like the compensation program, created expectations of automatic salary increases without regard to merit or performance. Even Xerox's organization chart militated against decentralized decisions and implementation—of the more than 100,000 people in Xerox's copier group, only one, David Kearns, had general management responsibility.

Such fundamental changes to the character of an organization far outstrip the capability of any single individual to achieve; presidential speeches and memos about the need for change could not, by themselves, modify the behavior of tens of thousands of people. Furthermore, three years without progress had sapped Kearns's strength. He looked beat, defeated, and tired. Kearns needed help and, by the latter part of 1980, he was finally ready to ask for it.

"Later that year," remembers Miller, the consultant, "Kearns kind of summoned us, and we had a meeting. It was clear that he'd crossed some kind of Rubicon. He said he'd decided he wanted to change the company and he wanted our help. We asked him if he was really serious this time, and he said yes. Then after thinking over how best to go about it, we decided that our earlier advice still held. He had to pick a group of movers and shakers, convince them he was serious, and then get *them*, not us, to figure out what to do."

The consultants asked Kearns to pick the twenty-five or so managers on whom Xerox would most depend for leadership over the next decade, then to charge that group with selecting and implementing a course for changing the company. The group itself constituted an important transition. Neither O'Neill nor

Sparacino could be part of it, and their exclusion signaled the decline of their authority within the company.

The new management team met several times in 1981. Out of their deliberations emerged a number of actions. First, they committed themselves to eliminating unnecessary jobs. Second, they created several general manager positions by dividing the copier organization into "strategic business units." Third, they replaced phased program planning with a system akin to the one Fuji-Xerox had followed with so much success. Fourth, they established a series of standards, called "benchmarks," by which the company could compare its performance against the offerings of competitors and the demands of customers. Most important, they promised, individually and as a group, to carry out their plan, and Kearns assigned them the organizational positions and clout to follow through.

None of the changes happened overnight, none without suffering. Thousands of people lost their jobs, and those who didn't lived in fear of the pink slip. Nevertheless, by late 1982, the new management organization—Kearns, his team, the strategic business units, the decentralized systems of responsibility and accountability—began to prove that disruption could have a worthwhile purpose and effect. That September, in quick succession, Xerox announced its acquisition of Crum and Forster, the insurance company, and the introduction of its "third generation" copiers known as the "10 Series." Even a year earlier the move into financial services might have depressed an already dispirited Xerox organization. But with the universal acclamation of the "10 Series" of copiers given by top management, analysts, and customers alike, company employees knew that insurance was not the top priority at corporate headquarters. After a decade without direction, Xerox had clearly taken the first earnest step toward reclaiming its legacy as the best copier company in the world.

Research:
The
Harvest
of
Isolation

Chapter

19

T hroughout 1980, as David Kearns resolved to change Xerox, he found comfort in a part of his corporation closer
to home than Fuji-Xerox: Dallas. For years, Dallas had
failed to meet expectations. Bob Potter would set targets with
numbers that appealed to Archie McCardell and Jim O'Neill, then
build high cost products that couldn't sustain the financial promises made on their behalf. After McCardell's departure, confidence in Potter faded. In 1978, the company combined Dallas
with other noncopier operations; Potter left to become Mc-
Cardell's chief technical officer at International Harvester. But
the reorganization flopped, and in 1979 Xerox reconstituted Dallas as the Office Products Division, appointing thirty-six-year-old
Don Massaro as president. Within months, Massaro and Dallas
offered Kearns a compelling glimpse of how much could happen
in how short a time.

Massaro did not immediately turn Dallas profitable. But he
injected a spirit of confidence and progress that Kearns could only
dream about finding in the rest of Xerox. He began by polishing
the self-image of the division's sales force, too few of whom called
on Fortune 500 accounts and too many of whom believed customer orders of one, two, or five machines were adequate. Massaro
pointed them toward large volume clients and promised them a
panoply of office products and systems to sell. He then challenged
engineering and manufacturing to deliver. Within a year of his
arrival, Dallas introduced its 860 word processor to replace the
disappointing 850, perfected two facsimile machines, announced
PARC's Ethernet as a product, backed an electronic typewriter
project, and threw support to the Systems Development Division.
In a company burdened by six- to eight-year product development
cycles, the pace was astounding and, to some, threatening.

"When I arrived in Dallas," Massaro recalls, "it took one hundred
eighty signatures on a product specification. Because the corporate staff had to sign off on everything, no single individual made
a decision. Everyone was safe. But also that was the problem—

there was no responsibility for risk taking. So I knew I had to break the back of the corporate staff.

"In one early meeting with Kearns, after I had taken on the Dallas assignment, Kearns asked me how things were going, and I said, 'David, I feel like the fucking Road Runner. Your corporate staff is like a pack of coyotes. They spend all their time setting traps, trying to get me.'"

Massaro's Office Products Division adopted the Road Runner cartoon character as their mascot. With an indomitable spirit, they repeatedly outsmarted the people in Stamford, infuriating the corporate staff while building an impressive record—in less than three years, Dallas brought out seven new products.

"That just blew the socks off David Kearns," says Massaro. "He saw that and said, 'That's what I want the rest of the company to do.'"

Massaro was unique. He had come to Xerox in 1977, when the copier giant paid $41 million to buy Shugart Associates, a computer disk drive company Massaro had cofounded. The Shugart success made Massaro rich, confirmed his appetite for risk, and marked him off from the ranks of executives he was about to join: "He's a real fireball," said one analyst who followed Xerox. "He is an entrepreneur, and you really don't find an entrepreneur in a big corporation."

Therefore, if any of Xerox's powerful managers could make a business of the Alto-inspired computer office system known as "Star" then under design by the Systems Development Division, it was Don Massaro. Nevertheless, Systems Development Division chief David Liddle was skeptical before meeting Massaro for the first time. For years Liddle had tried to win approval from Dallas management; for years Dallas had rejected him. "Xerox," had gone the constant refrain from Bob Potter, "shouldn't be in the systems business." But in November of 1979, at the request of another Xerox executive who appreciated Massaro's aggressiveness, Liddle packed an Alto and some Star software, and flew to Dallas one more time.

Thirty minutes into the demonstration, Massaro told him, "If you're trying to convince me about the utility and attractiveness of the technology, then turn off the machine. I'm already convinced."

The president of the Office Products Division spent the rest of the morning grilling Liddle about costs, weights, components, and other issues of manufacturability. Afterward, Massaro asked Xerox to transfer control of SDD to Dallas.

"Everyone had primed me that Star was a disaster, basically telling me to kill it once I got to Dallas," Massaro remembers. "I decided what the hell, to see for myself. No one else wanted to touch the product; they didn't understand what we had. No one was going to bet his career on this thing. And you weren't going to get it through the corporate staff because they were conventional thinkers.

"But I could do it. I had made a lot of money from the Shugart acquisition so I was betting the house's money. I had not spent twenty years of my life climbing the Xerox ladder rung by rung, playing according to the rules. I was prepared to fail. So I said, 'Fuck it! This is incredible technology, and we're going to bring it to the marketplace!' "

But when Massaro requested the $15 million required to make and sell the Star, Xerox said no. A few months of bargaining later, the answer remained no. Undeterred, Massaro volunteered to squeeze his own budget for the needed funds, and in February of 1980, David Liddle took hold of a group charged with introducing the Star by the spring of 1981. Five years from its start, Liddle's program had gained real business momentum for the very first time.

Liddle himself had joined PARC's Systems Science Laboratory in 1972 and had worked for two and a half years on the ill-fated POLOS project before George Pake suggested that he shift from research to development. Pake and Goldman wanted somebody to think about how Xerox might take advantage of PARC's technologies; Liddle had had industrial experience during graduate school; all parties agreed the assignment made sense. That modest effort inspired the Systems Development Division.

"SDD," explains Liddle, "started in part because people like George White, George Pake, and Jack Goldman in the research community—the left lobe guys in the company—wanted to persuade Xerox that there were ways of looking at front office systems which were different from and superior to the Dallas approach."

Liddle says "in part" for a reason—all development efforts required the approval of managers who usually shunned the product schemes of Jack Goldman. With respect to the Systems Development Division, however, the O'Neill-Sparacino wing had cause to say yes—in the mid-1970s, industrial rumors that IBM planned to introduce the first electronic copier compelled Sparacino to back a comparable effort within Xerox. The "architecture of information" and the multiyear investment in PARC to the contrary, SDD existed because of the mandate for an electronic copier; without the prospect of reinforcing Xerox's reprographics business, the computer development group would not have been funded.

Nonetheless, Liddle's contingent—which soon increased by a handful of former PARC researchers who included Chuck Thacker—saw opportunities that went beyond electronic copying to the kind of computing tools invented at PARC.

"I had complete confidence," Liddle says, "that the electronic copier could become the basis for other office systems. I told them to go ahead with building the xerographic engine, I would do the networking, the software, the processor, and the computer system to run it, and I would make it do other things as well."

So after Thacker started on the design of a processor powerful enough for an electronic copier, Liddle sallied forth with the first of many attempts to interest Bob Potter in a computer work station product. Potter ignored him, repeatedly.

The authority for the work station remained nebulous until the end of 1976 when the Display Word Processing Task Force, the same group who tried to recommend the Alto III over the Dallas 850 word processor, gave Liddle's program a boost. Having seen their Alto III proposal scorned, the task force insisted in their final report that Xerox migrate from Dallas-styled machines to systems more like Liddle's. Their findings endowed the SDD work station with official status and a code name—the "Janus" project was to "look forward to office information systems and backward to word processing."

Once again, the task force's conclusions raised eyebrows. This time executives at corporate headquarters voiced concern that the people on the West Coast might commit Xerox to the office automation business without the careful deliberation and participation of the company's broader marketing, planning, and finance communities. The high level hand wringing led to the appointment of yet another task force to study office information systems, or "OIS." To Liddle, the intent was obvious: powerful people at corporate headquarters wanted no part of a home-grown computer business. He claims their appointed representative on the OIS task force had explicit instructions to "torpedo" the Janus program, but the majority of the study group wouldn't let it happen.

"This is where I earned my driver's license," grins Liddle. "This OIS task force met every day, all week, every week for several months in the spring of 1977. We really slugged it out. In the end, I agreed to some compromises that weren't optimal. They were like riders on a Senate bill. But Janus was reaffirmed. The 'torpedo' was overcome."

For security reasons, Xerox changed a number of its project names after the Boca Raton conference in late 1977. "Janus" became "Star," and its development proceeded. Eventually, the Systems Development Division grew to more than 140 people split between Palo Alto and El Segundo. The northern California team worked on the Star's operating system and programming language; the southern California group designed user applications. Meanwhile, Chuck Thacker continued to build the computer processor, although the primary purpose of his hardware had shifted by then from an electronic copier to an electronic printer.

By late 1978, however, Thacker hit Liddle with a major technical dilemma—the Star could not run efficiently on the computer engine Thacker had designed. The "Dolphin," as Thacker had dubbed his machine, worked well for electronic printing, but was too complex and expensive to power the Star economically. Liddle needed another processor. He tried in vain to get engineering support from other parts of the company before ultimately turning to Butler Lampson for help.

He presented Lampson an odd challenge. Traditionally, hardware precedes software. Yet when Lampson answered Liddle's plea, much of the Star's software already existed. Moreover, because SDD's engineers wanted the Star simple enough for nonexperts, they burdened their software—and the hardware Lampson would have to create—with cumbersome technical constraints.

The most outstanding feature of the Star, like the Alto, was the so-called "user interface"—what a person actually saw on the screen and the tools he was given to interact with that image. SDD intended the Star to replicate a typical office setting by employing, among other things, pictures ("icons"), lists of action choices ("menus"), and multiple screen sections ("windows") to electronically re-create the desk top, file cabinet, telephone, in- and outboxes, wastepaper basket, and other features familiar to office workers. In addition, the Star's software sought to keep the user's work products—files, projects, calendars, etc.—available at all times.

Lampson had to force-fit the software into the design of his "Dandelion" computer processor. Although he succeeded, he believes the Dandelion's unusual origin as well as the overly ambitious objectives of the Star's software degraded the final product's performance.

"The root of the Star's difficulties," he notes, "arose from the fact that they designed and implemented this very grandiose piece of software. It was very complicated and it demanded a lot of memory and a lot of cycles from the hardware. Which eliminated any chance that it would run at a reasonable speed. The hardware, in a sense, was forced to buck."

With the Dandelion in place, Liddle reported to a PARC forum in June of 1979 that the Star remained on schedule for a 1981 introduction. But four years of organizational struggle and technical difficulty had taken their toll. Thacker was preparing to rejoin the Computer Science Lab; others had left SDD for Jerry Elkind's Advanced Systems Division; some openly questioned whether the Star would ever reach a customer. Several researchers blamed SDD for Star's apparent woes, citing the geographically split development organization, the backward history of the Dandelion, and the complex software design.

"In most development projects," charged Tim Mott, "the deadline is almost more sacrosanct than the actual project itself. But not at SDD. It was never really clear to me that the people in SDD wanted to make a product. They wanted to make a perfect system."

With neither concern nor curiosity from a business partner attuned to market requirements, SDD's engineers set their own schedule for product performance and completion. According to Lampson, this contributed to the "perfect system" syndrome. The Star, he says, "had a lot more innovation than necessary. It's the natural thing for engineers to do when they're not constrained. And they were not constrained."

While SDD's engineering team perfected the Star, Liddle continued to despair over the lack of support from the business side of Xerox. His doubts ran so deep that he questioned whether the enthusiasm Don Massaro expressed for the Star during their November 1979 meeting could withstand the anti-SDD opinion still reigning among those left over from the Potter regime in Dallas. But a few months later, Massaro dispelled Liddle's pessimism by providing the manufacturing and marketing resources to make Star into a product.

Only then, in early 1980, could Liddle savor a highly improbable victory: after four and a half years of institutional indifference and antipathy, he had maneuvered Xerox into promoting the personal distributed computing system invented at PARC. His was, lamentably, a singular achievement.

In April 1981, six years after the formation of SDD and eight years after the invention of the Alto, Xerox at last introduced the Star office system. Amidst the hoopla surrounding the announcement, a characteristically aggressive Massaro declared, "We're either on the verge of another huge success, or we're totally wrong—there's nothing in between."

Mostly, Xerox was wrong.

Unlike two decades before, when the company introduced its 914 to an industry that had languished while Haloid converted Chester Carlson's "electrophotography" into a xerographic office copier, Xerox brought the Star to a market bristling with alternatives. Significantly, the commercial and technical character of the competition differed from the "architecture of information" Xerox had closeted for so many years. Instead of "personal *distributed* computing" as invented at PARC and offered in Star, the industry belonged to the less robust, but extremely successful technology of "personal computing."

The Star provided distributed computing through a network of work stations, laser printers, and electronic filing cabinets. Personal computers, on the other hand, operated by themselves, typically connected at most to slow, poor quality printers on a one-to-one basis. Standing alone, the personal computers could not provide the communications capability considered so vital to Bob Taylor's team at PARC; the dialogue in personal computing was strictly between the person and his machine. Nonetheless, that interaction had been sufficiently enriched by 1981 to make personal computing a $2 billion market in just its seventh year.

The industry had started inauspiciously in January 1975—two years *after* PARC had conceived the Alto—when *Popular Electronics* proclaimed the world's first personal computer. Called the "Altair 8800," the primitive machine invented by a tinkerer from Albuquerque, New Mexico, could execute a limited set of operations that appealed to a comparably narrow audience.

"The only word which could come into mind was 'magic,'" commented the *Popular Electronics* editor describing the Altair. "You buy the Altair, you have to build it, then you have to build other things to plug into it to make it work. You are a weird-type person. Because only weird-type people sit in kitchens and basements and places all hours of the night, soldering things to boards to make machines go flickety-flock."

Not performance, but promise made the Altair famous: it demonstrated the reality of inexpensive computing. As integrated circuitry and microprocessors improved, subsequent machines could and did offer greater size, speed, and power. The most successful of them of course was the Apple II, announced to customers in July of 1977, four months before John Ellenby's "Futures Day" team tried to make the Alto "real" to Xerox executives in Boca Raton.

Yet personal computer hardware alone could not have fueled the expansion of computing beyond the realm of hobbyists. To paraphrase Chuck Thacker's comment about the first Alto prototype, computers without software are "no better than a hot rock—interesting but useless." Software is the reason people buy and use computers. And with the advances made in personal computing between 1975 and 1978, purchasers finally could program their machines to do something more than go "flickety-flock."

Among the first projects of any personal computer designer was to configure a programming language that could run on the machine. That permitted people who knew how to program, or were willing to learn, the opportunity to employ their computers as they saw fit. In this way, personal computer applications were said to be "open" to the imaginations of those who owned them; the user, not the hardware manufacturer, determined what tasks the technology would perform.

That arrangement proved essential to the growth of the industry. As personal computing became more popular, people shared programming ideas and results; as the number of applications expanded, so did the phenomenon of personal computing. Eventually, people who could program realized they had it within their power to make computing either entertaining or useful to those who could not. Even better, they could get paid for doing something they enjoyed. A cottage industry of software writers produced games, educational programs, data base management, word processing, and a wide variety of other applications to a growing base of consumers.

Of all the new software, the product most critical to the office market coveted by Xerox was the electronic spreadsheet, the first of which, called "Visicalc," appeared in 1978. Visicalc permitted managers without programming skills to look at numbers dynamically. Balance sheets, profit and loss statements, cash flows, break-even formulas, project budgets, marketing programs—any numeric management information could be recorded, modified, analyzed, and understood better with the aid of computer powered spreadsheets. For the first time, executives had a reason to buy computers for themselves. And it was that customer group—the managers—Don Massaro chose to target for the Star:

"With the introduction of its 'Star' desk top work station yesterday", *The Wall Street Journal* reported at the end of April 1981, "Xerox Corp. offered a novel way to include the nontyping professional in the 'office of the future.'

"Calling Star the 'keystone' of its piece-by-piece approach to automating the office, Xerox said Star was created for the business professional 'whose main job is to create, interpret, [and] manage information, and distribute the results to others in a convenient form.' "

To increase the productivity of managers, Star provided an array of tools that could compose and communicate words and pictures. The Star was the first personal computing system to incorporate the bit map screen, the mouse, high quality laser printing, "what you see is what you get" word processing, Alan Kay's advanced "Smalltalk" concepts, the Ethernet, and software that combined text and graphics in the same document. Moreover, the basics of the Star system could be learned in less than an hour. It was an impressive piece of technology. Nevertheless, as do most first-time products, the Star had flaws.

First, because of its ambitious software and cart-before-the-horse hardware development, the system operated more slowly than its stand-alone competitors, prompting one analyst to dub the Star "a jack-of-all-trades that does none really well." Second, despite targeting managers and executives, the Star software omitted a spreadsheet. Third, none of the electronic spreadsheets available in the market could run on the Star because, unlike "open" personal computers, the Star was "closed."

Xerox had neither made the Star compatible with other computers nor released its programming language to the public. Only Xerox employees could write applications for the Star, a self-inflicted burden that pinned the success of the machine's extraordinary tools—the bit map screen, the mouse, the communications, etc.—to how completely and how well Systems Development Division engineers could anticipate the software needs of their intended customers.

Any marketing or planning advisor familiar with the needs of those using personal computers, including the popularity of spreadsheets and the practice of cross-compatibility and "open" machines, could have argued forcefully against such product stratagems. But when David Liddle's engineers and technicians had designed and built the Star, they had received no such counsel. No one at Xerox had been interested.

The same Xerox habits and prejudices that for years had rejected ambitions like those of Jack Goldman and John Ellenby as the inadequate pipe dreams of researchers condemned David Liddle, a scientist and engineer, to select a product and business strategy without help from marketing or finance. Paradoxically, in a company whose copiers suffered in quality and timeliness because marketing and finance executives prevented copier engineers from exercising any meaningful technical liberty, the Star was conceived, designed, and built by engineers alone.

"All the while that I was running SDD," complains Liddle, "I couldn't get an operating division to agree to market and sell the product. We had to build it based on what we could see in terms of the use of the Alto within Xerox. And how we could best extrapolate that to the marketplace. We weren't getting professional marketing and professional planning feedback during that whole period of time. So we were mostly driven by what we had learned in research."

Left to himself, Liddle chose a business strategy more appropriate to the back office environment of mainframe computers than the emerging front office world of personal computers. Xerox would build a billion dollar business by offering an expensive system of proprietary hardware and software and releasing enhancements each year or so to customers who, because they neither could program the Star themselves nor look to third parties for software, were locked into Xerox. Each of those elements—the closed configuration of the machines, the paternal attitude toward users, the trap of "software lock-in"—mimicked the classic strategy of IBM.

"I saw it in maybe a grandiose way," Liddle admits. "I saw it that we were supposed to build a system architecture, kind of like a computer company does, that had a family of compatible processors and a programming language and a network and an operating system. And then a lot of products would be built onto that."

Ironically, when IBM itself entered the personal computer market in 1981, it did not pursue its own tried and true strategy. Unlike Xerox, IBM attacked the home and office computer opportunity as a business proposition that embraced development, manufacturing, marketing, and finance together. It paid close attention to the growth of the personal computer industry, and in mid-1980, after the market had passed the billion dollar point and software programs such as Visicalc had been introduced, IBM authorized a team to go after personal computing however they saw fit.

The IBM group broke completely with their company's past. They designed a machine comprised mostly of off-the-shelf components, they released technical specifications and programming languages to independent software houses to ensure a supply of user applications, and, in August 1981, when they brought out their "IBM PC" just thirteen months after beginning the project, they sold it through retailers instead of IBM's vaunted sales force.

"The results," went one account of the IBM story, "were extraordinary. Within two years of its introduction, the PC displaced Apple as the nation's top-selling personal computer."

The IBM PC was not, however, the first personal computer marketed by a Fortune 500 company. That honor belonged to . . . *the Xerox 820*. To his credit, when Don Massaro first saw the Star, he immediately knew it was far more elaborate than a personal computer. He funded a crash project to produce the Xerox 820 in order to fill out the Xerox product line. To Massaro's discredit, he proceeded without consulting the people at PARC. His impatient gamble failed; the designers of the Xerox 820 relied on obsolete technology to build a product 50 percent more expensive than its competition.

"In retrospect," says Massaro, "we should have had PARC design us a different product. It's the only thing I'm embarrassed about during my time in Dallas."

Some PARC researchers blamed the 820 fiasco on Massaro's conceit. At the same time, it is obvious that without Massaro's entrepreneurial vanity, the personal distributed computing system invented by those same researchers and embodied in the Star would not have found any commercial expression as early as 1981, if ever. The important question for Xerox was not what had happened to the 820, but whether the sophisticated Star system, despite its problems, could succeed.

Many thought not. "It was a technological tour de force," opined former Xerox executive Jack Crowley. "But it was too expensive, no one understood it, and no one wanted it."

"At a time when the market hardly understood stand alone computers," argued PARC researcher Jim Mitchell some years later, "the power and utility of a network system could not be sold."

Both Massaro and Liddle disagreed. By bringing the Star to the market, they had forced the product's blemishes into the open—just as Joe Wilson had done when he'd tested the Model A Copier. The Star's drawbacks—the "closed" system, the lack of a spreadsheet, the degraded performance due to the elaborate software and the twisted background of the Dandelion processor—could each be remedied with further development. In fact, in the opinion of Massaro and Liddle, the Star's primary handicap was not technical but organizational: Xerox had created a product its sales force couldn't sell.

"Our only disadvantage," Massaro explained, "was that we didn't have a systems oriented sales and distribution organization to sell Star. But we only realized this after we were committed to going forward."

Selling a complex computer system like the Star to executives differed from peddling copiers or nonprogrammable word processors to office administrators. Since the intended user of the Star was the "nontyping professional," several managers in a prospective customer's organization had to commit to the buying decision. Yet the vast majority of them were unfamiliar with, even apprehensive about, computers. Executives had only the vaguest notions about how they might use a Star-type system to improve professional productivity.

In addition, Xerox confronted its customers with an expensive choice. The Star work station by itself sold for $16,595, as much as five times the price of a stand alone personal computer. And given the distributed character of the Star system, a customer's complete system usually included many work stations, special filing systems, and at least one laser printer. It was not an easy purchasing decision; intrigued executives could experiment with stand alone personal computer alternatives for far less money.

Overcoming such obstacles demanded tremendous familiarity with how the Star could expedite and improve the office routines of professional workers. But as Massaro and Liddle quickly discovered, the Dallas sales force didn't understand any more than their prospective customers the many ways in which computers could improve professional productivity. Furthermore, having sold only nonprogrammable word processors, the Dallas salespeople had experience limited to the secretarial staff of their customers' organizations.

To compensate for the ignorance and inexperience of the sales force, the Office Products Division enrolled its best people in a crash course on the Star in September of 1981—four months after the product was introduced. A discouraging picture emerged from that training seminar.

"Primarily," summarized one of the computer engineers who taught at the conference, "these sales and service people have experience in selling hardware. This is what is called the 'box' business. They used to sell it by onesies and twosies to any customer who would buy 860s or earlier 850s, or 800s, or something like that. They were not accustomed to, and not trained to, or know anything about, selling whole systems to meet an entire organization's office needs. So they didn't know very much about selling what they are now selling.

"In addition, they were accustomed to a very short turnaround time. They were accustomed to waiting maybe ninety days between the time they first contacted a customer and the time they actually installed a piece of equipment. And to try and sell the Star in anything like under ninety days right now would be some kind of a record.

"They also were largely familiar with word processing and records processing kinds of applications—the sort of thing we refer to as automating the clerical workers rather than helping professionals do their job.

"The focus of the sales pitch that these people were accustomed to making was a competitive comparison of features and functions that our 'box' offers and their 'box' doesn't. And although that is obviously a complex subject, it's a little bit easier to compare this 'box' to this 'box' than it is to compare that blob of a system to some other blob of a system.

"In general, the broader issues of integrating all the functions in an office and recognizing the kinds of procedures and systematic ways of behaving that the customers already have in their offices and selling equipment that will help the customer improve that kind of work flow is not very well understood—either by our sales force or by many of us developers."

Massaro, however, confidently expected to mold a team capable of selling the Star. But Xerox denied him the opportunity. In 1982, a year after Dallas introduced the Star, David Kearns decided to integrate Massaro's sales force into the larger copier sales organization. Explanations for the move varied—jealousy among the copier salespeople because Dallas's computer sales force called on higher-ranking customer executives; a desire to present "one face" to the customer; a recent consolidation of sales forces by Kearns's alma mater, IBM; the continuing failure of Massaro's division to turn a profit.

Ironically, the decision was buttressed in part by the success of another Massaro scheme. In late 1981, he had persuaded Kearns to ask the copier sales force to push Xerox's new electronic typewriter, called the "Memorywriter," and by spring, the product was already a hit. Selling the Memorywriter, however, required practically no adjustment to the experience and training of the copier salespeople. "The Memorywriter's a simple product," said Jack Crowley. "An ape could sell that. It's not a system."

Massaro, who had been a model for Kearn's decision to reorganize the copier group around strategic business units headed by their own general managers, now saw the Office Products Division stripped of its valuable sales function. It was too much. He told Kearns he was quitting. "I didn't want to lose my salesmen," he explained later. "That was basically the reason why I left Xerox, the fact that they were combining sales organizations."

Many people in Stamford cheered; they had never liked Massaro, and in their still too political world, Kearns's persistent praise for the Dallas executive made them despise Massaro even more. The news disheartened Massaro's supporters. At his farewell party in Dallas, they presented him with a bronze statue of the Road Runner. Said Massaro, "These were three of the best years of my life. In the first two, I was a hero; in the third, I fell on my sword, and so I was an asshole."

Chapter
20

D avid Liddle resigned soon after Don Massaro, and together they founded their own company to pursue systems
applications for personal distributed computers. They were
not, however, either the first or the last employees to leave Xerox
because of disappointed computer expectations. By 1983, more
than a dozen key contributors had taken their knowledge and
experience elsewhere. Some former PARC scientists, like Alan
Kay, Tim Mott, and Charles Simonyi, assumed research or product development posts in established firms; others, including John
Ellenby, Patrick Baudelaire, Chuck Geschke, and Robert Metcalfe,
raised venture capital to start new enterprises. Meanwhile, with
each departure, Xerox lost a measure of control over the ideas
that made its "architecture of information" so special.

At times, Xerox was bizarrely generous with its computer inventions. For example, in late 1979 one of the company's investment arms contacted Steven Jobs of Apple Corporation about a
possible deal. Jobs, who for years had heard about the fabled
accomplishments of Xerox PARC, asked for and received a tour
of the research center. According to Larry Tesler, who conducted
a demonstration of the Alto for Jobs, the young entrepreneur
immediately grasped what had eluded Xerox executives for more
than half a decade.

" 'Why isn't Xerox marketing this?' " Tesler recalls Jobs demanding. " 'You could blow everybody away!' "

Ensuing discussions between Xerox and Apple fizzled. But
within months of Job's visit, Tesler left Xerox for Apple, and Jobs
ordered an Apple team to design the "Lisa," a computer introduced in 1983. The Lisa replicated many features invented at
Xerox, and because of Apple's strong presence in the personal
computing market, the Lisa seemed to steal a march on Xerox's
Star.

"Office equipment analysts have started referring to PARC-
style systems as 'Lisa-like,' not 'Star-like,' " noted a reporter.
"Apple's next computer, MacIntosh, scheduled to ripen into a
commercial product by the end of this year, could further identify

Apple with PARC's ideas. The engineering manager for Mac-
Intosh came from PARC, where his last big project was a personal
computer."

The Jobs boner upset a number of PARC people who believed
the Xerox investment group should have been looking for ways
to invest in developing, not disclosing, PARC's ideas.

"I was just as incensed at them for not taking advantage of
the things that were here as I had been with Bob Potter for ignoring them," said George Pake. "To allow Jobs to see the power
of the system and gain access to bright people was a dumb thing
to do. And he did make off with Tesler. Once he saw it, the damage
was done; he just had to know that it was doable. Just like the
Russians and the A-bomb. They developed it very quickly once
they knew it was doable."

The defections of both people and ideas caused a lot of embarrassment for Xerox; Pake's friends teased him about PARC
being a "national resource." In September of 1983, *Fortune* ran a
major article entitled, "The Lab That Ran Away From Xerox."
Featuring Ellenby, Simonyi, and Tesler, the piece criticized Xerox
both for letting so many talented researchers escape and for failing
to profit from the computerized office systems invented at PARC.

In one respect, though, the *Fortune* account missed its mark
—the most productive of Xerox's computer scientists remained
at PARC. Bob Taylor, Butler Lampson, Chuck Thacker, and others who had created personal distributed computing still preferred research to commercial opportunity. Since the mid-1970s,
they had designed a new processor, called the "Dorado," which
was at least ten times as powerful as the Alto, then had employed
it to develop a variety of pathbreaking operating systems, programming languages, and other software, all of which had perpetuated PARC's distinction as among the very best computer
science establishments in the world.

Nevertheless, PARC had drifted from the tranquil intellectual
retreat Jack Goldman and George Pake had founded thirteen
years earlier. In 1983, tensions threatened to break the center
apart. And at the root of the unhappiness—like so many of PARC's
attainments—was Bob Taylor's obsession with interactive computing.

From the beginning, contradictions had beset Taylor's position
at PARC. George Pake had coveted Taylor's access to the finest
young computer minds in the country, but not imagining that

such talent would expect and depend upon Taylor's guidance, had withheld the Computer Science Lab manager's job from the former ARPA official, citing Taylor's inadequate personal research track record. Rather than confronting Pake with the misunderstanding, Taylor had contrived the artificial "Mr. Outside/Mr. Inside" plan that had led to Jerry Elkind's appointment as manager of the Computer Science Lab. Although Taylor and Elkind had forged a modus vivendi, the two men could not shield the strains in their relationship from others at PARC.

"Jerry came thinking it was a real job," said one PARC administrator. "He started behaving like someone who was going to manage CSL, and that immediately put him in conflict with Bob."

Despite Elkind's title, the crucial organizational attributes of the Computer Science Lab—collaborative hiring, flat structure, constant communications, and habitual use of the systems invented—each bore Taylor's stamp. Scientists cleared their budgets, project plans, and other decisions through Elkind, but most of them discussed the issues at length with Taylor first. The reality of their respective positions frustrated both men.

"Eventually," said Ed McCreight, a researcher, "I came to notice that Elkind was not giving Taylor much rope, and I didn't think Bob was enjoying it, although Taylor always seemed to keep things about himself to himself."

Apparently, Elkind's personality further diminished his authority within the lab. In contrast to Taylor's contemplative and solicitous manner among the researchers, Elkind tended to attack people and their ideas. Although some scientists thrived on his belligerence, many more were disheartened, driving them further into Taylor's camp.

"Elkind had an awful shorthand," comments McCreight. "He would say, 'Explain why what you're doing is important!' in a way that implied he didn't think it was important. I came from a small town in Pennsylvania where that kind of tone bordered on an attack. So I would think that maybe my stuff really was dreck. Later I learned in my head not to interpret it so negatively. But my gut reaction always overwhelmed my mind. I was really getting down on myself."

Agrees Severo Ornstein, who worked for Elkind at Bolt, Beranek and Newman as well as at PARC, "Jerry just didn't know how to encourage people."

In mid-1976, Elkind took a leave of absence to serve on Bob

Sparacino's technical staff for a year. The awkwardness of serving two bosses dissolved. So many researchers appreciated the improved atmosphere that, just prior to Elkind's return in late 1977, a handful of them petitioned George Pake to arrange for a different assignment for Elkind.

"I had lunch with George," recalls Ornstein, "and told him that the lab just operated better under Bob than Jerry, that Bob was easier to work with. When I said that, George looked off into the distance, his eyes glazed over, and he said, 'Taylor can be pretty hard too.'

"Then George said he had promised Jerry his job would be held for him at the time he took the leave and that he wouldn't go back on his word. So a number of the senior people in CSL took our courage in both hands and went to Jerry and told him we'd rather he didn't come back, that we liked it better with Bob in charge."

In the words of one participant at that meeting, the scene was "surrealistic"—Elkind, who in effect had been hired by his subordinates in the Computer Science Lab was now informed by the same group that they no longer wished to report to him. All agreed that Elkind handled the situation well. Although he did not resign, he left the Computer Science Lab a few months later to manage Xerox's new Advanced Systems Division. Thus, by early 1978, Bob Taylor finally gained in name what had been his in fact for seven years: the job of managing the Computer Science Laboratory at PARC.

George Pake found the Elkind coup attempt distasteful; according to Jim Mitchell, Pake unfairly charged Taylor with engineering the event. Though unsubstantiated, Pake's suspicions could not have surprised anybody at PARC. Almost from the beginning, he had considered Taylor a zealot who fostered an "orthodoxy" within the Computer Science Laboratory.

"CSL under Taylor," charges Pake, "was not hospitable to differing points of view. You could get shot down so fast if you didn't agree with the party view."

Taylor's single-minded pursuit of interactive computing threatened the most basic premise of Pake, the university man—truth's dependence on diversity of opinion. Yet those who defend Taylor claim that Pake's standard for research, formed by decades as an academic physicist, misconstrued the nature of computer science. Unlike physicists, computer scientists don't assemble tools to verify hypotheses about the world. Rather, they build software and hardware because they believe, in Chuck Thacker's words, such constructs "will be a good thing to have." Specific engineering goals, not truth, governed the Computer Science Laboratory; where Pake feared orthodoxy, Taylor's partisans saw only effective management.

"The fundamental ethos in a university," comments Butler Lampson, "is that the professor is an independent agent. A department or a school derives its strength from individual achievements and not from the fact that they work together. The thing that's good about it is that anybody who has a new idea can pursue it without being affected by the group.

"We didn't run CSL that way. We promoted a substantial amount of group thinking. What that means is that we didn't hire people whose thinking was too far afield from the main line of the group.

"The reason we ran CSL that way was that it was our view that if you were going to do systems research, you had to get people to work together to a considerable extent or else you couldn't get the kind of synergy that was necessary. In order to do that, you had to have good planning, because if everyone did their own thing, then there would be no way to get those things to work together. That was why we enforced that. There was a corresponding danger. There was a hazard. But we didn't miss too many good things, too many good people as a result."

Without question, CSL achieved the goals they set for themselves. Most of the researchers in the Computer Science Lab unanimously credit Taylor for their mutual success. "I've never worked for anybody better in my life," said one; "He's been in many ways the best manager I've ever seen, let alone worked for," agreed another. Still, Taylor's monomania and the "group thinking" Lampson described could and did ostracize some CSL scientists who, for whatever reason, sought independence.

"Being inside CSL and being on Taylor's good list was like heaven," says Ed McCreight. "You could do anything, and really conquer the world. Bob really cared about you as an individual, and if you had any problem with Xerox, Bob would take care of it. You felt entirely supported.

"But it was bimodal. If you weren't on his good list, it must have been like hell."

Some disgruntlement stemmed from the inevitable hierarchy that crept into CSL's organization notwithstanding Taylor's preference for a "flat" structure. As the age, tenure, talents, and friendships of several of the researchers matured, people like Lampson, Thacker, Mitchell, McCreight, and Ornstein emerged as the opinion makers to whom Taylor looked for technical guidance. The group even had a name, the "Graybeards," and their influence rattled some of the lab's younger members who felt they didn't get enough time and attention from the boss.

Other dissatisfied researchers lost out in labwide decisions over technical direction; a few simply disliked Taylor or Lampson, the lab's major technical presence. As one malcontent is reported to have complained, "I don't want to be told all the details of my personal life by Bob Taylor, and I don't want to be told all the details of my professional life by Butler Lampson."

All the outcasts found their way into George Pake's office, confirming Pake's fears about the dangers of orthodoxy. Equally unsettling to Pake, Taylor appeared set on spreading the CSL view of PARC's objective to the research center as a whole: he placed "agents" like Alan Kay in the Systems Science Laboratory; he criticized the series of men who managed SSL; he belittled the accomplishments of the physicists in the General Science Laboratory; he questioned Pake's judgment and understanding of the computer research conducted at PARC. The Bob Taylor seen by George Pake in the PARC-wide context differed from the calm, understanding, and supportive manager of creative egos resident in the Computer Science Lab. Instead of the image of a reassuring ear, the metaphor Pake and other PARC managers prefer is that of a fanatic, vituperative mouth. To them, Taylor would stop at nothing to get his way.

"One of the things that makes Taylor so powerful," says Frank Squires, a longtime advisor to Pake, "is that he can focus so strongly on narrow goals and never be distracted. He never has to worry if he's right because he never has to consider anything beyond his narrow focus. One aspect of this was to take to attacking other activities outside CSL. He managed CSL by circling the wagons; everyone inside is great, and everyone outside is a turkey. It led to a whole series of actions—some above the table and some below—that were critical to other groups. And that was the beginning of the end of his relationship with Pake."

Taylor scoffs at such complaints. He contends that the PARC achievements most consistent with Peter McColough's original "architecture of information" charter were produced by those scientists who, whether officially part of CSL, SSL, or other labs, cooperated within the vision of personal distributed computing. Throughout the 1970s and early 1980s, Taylor laments, those people constituted less than a fourth of the center's budget, an allocation of resources that he claims precluded Xerox from enjoying even greater accomplishments. In his opinion, Pake's even-handed university ethic veiled an unacceptable ignorance—both about the nature of computer science and the best interests of Xerox.

"I came to Xerox," asserts Taylor, "driven by a vision and set of objectives, and having decided to devote my life to work that was going to make a difference. Pake is motivated differently than I. I'm a content guy. Pake's more of a process guy. From my perception, he simply wasn't interested in the content of what we were doing.

"We were exploring a new space: personal distributed computing. That space was huge, in terms of the number of unknowns that were associated with it, the number of problems one ought to have worked on if you were really to have explored that space. We never had the resources to explore the way we should have. And the reason that we didn't is that because from our management on up there wasn't a sufficient understanding of what the nature of that problem space was.

"When we talked to Goldman or Pake about the importance of programming technology, for example, they would nod their heads. But as soon as any issue would come up where we wanted to increase our *investment* in programming technology, in one way or another, the answer would always come back, 'Not at the expense of physics!' "

Taylor conceived of PARC solely in terms of interactive computing; he rejected as misguided any activity not in furtherance of his goal. Consequently, he persistently criticized Pake's support for the research being conducted by other PARC laboratories into the physics of optics and materials. All major breakthroughs in interactive computing after the invention of the integrated circuit, Taylor argued, had depended, and would continue to depend, on solving the mysteries of design and programming logic instead of the physics of light, electricity, or matter.

"The complexities that we had to work out to do what we did were *not*," he stressed, "in physical science."

Unfortunately, Taylor packaged his profound differences with

Pake in a series of wild charges and unrealistic demands. Every time Pake refused to sacrifice physics research in favor of Taylor's activity, the screams about underfunding would fly. To Pake, Taylor's relentless complaint about resources must have seemed like a wolf on the wrong side of the door. That such operating groups as Scientific Data Systems and the engineering division led by O'Neill and Sparacino would grab for research money was, perhaps, predictable; but that one research manager would so blatantly demand the budgets of his peers deeply offended Pake.

Nonetheless, as long as Pake directed PARC, Taylor's stridency was kept in check. In 1978, however, Pake unexpectedly relinquished day-to-day control of the West Coast research center. That spring, to protect the research function's corporate reporting status from an assault by Sparacino and O'Neill, Pake had agreed to replace Goldman as the company's chief of research. Bob Spinrad, a man with a computer engineering background, assumed Pake's position at the head of PARC. The switch pleased Taylor and troubled his enemies in equal measure.

"Spinrad and Taylor got along," according to Bert Sutherland, the manager of the Systems Science Lab, "because Taylor found in Spinrad a computer guy who shared his world view. The word around PARC became, 'When Spinrad needs to know what to do, he asks Taylor.' "

A year after Spinrad took control of PARC, Xerox headquarters asked each of the research centers to provide a long-term assessment of direction and related budgetary requirements. Taylor contends that Spinrad diligently reviewed the technical priorities of each of PARC's laboratories, including the strengths and weaknesses of their respective scientists, before recommending any action.

"This was a job that had never been done before," claims Taylor. "Pake certainly never did it. After about a year and a half of reviews, Spinrad started a series of final meetings designed to build a five-year plan for PARC. The plan that emerged would have gradually changed PARC's investment profile over the period of the plan, enlarging the computer investment at the expense of the physics investment."

The physicists immediately complained to their fellow physicist Pake, who was already unhappy with Spinrad for a separate reason. Shortly after Pake had assumed Goldman's corporate responsibilities, he had persuaded Kearns—over Sparacino's bitter objections—to add an integrated circuit laboratory to PARC. Despite repeated admonishments from Pake, however, Spinrad had failed to hire a manager for the new lab. Now Spinrad's five year plan, no doubt under Taylor's spell, devalued other research efforts Pake considered important. Therefore, to get action on the integrated circuit lab and to protect his vision of PARC, Xerox's head of research intervened.

"I was unhappy with Spinrad's report," explains Pake. "Not only the substance, but also the way it was handled. It was no way to inspire creativity to tell people they had no future. In some of the labs to be deemphasized there were good people and good projects making progress, all of which I believed Xerox should keep.

"There was also the second problem. We had the approval for the integrated circuit lab, and we had to get a first-rate manager. Bob Spinrad had been interviewing without success, and, to his credit, admitted as much in his performance review that year.

"So I took the artificial step of splitting PARC into two. One part, called the 'Systems Center,' reported to Bob Spinrad, and the other, the 'Science Center,' to Harold Hall."

Pake put the new integrated circuit lab, the threatened physics lab, and certain computer science groups that were out of favor with Taylor into Harold Hall's Science Center, intentionally restricting Spinrad's control to those activities supported in his long range plan. Pake admits that his action bore an obvious message for Taylor.

"There was a method to my madness. I wanted a plurality of viewpoint and did not want everything done here within what I called the orthodoxy of CSL. There is no question it was a brilliant lab. But it did not have to be so dominant."

Buildings, however, do not divide as easily as organizations; the scientists of Hall's Science Center and Spinrad's Systems Center continued to park in the same lots, walk the same halls, and eat in the same cafeteria. But their mutual enmity rapidly spoiled the common atmosphere. According to Bill Spencer, the man Hall hired away from Bell Labs to run the integrated circuit lab, Xerox's West Coast research "Centers" suffered from a social pathology —people went out of their way to physically avoid and verbally assault their antagonists. Taylor supporters accused Pake of double dealing; Pake's allies labeled Taylor a malevolent "Reverend Moon" who had mesmerized researchers within and beyond CSL to accept his word as gospel. Moreover, they claimed Taylor had begun an effort to "sell" his entire research group to other companies.

Spencer, the new integrated circuit lab manager, got to know Taylor quite well. The two men played tennis nearly every Saturday throughout 1981 and 1982. "After every tennis session," says Spencer, "we would have drinks—Taylor a Dr. Pepper and me a beer. He was a man of very deep habits, and very strong feelings. Most of my views about PARC were very much influenced by Taylor. Taylor would say over and over again, 'We've pulled together a group of outstanding people, and we've demonstrated we can build things. The whole world says it's great stuff, yet Xerox hasn't made a success of it. We now need more funds, and if we could only get rid of other parts of PARC, we could go on and do more great things.'"

Based on his twenty years of experience at Bell Labs, Spencer concluded that Taylor's group had an inflated opinion of themselves. Nevertheless, he appeared to win Taylor's friendship without succumbing to Taylor's orthodoxy, a feat that persuaded Pake to tap Spencer to put PARC back together again in the spring of 1983.

"There was an artificiality about the two 'Centers,'" explains Pake. "And I believed Spencer was strong enough to think through the future of PARC in ways that would not arbitrarily curtail any segment of it. Taylor had always been a big managerial problem, and I thought it was important that they be able to get along. I thought Spencer was the ideal man to run the lab because he and Bob played tennis together and got along great."

Spencer avoided Bob Spinrad's error. Rather than buying into the Taylor line, PARC's new director turned his full attention to an issue he considered far more critical to the research center's long-term viability. He made clear that he believed Xerox and PARC had failed to join scientific invention to commercial innovation and that at least half the blame belonged to the research center. To improve results, he asked PARC's lab managers to get to know their "customers" elsewhere in the corporation. "Fifty percent of their performance reviews," Spencer decreed, "would be based on how successfully they achieved it. What I was looking for was to see if you could couple PARC closer to the organization and still keep it as creative as it had been in the past."

Spencer's independence quickly cooled his relationship with Taylor. The two men stopped their game of tennis and, ominously, quit talking. Reflecting bitterness over what happened, Spencer says, "It wasn't my tennis elbow. Bob feels threatened by technical people who want to move into management. He's an interesting guy to have come as far as he has without the academic trappings people usually have in those positions. It would have been hard for him to have been an individual contributor."

From Taylor's perspective, George Pake appeared to have cloned himself—right down to Spencer's retreat to credentialism. Taylor was wrong. Significantly, Bill Spencer lacked the depth of Pake's conviction about pluralism. For years, those who had objected to Taylor's ethics and behavior had advised Pake to fire the CSL strong man. To have acquiesced, however, would have struck at the core of Pake's principles. Although Pake may have considered Taylor obnoxious, as long as CSL's "orthodoxy" was kept at bay, Taylor had an equal right to pursue research in George Pake's organization.

Pake and Taylor coexisted for more than a decade; Spencer, as PARC director, confronted Taylor within months. In late August of 1983, Spencer summoned Taylor to his office, briefly delineated their differences, then handed Taylor a memorandum of their "understanding." In it, Spencer accused and forbade Taylor from attempting to induce employees to leave the company, gave him three weeks to reorganize CSL into several subgroups, directed Taylor to share managerial responsibilities with others in CSL, commanded CSL to improve its contacts with the rest of Xerox, announced that Spencer himself would attend CSL staff and planning meetings, and ordered Taylor to stop bad-mouthing other PARC programs and labs.

The Spencer note ended with an ultimatum: "Bob, it is my desire that as the result of our discussions that you will make the necessary corrections in your behavior and actions to be a valued member of my staff. However, it is important for you to understand that any failure to comply with these action items, or the confidentiality of this memo, will result in disciplinary action that may include your termination."

Spencer threatened Taylor with much more than a lost job. To re-create CSL's computing environment, even with the same people, would take several years because, while many researchers might join a fired Taylor elsewhere, their technology—blueprints, programs, and manuals for the personal distributed computing hardware and software advances of the past decade—would remain at Xerox. They could pack their ideas and experiences, but to reach the same interactive computing frontier in a different setting, a Taylor-led laboratory would have to retake much of the ground already conquered. No one as creative as Taylor or his colleagues likes to reinvent old wheels.

Nevertheless, Taylor refused to back down. A week after Spencer had read him the riot act, CSL's manager submitted a lengthy defense of his conduct at PARC. He wrote for the record that he had spent his entire Xerox career recruiting talented people to join, not leave, PARC, that his organization worked effectively without subunits, and that senior people in CSL either preferred research to management or rejected managerial opportunities because of "the management environment immediately over me." Taylor was dismayed by Spencer's charges, but remained, true to form, unbowed:

"The PARC research investment strategy," he argued in his memo to Spencer, "has not been one of building upon our strengths to maximize synergy, but rather to let many disjointed flowers bloom. This investment strategy is most unwise for computing research in particular.

"The important issue here and implied throughout your entire memo, is the successful transfer of technology within Xerox, is it not? This is what we all want! Indeed, that is why all the people in CSL joined CSL. We recruited to the dream that Xerox, using the technology we believed we could create, would significantly change and enhance the information world for millions of Xerox customers. We intended from the beginning to put the technological flesh on the bare bones of Peter McColough's phrase, 'the architecture of information.' That is what we came here to do, and we have made a very good beginning; certainly better than any other group in the world, large or small, over the past thirteen years. This is especially remarkable when one realizes that we have worked with less than one-fifth of the total resources of PARC from the beginning through to the present.

"We have transferred an enormous amount of technology. But the real challenge has been the transfer of an entirely new and quite different framework for thinking about, designing, and using information systems. *This is immensely more difficult than transferring technology.* Opportunities for pioneering completely new ways of thinking about large collections of ideas are rare. Most people spend a lifetime without any such opportunities. Over the past twenty years, I have been fortunate to have been a leader in three: timesharing; long-distance, interactive networking; and personal distributed computing. Each of these required large upheavals in the way people think about information systems. I learned a great deal from these experiences."

Though Taylor knew his PARC days were numbered, he insisted that his note to Spencer was not a letter of resignation. Before taking that final step, Taylor wanted the chance to discuss his position with his senior colleagues—the "Graybeards"—as well as David Kearns. Spencer okayed a Taylor-Kearns meeting, but officiously refused to lift his ban against disclosure of the situation to anyone at PARC. After failing to win any comfort from Kearns, Taylor informed the Graybeards that he would resign.

On September 19, two weeks after publication of "The Lab That Ran Away From Xerox," the curtain rose for the final part of the drama missed by the article in *Fortune*. Taylor convened the Computer Science Lab for the last time. In a brief address to an audience that included Bill Spencer, he reviewed the circumstances of the previous weeks, announced his resignation, and, before leaving, thanked the researchers for enriching both his life and the world with their many accomplishments. The scientists were stunned.

According to Jim Mitchell, "Spencer stayed on after Taylor departed and tried to be upbeat. But no sooner did Spencer begin talking than Chuck Thacker stood up and publicly resigned. That stopped Spencer cold. He recovered to tell Thacker that he knew things were emotional, that nothing was irreversible, and why didn't they talk the next day, et cetera. But the next day, Thacker was gone."

The other Graybeards went directly to Pake to tell him they thought a terrible mistake had been made. They warned him that Xerox might lose much of the lab unless Taylor was reinstated. Pake explained that he had no desire to see CSL dissolved, but that, in Spencer's opinion, Taylor had become intractable, creating a crisis in the management of the center. To the Graybeards, it sounded as though Pake disclaimed any part in the decision to fire Taylor. They weren't convinced.

"Spencer may have been the hit man," one of them remarked, "but I know who the godfather was."

Over the next few months, the group tried without success to persuade Pake, Spencer—even David Kearns—to invite Taylor back. Meanwhile, Taylor received an offer from Digital Equipment Corporation to build a computer research center in Palo Alto. Word about Taylor's deal spread through PARC with the same effect that the news of Taylor's move from Utah to PARC had had on the scientists of Berkeley Computer Corporation more than a decade before. Lampson immediately resigned to join Taylor and Thacker at DEC, and more than a dozen top researchers followed. When they arrived, they found a relieved Bob Taylor.

"It's great," he exclaimed, "to finally work for a computer company!"

For George Pake, the crisis had come just when PARC seemed to have earned a more active role in the corporation. In 1983, the PARC inspired laser printer business continued to grow rapidly, Xerox headquarters approved plans to back product developments in the high density memory disk and solid state laser technology pioneered at PARC, and, perhaps most important, PARC's Ethernet had been modified and installed in Xerox's successful "10 Series" of third generation copiers.

"Xerox researchers can be very proud," Pake wrote, "that there is no current or projected major Xerox product which is not enabled in some technologically essential way by a result from the research laboratories."

As for the Alto and the Star, the optimistic Pake refused to mourn the personal computer opportunity that had bypassed Xerox. Showing that he remained more physicist than businessman, Pake asserted that, if anything, Xerox had introduced personal distributed computing in the Star too soon.

"The public," he claimed, "wasn't ready."

Epilogue

January 1988

Patrick Baudelaire is chairman of Tangram, a French computer technology company.

David Boggs is a researcher at the Western Research Laboratory of Digital Equipment Corporation.

Jerry Elkind is vice president of systems, integration, and technology for Xerox.

John Ellenby has left GRiD Systems Corporation, the personal computer company he cofounded, and is reported to be living in California.

Chuck Geschke is cofounder and executive vice president of Adobe Systems, Incorporated.

Jack Goldman is president and chief executive officer of Cauzin Systems, Incorporated.

Bill Gunning is a senior research fellow at Xerox PARC.

Michael Hughes is chairman and chief executive officer of Business Exchange International, Inc.

Alan Kay is an Apple Fellow for Apple Computer, Inc.

David Kearns is chairman and chief executive officer of Xerox.

Butler Lampson is corporate consultant engineer at the Systems Research Center of Digital Equipment Corporation. Along with Taylor and Thacker, he received the 1984 Software System Award from the Association for Computing Machinery for the invention of personal distributed computing.

David Liddle is cofounder and chairman of Metaphor Computer Systems.

Don Massaro is cofounder and president of Metaphor Computer Systems.

Archie McCardell is retired and living in Connecticut.

Peter McColough is living in Connecticut. Following McColough's 1987 retirement from active service to the corporation, Xerox paid tribute to him, in a letter to company shareholders, by summarizing his career as follows: "In 1966 Mc-Colough was elected President of Xerox. In 1968 he succeeded Joseph C. Wilson as Chief Executive Officer. During his tenure as CEO, Xerox revenues grew almost tenfold, from $896 million to over $8.5 billion in 1981, his last full year as CEO. While he headed the Company, Xerox acquired operating control of Rank-Xerox, settled complex litigation issues and began its move into systems and digital technology while also exploiting its heartland strengths in copying and duplicating. Also, Xerox became widely respected for its social consciousness and for its sponsorship of quality television."

Ed McCreight is a senior research fellow at Xerox PARC.

Robert Metcalfe is cofounder and senior vice president of technology of 3-Com Corporation.

Jim Mitchell is director of the Acorn Research Center of Acorn Computer Company.

Tim Mott is senior vice president of United States Publishing for Electronic Arts.

Jim O'Neill lives in Connecticut.

George Pake is retired from Xerox and serves as director of the Xerox sponsored Institute for Research on Learning. In 1987, citing PARC's many accomplishments, President Reagan awarded Pake the National Medal of Science.

Bob Potter is president and chief executive officer of Data Point Corporation.

Ron Rider is vice president for systems research at Xerox.

Charles Simonyi is chief architect of the Applications Division of Microsoft Corporation.

Bob Sparacino is president and founder of Sparacino Associates in Connecticut.

Bill Spencer is corporate vice president of research for Xerox.

Gary Starkweather is a project leader at Apple Computer, Inc.

Bob Taylor is manager of the Systems Research Center of Digital Equipment Corporation. Along with Lampson and Thacker, he received the 1984 Software System Award from the Association for Computing Machinery for the invention of personal distributed computing.

Larry Tesler is vice president of advanced technology for Apple Computer, Inc.

Chuck Thacker is a senior consultant engineer at the Systems Research Center of Digital Equipment Corporation. Along with Lampson and Taylor, he received the 1984 Software System Award from the Association for Computing Machinery for the invention of personal distributed computing.

George White is vice president for research, University of Pittsburgh.

Notes

Marketing: The Architecture of Information

Page No.
Chapter 1

23   "to keep our momentum": McColough, quoted in *New York Times*, May 26, 1968.

24   "Look we're only communicating": Wilson, quoted in Jacobson and Hillkirk, *XEROX American Samurai* (New York: Macmillan, 1986), p. 214.

25   "I went to get my papers": McColough in *New York Times*, May 26, 1968.

25   "He was home sick": McColough in *New York Times*, May 26, 1968; and *Time*, May 24, 1968.

26   "Our machines are too big": McColough, quoted in Dessauer, *My Years With Xerox* (New York: Doubleday, 1971), p. 98.

26   "To sell machines": McColough in Dessauer, op. cit., pp. 98–99.

27   "The younger guys": McColough in Jacobson and Hillkirk, op. cit., p. 64.

27   "We shipped our first": Ibid., p. 62.

28   One chronicler of the copying madness: Brooks, "Xerox, Xerox, Xerox, Xerox," *The New Yorker*, April 1967, pp. 57–58.

29   "The company was exploding": McColough in Jacobson and Hillkirk, op. cit., p. 206.

30   "The pressure was on": Ibid., p. 216; and *Forbes*, August 15, 1972.

30   The deal was done in less than two weeks: Dessauer, op. cit., p. 213.

Chapter 2

34   "The familiar cartoon": Goldman, "Innovation in Large Firms," *Research on Technological Innovation, Management and Policy*, Vol. 2, p. 2.

36   "Of course it's got a million miles": Wilson in Dessauer, op. cit., p. 42.

39   "Xerography went through many stages": Owen, "Copies in Seconds," *The Atlantic Monthly*, February 1986.

40   "Peter told me": Goldman in *Forbes*, July 1, 1969.

Page No.

Chapter 3

45 "If you're talking about diversification": Dessauer, op. cit., p. 164.

46 "Look, unless we work in Rochester": Jacobson and Hillkirk, op. cit., p. 204.

48 "There was a goal": McColough in *U.S. v. IBM*, Document #3157, p. 54.

48 In March of 1970: "XEROX: Searching For An Architecture of Information," an address by C. Peter McColough, President, Xerox Corporation, before the New York Society of Security Analysts, March 3, 1970.

Research: The Creation of the Alto

Chapter 4

55 "Little success is likely": Pake, "Research at Xerox PARC: A Founder's Assessment," *IEEE Spectrum*, October 1985.

56 "I spoke to leading professors": Ibid.

58 "It is often said that programming": Licklider, "Man-Computer Symbiosis," *IRE Transactions on Human Factors in Electronics*, March 1960.

60 "Our rule of thumb": Taylor in Rheingold, *Tools for Thought* (New York: Simon & Schuster, 1985), p. 207.

Chapter 5

65 He also scorned traditional education: Rheingold, op. cit., p. 233.

66 "an interactive tool which can aid": Kay, *"The Reactive Engine,"* University of Utah Ph.D. thesis, 1969, p. 75.

67 "I studied physics at Harvard": Lampson in Lammers, *Programmers at Work* (Redmond: Microsoft, 1986), p. 26.

73 "A research manager": Pake, op. cit.

Chapter 6

76 "The people here all have track records": Kay in Brand, *II Cybernetic Frontiers* (New York: Random House, 1974), p. 65.

77 "CSL was a flat organization": Thacker, "Personal Distributed Computing: The Alto and Ethernet Hardware," *ACM Conference History of Personal Workstations*, January 1986.

82 "The prevailing attitude": Lampson, "Personal Distributed Computing: The Alto and Ethernet Hardware," op. cit.

83 In 1962, an integrated chip containing: Reid, *The Chip* (New York: Simon & Schuster, 1985), p. 122.

84 "making it possible to produce": Lampson, "Guest Editorial," *Software —Practice and Experience*, Vol. 2, 1972.

Page No.

84   "Millions of people will write": Ibid.

85   "Imagine having your own self-contained": Kay and Goldberg, "Personal Dynamic Media," *Computer,* March 1977.

Chapter 7

87   "Timesharing systems had made computing": Thacker, "Personal Distributed Computing: The Alto and Ethernet Hardware," op. cit.

87   Four years later, in a seminal event: Rheingold, op. cit., pp. 188–193.

88   "Only one technique": Thacker, McCreight, Lampson, Sproull, and Boggs, "Alto: A Personal Computer," in Siewiorek, Bell, and Newell, *Computer Structures: Principles and Examples* (New York: McGraw-Hill, 1982), p. 556.

90   "Fortunately, surprisingly good images": Ibid.

90   "preserve the recognizable characteristics": Ibid.

Chapter 8

95   "In a few years, men will be able": Licklider, Taylor, and Herbert, "The Computer as a Communication Device," *Science and Technology,* April 1968.

Chapter 9

106   "The summation of human experience": Bush, "As We May Think," *The Atlantic Monthly,* July 1945.

106   "A memex is a device": Ibid.

107   "wholly new forms of encyclopedias": Ibid.

107   Following the war, Engelbart earned college: Rheingold, op. cit., Chapter 9.

107   "adopted some years ago": Engelbart and English, "A Research Center for Augmenting Human Intellect," *Fall Joint Computer Conference,* 1968.

108   "3c4 The basic validity": Ibid.

111   "There is a story, probably apocryphal": Shore, *The Sachertorte Algorithm* (New York: Penguin, 1985), p. 113.

Finance: The Rejection of the Alto

Chapter 10

117   "Office automation has emerged": *Business Week,* June 30, 1975.

118   "is almost impossible to understand": McColough in *New York Times,* May 25, 1973.

Page No.

119   "Patents are not as important": McColough in *New York Times*, December 1, 1974.

119   "to occupy himself with the international": Dessauer, *My Years With Xerox* (New York: Doubleday, 1971), p. 101.

121   The press has long since: *Forbes*, August 15, 1972.

122   "We sold them a dead horse": Palevsky in DeLamarter, *Big Blue* (New York: Dodd, Mead, 1986), p. 100.

122   "Xerox didn't do it right": Rock in Levering, Katz, and Moskowitz, *The Computer Entrepreneurs* (New York: New American Library, 1984), p. 457.

122   "In big miltidivision companies": Norris in Doerflinger and Rivkin, *Risk and Reward* (New York: Random House, 1987), p. 200.

122   "I don't subscribe to the idea": McColough in *Forbes*, July 1, 1971.

123   "Once an IBM customer": DeLamarter, op. cit., p. 44.

124   In the opinion of an expert witness: Ibid., p. 353.

126   "The thought was that [SDS]": McColough in *U.S. v. IBM*, Document #3157, pp. 17–18.

127   "The effect was adverse": Currie in *U.S. v. IBM*, Document #3097, p. 58.

127   "We tracked what we characterized": Ibid., p. 67.

127   "Morale in the field": McKee in Sobel, *IBM vs. Japan* (New York: Stein and Day, 1986), p. 75.

128   "In retrospect": McColough in *New York Times*, July 22, 1975.

Chapter 11

130   "When I was made president": McColough in Jacobson and Hillkirk, *XEROX American Samurai* (New York: Macmillan, 1986), p. 193.

130   "Under Mr. Wilson's influence": Ibid., pp. 194–195.

131   "This is the worst time": McColough in Dessauer, op. cit., p. 232.

131   "I happen to like politics": McColough, "The Corporation and Its Obligations," *Harvard Business Review*, May–June 1975.

133   "walked into a brand new airplane": McCardell in Marsh, *A Corporate Tragedy* (New York: Doubleday, 1985), p. 178.

133   "Archie has a manner of interfacing": Marsh, op. cit., p. 174.

Chapter 12

150   "There is absolutely no question": Pake in *Business Week*, June 30, 1975.

Chapter 13

153   "McCardell recognized right off": Goldman in Marsh, op. cit., p. 185

Page No.

Chapter 14

166   "The automatic typing and text": *Word Processing Management*, December 1973.

170   "Featuring a speedy typing mechanism": *Administrative Management*, November 1974.

170   "Within eighteen months": *Fortune*, March 13, 1978.

171   "Moving to the office of the future": Potter in *Business Week*, June 30, 1975.

171   "The bean counters": *Fortune*, March 13, 1978.

175   "We had to rush": Wang, *Lessons* (Reading: Addison-Wesley, 1986), pp. 182–183.

Marketing: The Reaffirmation of the Copier

Chapter 15

181   "If we ever get to be afraid": McColough in *Forbes*, August 15, 1972.

181   "The premium is on political maneuvering": Jacobson and Hillkirk, *XEROX American Samurai* (New York: Macmillan, 1986), p. 180.

184   Xerox, creators of the first and second: *Fortune*, March 13, 1978.

185   For example, one Savin ad: *Advertising Age*, April 11, 1977.

185   "We are where Xerox used to be": Jacobson and Hillkirk, op. cit., p. 135.

186   At the end of a full day of discussing: Ibid., p. 124.

187   "XEROX having spent a decade": Freberg, "The Eventual Arrival of Ardri," unpublished manuscript, pp. 2–4.

188   "You want the problem in a nutshell": Ibid., p. 44.

188   By the end of 1977, Xerox had placed: *Fortune*, March 13, 1978.

190   According to one source, Carter did ask: Jacobson and Hillkirk, op. cit., p. 191.

190   "You know that McColough's going to be there": Marsh, *A Corporate Tragedy* (New York: Doubleday, 1985), p. 6.

190–191   "McCardell was willing to stay on": Goldman, "Book Review," *IEEE Spectrum*, July 1987.

Chapter 16

198   "We had nothing but refried beans": Jacobson and Hillkirk, op. cit., p. 70.

Chapter 18

218   Xerox euphemistically described the 3300: Xerox 1980 Annual Report, p. 9.

Page No.

218   others were less charitable: *Dun's Business Month*, May 1983.
219   "We are determined to change significantly": Kearns in Jacobson and
         Hillkirk, op. cit., p. 171.
222   " 'We did,' the five said": Jacobson and Hillkirk, op. cit., p. 314.

Research: The Harvest of Isolation

Chapter 19

228   "He's a real fireball": *New York Times*, May 3, 1981.
233   "We're either on the verge": Massaro in *Business Week*, October 12,
         1981.
233   "The only word which could come into mind": Levy, *Hackers* (Garden
         City, NY: Doubleday, 1984), p. 185.
235   "With the introduction of its 'Star' ": *Wall Street Journal*, April 28,
         1981.
235   "a jack-of-all-trades": *Dun's Business Month*, May 1983.
237   "The results were extraordinary": *New York Times*, July 7, 1985.
240   "I didn't want to lose my salesmen": Massaro in *Wall Street Journal*,
         May 9, 1984.

Chapter 20

241   "Office equipment analysts": *Fortune*, September 5, 1983.
254   "Xerox researchers can be very proud": Pake, "From Research to
         Innovation at Xerox: A Manager's Principles and Some Examples,"
         to be published in R. S. Rosenbloom, *Research on Technological Inno-
         vation, Management and Policy*, Vol. 3.

Epilogue

257   "In 1966 McColough was elected": Xerox Third Quarter Interim
         Report, September 30, 1987, p. 4.

Index